A Weekend With the Great War

PROCEEDINGS OF THE FOURTH ANNUAL GREAT WAR INTERCONFERENCE SEMINAR LISLE, ILLINOIS

16–18 SEPTEMBER 1994

Contributors:
George Anastaplo, Robert Cowley, Gerard J. Demaison, Aleks A. M. Deseyne, Paul Fussell, Sergey V. Listikov, Viktor L. Mal'kov, Philip Markham, Daniel Moran, Desmond Morton, Edward F. Murphy, Dennis E. Showalter, Richard B. Spence, Betty Miller Unterberger, Dale E. Wilson

Sponsored by the Great War Society and
the Western Front Association
Hosted by the Cantigny First Division Foundation and
Robert R. McCormick Tribune Foundation

EDITED BY

STEVEN WEINGARTNER

Published by the Cantigny First Division Foundation and
White Mane Publishing Company, Inc. with the Great War Society and
the Western Front Association

The Cantigny Military History Series
A Weekend With the Great War
Proceedings of the Fourth Annual Great War Interconference Seminar

Published by the Cantigny First Division Foundation and White Mane Publishing Company, Inc. with the Great War Society and the Western Front Association

The Cantigny First Division Foundation
1 South 151 Winfield Road
Wheaton, Illinois 60187
708-668-5185

This White Mane Publishing Company, Inc. publication
was printed by
Beidel Printing House, Inc.
63 West Burd Street
Shippensburg, PA 17257 USA

In respect for the scholarship contained herein, the acid-free paper used in this book meets the guidelines for permanence and durability of the Committee on Production Guidelines for Book Longevity of the Council on Library Resources.

For a complete list of available publications
please write
White Mane Publishing Company, Inc.
P.O. Box 152
Shippensburg, PA 17257 USA

Library of Congress Cataloging-in-Publication Data
Great War Interconference Seminar (4th : 1994 : Lisle, Ill.)
    A weekend with the Great War : proceedings of the Fourth annual
Great War Interconference Seminar, Lisle, Illinois, 16–18 September
1994 / edited by Steven Weingartner : contributors, George Anastaplo
... [et al.] ; sponsored by the Great War Society and the Western
Front Association : hosted by the Cantigny First Division
Foundation and Robert R. McCormick Tribune Foundation.
        p.   cm.
    Includes bibliographical references and index.
    ISBN 1-57249-062-4. -- ISBN 1-57249-068-3 (pbk.)
    1. World War, 1914–1918--Congresses.   I. Weingartner, Steven.
II. Anastaplo, George, 1925   .   III. Great War Society.
IV. Western Front Association.   V. Title.
D504.G75   1997   96-37490
940.3--dc21   CIP

PRINTED IN THE UNITED STATES OF AMERICA

The Cantigny Military History Series is sponsored by the Robert R. McCormick Tribune Foundation. The series presents conferences and related publications that address issues consonant with the foundation's mission.

The conferences are hosted by the First Division Museum, located on the grounds of Cantigny, the McCormick Estate, located in Wheaton, Illinois, approximately 30 miles from Chicago.

Contents

v

List of Illustrations

Foreword

In 1992 Ken Finland and Flip Carroll—representing, respectively, the Western Front Association and the Great War Society—first approached me about hosting a joint annual meeting of the two organizations. Their concept was to invite scholars and authors of the history of World War I to gather in Wheaton, Illinois, in the fall of 1994 for a weekend of presentations and discussions.

Papers were presented at the Hilton Hotel in Lisle, Illinois; other events, including the grand banquet, were held in the First Division Museum at Cantigny, the estate of the late Colonel Robert R. McCormick, a former publisher of the *Chicago Tribune* and a veteran of the Great War. Most of the papers presented that weekend have been edited to be included in this volume, which represents the accumulated results of the weekend activities. The final result is the excellent work of Steven Weingartner, our editor, and White Mane Publishing Company, Inc., our publisher. The Cantigny First Division Foundation took on the task of organizing the publication effort, to include funding, as part of the Cantigny Military History Series.

The fifteen selections included in this volume illustrate the continuing interest in the First World War by academic historians and others whose intellectual passion is greater understanding of one of the most persistent of human activities—war. The papers cover a diverse group of subjects, but each represents serious scholarship and an abiding desire to explore new horizons. We have grouped the papers topically rather than in the order they were presented during the conference and have limited the question-and-answer discussions and the critical commentary held at the end of each day to short edited passages. In most instances those discussion sessions provided additional information that was debated long into the night in other venues of the hotel. The conference was well organized by the staffs of the two host organizations and included the showings of important films and exhibitions of new books in the field.

Although the Western Front Association and the Great War Society chose to go their separate ways for future annual meetings, this last joint gathering was productive and interesting. We are pleased to be able to share the fruits of that collaboration with you in these conference proceedings.

John F. Votaw, Ph.D.
Executive Director
Cantigny First Division Foundation
February 1997

Editor's Preface

Several of the essays in this volume were originally crafted as formal papers with notes included or appended later. Others were derived from the tape transcripts of presentations which the contributors subsequently shaped into essays, without notes. Paul Fussell's essay, "The Great War and Cultural Modernism," was adapted from his speech at the Grand Banquet on the second night of the conference.

Each presentation was followed by a question-and-answer session. Highlights of the sessions, edited for clarity and content, appear after the essays. They are followed by comments, similarly edited, made during the panel discussions that closed out each day. The panelists are identified with their comments and, where possible, audience members who participated in the discussion are identified as well. Where names could not be attached to speakers, however, the latter are simply identified as "Audience Member." Readers are reminded of the off-the-cuff nature of the discussions, and that what is said is often, if not always, meant as an exploration of ideas and themes rather than statements of fact or belief.

Papers by two contributors, Donald Abenheim and Douglas Porch, were not available for publication. Remarks by Donald Abenheim included in the comment segments reflect his further participation as a panelist.

Finally, a note on inconsistencies in the spelling of some foreign-language terms and proper nouns. Most of these are romanized words of Cyrillic-Russian origin. There being no hard and fast rules governing such conversions—all of them the result of an inherently imprecise process—it was decided to let individual choice and preference determine the outcome. Hence, the difference in first-name spellings between Sergey Listikov, a contributor to this volume, and Russian Foreign Minister Sergei Sazonov; or, similarly, the *nom de guerre* of Lev Davidovich Bronstein appearing alternately as Trotsky and Trotskii.

Steven Weingartner
Editor

PART 1

OVERVIEW

Did Anyone "In Charge" Know What He Was Doing? Thoughts on the Thirty Years' War of the Twentieth Century

George Anastaplo

Argument has little chance after war has once got under full way. As John Adams put it, in 1776, a Torrent is not to be impeded by Reasoning, nor a Storm allayed by Ridicule. [John] Bright said something of the same kind after the Crimean War, when his wisest utterance did not shake public opinion by a hair's breadth. The sensible saying, *Inter arma silent leges*—grossly misconstrued as it is by war governments— has an application of its own to the platform. That is the worst of war: it ostracises, demoralises, brutalises reason.

—John Morley[1]

I.

The First World War is considered by many historians to be the most important event of the twentieth century. The importance assigned to this event recognizes the far-reaching consequences of the Great War. It was, in critical respects, a senseless war that almost wrecked European civilization. One of its consequences was to open the way for unprecedented tyrannies in both Germany and Russia.[2]

Still another consequence, of course, was the Second World War. Renewed fighting was anticipated by some, including by the strong-willed commander in chief of the Allied armies who said, upon hearing of the signing of the Peace Treaty of Versailles, "This is not Peace. It is an Armistice for twenty years."[3] Winston Churchill, in the preface to his 1948 history of the Second World War, observes that this work, together with the history he had written of the First World War, provides "an account of another Thirty Years' War."[4]

There are precedents for thus combining a series of wars. Thucydides, for example, presented the repeated conflicts among the Greeks of his time (in the fifth century B.C.) as all one war. Fundamental differences, primarily between Athens and Sparta, worked themselves out over three decades, with a peace of a few years being little more than an opportunity to prepare for still more war. This led eventually to the decline of the longstanding Greek

3

domination of the peoples bordering the northern Mediterranean and thereafter to the ascendancy of Rome.[5]

We can well wonder whether the series of European wars of the seventeenth century that we know as the Thirty Years' War was recognized by its participants as indeed one war lasting thirty years. That war, for which Germany provided the principal battlefields, ended with the Treaty of Westphalia in 1648.[6] This was three centuries before the end of the Thirty Years' War of the twentieth century.[7]

The Thirty Years' War of the seventeenth century led to the establishment of the modern arrangement of sovereign states in Europe. "The ancient notion of a Roman Catholic empire of Europe, headed spiritually by a pope and temporally by an emperor, was permanently abandoned . . ."[8] The Thirty Years' War of the twentieth century led to the beginning of a repudiation of the European system of sovereign states established three centuries earlier.

One's effort to understand a conflict is likely to be furthered if one can grasp the whole of which that conflict is a part. One is helped to see the underlying causes, as well as the extended consequences, of a conflict if the relevant whole is considered. I say *relevant* because there may be an art to determining how much of the history of an age matters in dealing intelligently with any event. If the whole that one works with is too small, the event is not seen in its origins, context, and consequences; if that whole is too large, it can be impossible to grasp it in its entirety. What truly constitutes a "whole" can be difficult to be sure about. The Cold War, for example, now looks quite different to many people from the way it looked as recently as ten years ago.[9]

Or is it an Eighty Years' War that we have had in the twentieth century, with the Cold War's fifty years intimately related to the thirty years of the First and Second World Wars? The Cold War included not only the struggle between the United States and the Soviet Union, but also the colonial wars of liberation influenced by that struggle.

We may better grasp what happened during the three decades before 1945 by examining what has happened since then. It may be useful to recall how things could look in 1946 to comfortably unsophisticated Americans. This is a perspective that I happen to have reliable access to because of a letter of mine that a ninety-year-old former high school teacher recently returned to me. Dated September 20, 1946, it is a long letter, from Paris, in which I (as a cocky twenty-year-old flying officer from Carterville, Illinois) reported on trips I had been taking to Berlin, Rome, Tripoli, Cairo, and Saudi Arabia. Of particular interest for this discussion is the following excerpt (modified slightly in its style):

One thing that has struck me has been the attitude about Russia among people all over the parts of Africa, Asia, and Europe I've visited. That there will be a war between Russia and an Anglo-American coalition is as certain to them (almost) as the daily sunrise. The question is, "How soon?" Within a year doesn't seem too improbable to many that I've met.

      Egypt left a strong impression upon me. Nowhere have I "felt" such hatred as is directed there by the Arabic peoples against the English—and indirectly against all whites. . . . The Arabs may want the British troops to evacuate Egypt—but their fervor doesn't match that of the various white races there who want them to remain—"For God's sake, they'll slaughter us if the Tommies and you Yanks pull out," was a comment I heard many times (even though we "Yanks" are there only in small numbers).[10]

The "white races" I referred to in 1946 included the Greeks and other Europeans I had gotten to know in Cairo, some very nice people whose merchant families had lived in Egypt for generations. Most of them left Egypt during the following decade because of the takeover by Gamal Abdel Nasser and his followers. I will return to these matters, but I mention in passing that American responses to colonial struggles since 1945 have exhibited a range that extended from an orderly retirement from the Philippines to a nightmare involvement in French Indochina.[11]

II.

      The history of the Thirty Years' War of the twentieth century is in large part the story of my own generation here and abroad. In the United States we had parents who were very much shaped by the First World War, its prelude, and its immediate repercussions. My father, for example, left Greece (never to return) before the First World War, an emigration related to the Balkan wars and to the prospect of an even greater war. My mother (from the same mountain village in Arcadia) was in the last great wave of emigration to the United States from Europe, immediately after the First World War.

      I, as someone born in St. Louis ten years after the Great War began, grew up in Southern Illinois where there were local recollections of that conflict. Every year there would be in Carterville the sale of poppies by the American Legion, with school programs in which a poem would be recited about the Flanders military cemeteries where those flowers grow. Veterans of the war were generally known. Every county had visible reminders of the war in the form of the crippled, including the permanently shell-shocked. Then there were the names on land—on war memorials, and in the names of streets such as Pershing Road in faraway Chicago. There were also the pulp stories about the war to be relished. One favorite of mine was *G-8 and His Battle Aces,* which may have influenced my 1943 decision to enlist in the Army Air Corps when I was seventeen years old.

The First World War *was,* in my childhood, very much the Great War, however vague we may have been about what had really caused it or what it had been all about. We knew that it had had something to do with the killing of someone in a place with the exotic name of Sarajevo, a name that has once again become dreadfully familiar (if not even ominous) to us. We also knew that it was the war to end all wars, a war that would at last "make the world safe for democracy."[12]

III.

It is still uncertain whether it was Germany's fear of encirclement more than her ambition that unleashed the First World War.[13] A study of the diplomatic exchanges and ministerial minutes of July 1914 can be engrossing. These maneuvers and reflections are worthy of a Thucydidean analysis, reaching back decades (if not centuries) to explain what led to impasse and war. In this respect, the beginning of the First World War is more interesting than the beginning of the Second World War. Churchill, for one, regarded the Second World War as having been far easier for people of good will to prevent than the First World War had been. Economic interests (including access to markets) and Germany's desire for colonial expansion were underlying factors leading up to the Great War, but they may not have been paramount in the July 1914 maneuverings. More immediately evident were the not-unnatural strivings of Central European ethnic groups to assert their separate identities. Both Germany and Austria-Hungary were troubled by the nationalistic ferment represented and agitated by Serbia.[14]

It is instructive, in reviewing the record of July 1914, to see what diplomatic protocol required in communications, how gentlemanly everyone could be in personal relations, and what moral standards were implied by the deliberations of that day. It was sad to see much of this destroyed, or at least severely compromised, by the war and thereafter by disillusionment, by the influence of the mass media, and by demagogic governments.

Hidden behind the polished veneers of 1914, however, were passions that "had" to be acted upon in this way—or so it can seem to the reader of the July 1914 record, a record that shows intelligent and polished men determined to have themselves a war.[15] Is there, one can speculate, something suicidal at the core of the West, perhaps even a yearning for collective martyrdom? In the course of the July 1914 crisis, an English official in effect asked (and he would no doubt have been seconded in this stance by his counterparts in other countries), "What is an army for if we don't intend to use it?"[16]

One can see in the July 1914 exchanges what a handful of talented men in a half dozen countries, who mostly knew each other, were able to set in motion. The character of our Thirty Years' War, as it developed, was anticipated by the profound irrationality of its onset, illustrated by such things as the complexity and even inexorable character of the various mobilization plans that were triggered by the Austro-Hungarian ultimatum (of July 23, 1914) to Serbia.[17]

The principal instigators of the war, on all sides, knew far less than they believed themselves to know, however talented and efficient many of them were.[18] The ultimate inefficiency of the efficient—that is, an institutionalized thoughtlessness—may be seen particularly in the complicated German mobilization plan, which included a near-automatic invasion of France, no matter what France happened to be doing or even planning to do at the moment. It is intriguing as well as sobering to realize how things could get out of control because of a high level of organization and coordination. We may even have here an image of the social, political, and spiritual effects of the Industrial Revolution in the West and perhaps worldwide. In a sense, that is, the First World War was two to three centuries in its making.[19]

A remarkable feature of the July 1914 exchanges is that the United States did not seem to figure at that time in European calculations, reminding us of how unpredictable such great movements as wars can be in their long-run consequences. Even England was on the periphery of much that was happening that fateful July.[20]

IV.

The high level of personal nobility and of soldierly self-sacrifice, exhibited on all sides in the course of the First World War, should never be forgotten. Even so, dedication to a cause cannot suffice to justify or explain deeds of this scope. The standard to be brought to bear here is suggested in comments by Ulysses S. Grant upon Robert E. Lee:

> When I went into the house [at Appomattox Court House] I found General Lee. We greeted each other, and after shaking hands took our seats. . . . What General Lee's feelings were I do not know. As he was a man of much dignity, with an impassible face, it was impossible to say whether he felt inwardly glad that the end had finally come,

or felt sad over the result, and was too manly to show it. Whatever his feelings, they were entirely concealed from my observation; but my own feelings, which had been quite jubilant on the receipt of his letter [offering to surrender his army], were sad and depressed. I felt like anything rather than rejoicing at the downfall of a foe who had fought so long and valiantly, and had suffered so much for a cause, though that cause was, I believe, one of the worst for which a people ever fought, and one for which there was the least excuse. I do not question, however, the sincerity of the great mass of those who were opposed to us.[21]

Bad as getting into the First World War was, the way it was fought once it began was even worse, leading as it did to appalling casualties over four years and horrendous repercussions in the decades following. It is here that a latent suicidal element became manifest. One does not have to know much about that war to appreciate the characterization of it, by one of my law school professors (himself an airman of the First World War), as an instance of "governmental insanity."[22]

The spirit of dedication which made the First World War even worse than it might otherwise have been is suggested in the literature of the period. One example is John Buchan's *The Thirty-nine Steps*, an exciting novel published in September 1915.[23] The perfidy of the Germans and the highmindedness of the British were dramatized. Comparable stories were also being read in Germany with the nationalities of the villains and heroes reversed, of course.[24]

The almost incredible folly of the war, with its mad and maddening destruction of the flower of European youth, is suggested most graphically for us perhaps in C. S. Forester's novel, *The General*, published in 1936. Englishmen, we are told by Forester, died far faster during the great offensives on the Western Front than they had in the Great Plague.[25] Symptomatic of how a remarkably devastating war was settled into by the belligerents, with their principled antipathy to a negotiated settlement and with their reliance upon one "final great push" after another, is that the network of trenches on the Western Front could be accurately described at that time as the world's largest metropolis.[26]

Wartime can lead to an engaging heightening of sensibilities. Everything is felt much more intensely than in ordinary times— and this can be exhilarating, allowing those caught up in the heroic adventure, especially the young and the young at heart, to believe that at last they are truly living.[27] Of course, this heightening of spirits can also lead to the most disturbing disillusionment if things should turn out to have been, and to be, far different from what they had seemed.

The highmindedness exhibited during the Great War, at least in its first stages, was carried over from the nineteenth century, when the way European wars were fought was still "primitive" enough to keep losses down, no matter how high the level of dedication. Forester observed in *The General*, "It might have been—though it would be a bold man who would say so—most advantageous for England if the British Army [and the same could be said, I presume to add, for France, Germany, and Russia and their respective armies] had not been quite so full of men of high rank who were so ready for responsibility, so unflinchingly devoted to their duty, so unmoved in the face of difficulties, of such unfaltering courage."[28] Further on in his novel Forester reported:

> The men who were wanted [in command at all levels] were men without fear of responsibility, men of ceaseless energy and of iron will, who could be relied upon to carry out their part in a plan of battle as far as flesh and blood—their own and their men's—would permit. Men without imagination were necessary to execute military policy devoid of imagination, devised by a [commander in chief] without imagination. Anything resembling freakishness or originality was suspect in view of the plan of campaign. Every general desired as subordinates officers who would meticulously obey orders undaunted by difficulties or losses or fears for the future; every general knew what would be expected of him (and approved of it) and took care to have under him generals of whom he could expect the same. When brute force was to be systematically applied only men who could fit into the system without allowance having to be made for them were wanted.[29]

Another way of putting all this is to say that generals were entrusted from the outset with the direction of the war. This meant that truly political skills were not brought to bear upon assessing and guiding how the war would be fought and what the objectives were for which such a price was being paid as was being routinely exacted on both the Eastern and the Western Fronts. How generals tended to see the war is suggested by a prayer which could be attributed to Marshal Foch, that the Allies would smash (and, of course, sacrifice) their way to victory before the arrival of the Americans with whom the French and the English would have to share the glory.[30] The generals were permitted to have their way for so long in large part because of the governmental ineptitude that permitted the war to begin when and where it did. David Lloyd George said in 1920 that "all nations had tumbled into war."[31] Thereafter, it can also be said, they tumbled into the awful way they fought their war.

Again and again, students of the Great War can see confirmation of the ancient teaching that only those human beings who know what they are doing, and who do the right thing, are truly in charge.[32]

V.

No human action can be properly assessed without sensible investigation of what the alternatives were at the time.[33] It remains difficult for us to see what so deeply divided Europeans at the beginning of the war in 1914. Barbara Tuchman begins *The Guns of August* with the funeral, in 1910, of Edward VII, which was held in London and attended by most of the crowned heads of Europe, and at which Kaiser Wilhelm II was the most honored guest.[34] There were many times in the 1930s and the 1940s (and during the Cold War as well) when the enemies of 1914–1918 seemed (despite their intermittent First World War atrocities) much to be preferred to the monsters with whom the world had later to contend.[35]

Did the war "have" to be fought the way it was on the Western Front, the theater of the war that proved most critical to the long-term effects of the war? (The "needs" of the Allies on the Western Front led, for example, to the politically suicidal sacrifices of the Russians on the Eastern Front.) Perhaps the most articulate critic at that time (among the belligerents) of the way the war was being fought in Western Europe was Winston Churchill. A consequence of his criticisms was the Dardanelles operation, which was undertaken in part to relieve the pressure on the Russians. Debates have been heard ever since about whether the British, if better organized and supplied, could have accomplished there what Churchill had intended.[36]

Unfortunately, Churchill's somewhat unconventional approach to war did not seem to extend to questioning the original British decision to go to war, not even after he saw how the war "had" to be fought. Should the ferocity of this war have been foreseen? Some *had* warned that the war would be fierce, perhaps even mortal for European civilization. Churchill himself had been enthusiastic at the outbreak of war.[37] Impressive though this remarkable man was, especially as the voice of freedom during the Second World War, his limitations were all too often those of his age. It has been said of him that at times "his dynamism was too strong for his statesmanship— and his strategy."[38] Perhaps the same can be said as well, if not even more, of other influential European statesmen in 1914.

VI.

I have suggested that the underlying causes of the Great War may have been the outcome, perhaps the natural if not inevitable outcome, of developments in the eighteenth and nineteenth centuries. The serious student of the war must yearn for an understanding of the philosophical opinions and states of mind which led to and permitted, if they did not even require, the Great War.[39]

The nineteenth-century state of mind that bore the bitterest fruit in the First World War is dramatically presented in Alfred Tennyson's most familiar poem from the 1850s, *The Charge of the Light Brigade*. Into the valley of death, we are told, rode the six hundred. Although it was apparent that someone had blundered, this cavalry brigade nevertheless threw itself against the cannon that easily cut it down. Similar deadly heroics could be celebrated in other countries. By the time of the First World War, memories may have faded as to how badly generals could blunder. Contributing to the desire to forget may have been the inspiring American Civil War, which showed the world that great sacrifices could lead to great advances in the cause of humanity.[40]

The Second World War generated similar inspiration among my generation, a legacy that was eventually squandered in Vietnam.[41] But it is prudent to notice, even with respect to the Second World War, that the Czechoslovaks who were abandoned by the Allies in 1938 suffered far less during the war than the Poles for whom the Allies went to war in 1939. It is also prudent to notice that the course of European history in the twentieth century would probably have been far saner than it was if the Belgians had quietly capitulated to German demands in the summer of 1914 and the Germans had taken Paris in the opening months (or even weeks) of the *First* World War, however unseemly all that might have been.

The French Revolution, following upon the Age of Enlightenment, began to play itself out in the Napoleonic Wars and their colonial aftermath throughout the nineteenth century, culminating (in a sense) in the Bolshevik Revolution in Russia. It has been noticed that the first half of the nineteenth century, "like ours, was one of post-war change and uncertainty, for the Napoleonic Wars seemed just as shattering as our world wars have seemed to us."[42] Something was evidently very much wrong in the European soul by the beginning of the twentieth century that did need to be worked out.[43]

In a way, C. S. Forester's First World War general, Herbert Curzon, is a professional albeit perverse descendant of Forester's hero of the Napoleonic Wars, Horatio Hornblower. One critical difference between Curzon and Hornblower is that the latter was an excellent card player. This meant, among other things, that Hornblower knew how to count—and, even more important, what to count. He can be considered in the tradition of Wellington, who always tried to conduct his campaigns with far fewer casualties than others thought justified.[44]

The British did finally come to terms with the French whom Hornblower fought so often, but in such a way as to help make an insecure Germany more fearful than that new nation might otherwise have been. That France and Germany (or Prussia) were regarded by many Europeans as natural enemies may be seen in Karl von Clausewitz's classic on war ends. He sketches plans, in the decade following his service with the Russians against the French during the Napoleonic Wars, for further conflict between his Prussia and France.

One salutary consequence of our Thirty Years' War does seem to have been to make countries such as Britain, France, Germany, and even Russia recognize how much they truly have in common.

VII.

The risks of nuclear war, as well as the 46 million military and civilian deaths caused by the Second World War, have no doubt had a restraining effect since 1945 on the more advanced nations of the world (as distinguished from those desperate, sometimes hate-ridden, peoples who depend upon revolution or its ugly variant, terrorism, to advance their causes). But it is evident from my instructive letter home in 1946 that the restraints that had already developed by then for both the Russians and the Americans, and that would limit the Anglo-American struggle with Russia to wars between proxies, were not yet generally apparent, at least in the West.

Is the Cold War, and hence our Eighty Years' War, really over?[45] It should be remembered that Alexis de Tocqueville predicted, in the 1830s, that the great powers of the twentieth century would be Russia and the United States. I suspect that the full power of the Russian people has yet to be encountered by the world at large. Marxism in Russia, however effective it may have sometimes been in promoting certain salutary social developments in an extremely backward country, probably hobbled the full industrialization and hence empowerment of the Russians.[46] The Soviet Union was never as formidable as it was made out to be during the Cold War.[47] The twenty-first century may yet see the Russians as the primary counterpoise to the United States that Tocqueville anticipated. China, too, will have to be reckoned with, perhaps by the middle of the twenty-first century—but its ancient continental culture and its commercial aptitude are such as to make it less of a threat to the United States than, say, a beleaguered Japan has been at times.[48]

Even so, our most profound problems have never had their sources abroad. The Cold War permitted postponement of a proper consideration of enduring issues among us. The condition of the

American soul—or rather the condition of the souls of Americans—is what has to be addressed properly in the coming decades. What, for example, are the expectations and the illusions that we have now—and what can and should be done about them, and by whom?[49]

Q&A

Q. *Do you believe the war could have been shortened if the U.S. had been more aggressive? If there had been a forceful push by the U.S., Britain, and France earlier than the autumn of 1918, would Germany have quit fighting?*

A. What you said echoes in a way several passages in the E. M. Forster novel where everybody talks about how one more big push would "do it." Churchill at least could see that this approach wasn't going to work, and he tried with the Dardanelles offensive to get around the problem. What he didn't do was step back and say it was all a dreadful mistake from the beginning. That's also a problem. Attempts to negotiate an end to the war were very difficult to make. The risk of being called a traitor was very high. In England, for example, it was difficult for people, even people of standing, to publish, say, letters in the newspapers calling for negotiations to end the war.

Q. *In July 1914, all those involved in diplomatic efforts to defuse the crisis that started at Sarajevo made a genuine effort to avoid war. All save one: Count Leopold von Berchtold, Austria's Foreign Minister, was eager for war and both consciously and unconsciously sabotaged all the efforts to preserve peace. Could you comment on that?*

A. It's hard to think of the Austrians as being the prime instigators, partly because they were the weakest of all the powers involved except Serbia. Unless they had certain assurances from Germany, they weren't going to move. Maybe there was something about the character of Berchtold particularly to be regretted. But it does seem that the Austrians were almost pawns of the Germans. So I just don't think Berchtold was a critical factor. The real decisions were being made by the Germans. The German mobilization plan called for an immediate attack upon France; it was not a matter of getting ready to do something, but actually moving. And this was in response to the Russian mobilization plan which everyone knew to be inefficient. It would take days and days for the Russians to mobilize, and the plan did not end with an automatic attack on Germany or Austria.

There's an element of high comedy in all this. The German mobilization plan is a response to the Russian mobilization which
is a response to Austria-Hungary's ultimatum to Serbia; but
the German plan for an attack upon France not Russia. Something odd going on here.

Q. *If Germany had not invaded Belgium, would Britain have entered the war?*

A. I gather that the English were too much bound to the French to
stay out of the war simply because Belgian neutrality remained
inviolate. The invasion of Belgium certainly affected British
public opinion, but I don't have the impression that it was decisive. But I also have the impression, as many of you probably
do, that Sarajevo ultimately didn't matter, that something else
would have triggered the war. People were itching to fight for
some reason. They were purging themselves of something or
other—certain conditions of the soul.

Comment

Tim Travers: Before August 1914, politicians and soldiers alike
expected a short war. Had they known what would have happened
over the next four and a half years, they might have thought twice
about beginning the war. There's no question about that. So there
was a very strong short-war syndrome operating. I think that should
be factored into any consideration about the causes of the war.

Paul Fussell: I'm fascinated by the whole concept of a thirty years'
war. At one point in the winter of 1944–45, my unit was defending
against the Germans, and the place we stayed to keep alive and
warm was a bunker made of concrete which had served exactly the
same function thirty years before. When you look at the two world
wars as one great event with two major acts, you begin to see that
there is a plot in it, almost a literary plot. The plot is one of humiliation and revenge with both the Japanese and the Germans. The
Japanese were humiliated by the Oriental Exclusion Acts and took
their revenge at Pearl Harbor; and America took its revenge, finally, at Hiroshima for the humiliation visited upon it on December 7. The Germans, of course, were humiliated by the Treaty of
Versailles and pursued their own kind of revenge.

In one of his poems, W. H. Auden wrote a line which I think might
shed light on this whole plot of humiliation and revenge: "Those to
whom evil is done, do evil in return." And that prompts us to wonder how much evil was built into the Treaty of Versailles.

Robert Cowley: Professor Anastaplo's paper makes the valid point that the Armistice truly was an armistice. It was just an intervening period of twenty years, exactly what Marshal Ferdinand Foch had predicted.

It's interesting, too, that what started in 1914 as basically a European civil war turned into something so much bigger. No one knew how much bigger it would get, and that the whole European system would come apart by 1945.

Tim Travers: Before the war started, there were some politicians—Kitchener, for example—who thought it would last a long time. But most people believed it would be a short war. There was considerable precedent for this belief. If you look back at, say, the Franco-Prussian War, you find that the duration of fighting was quite short. With regard to the Great War, it was thought at the beginning that the nations involved did not have the industrial resources to keep it going for very long. It was also thought that, because all nations had very strong offensive plans, offensives would succeed quickly. And so there was a great rush to get into the war because, supposedly, it was going to be over so soon.

Robert Cowley: I would add that, not only did the leaders think it was going to be a short war; the common soldiers did too. I think of the journals of the French historian, Mark Bloch. He was in the Argonne in 1914. He writes that, early on, he and the men in his unit were absolutely convinced it was going to be a short war; then, in October, they were issued great coats. That's when they knew they were not going home before the leaves fell.

Dennis Showalter: Something that's often overlooked is that not only were the fighting forces of Europe symmetrical—that is, they were armed alike, trained alike, and fought alike—but each one was much more conscious of their weaknesses vis-à-vis the others' strengths. Their leaders see, you might say, the beams in their own eyes rather than the motes in their eyes of their enemies. This makes them kind of like a fighter with a glass jaw or a short, skinny guy in a tough bar. If you've got time to throw only one punch, you'd better make it a good one.

Arguably, the BEF was the only force that didn't have that sense of its own weakness. The British army was greatly improved since the Boer War and had a lot of confidence in its capabilities. But we tend to see the war through British eyes, as opposed to looking at it from the perspective of the French, Germans, Russians, and Austrians. And these states were all too aware of their own weaknesses relative to the strength of their potential enemies.

Audience Member: I've always been of the opinion that Britain and Germany enjoyed fairly good relations in the years preceding the war. This may have had some influence on the thinking of German military planners, leading them to believe that Britain might stay out of the fighting just long enough for the German army to deliver a knockout blow against France. It would also have occurred to them that Britain might remain on the sidelines indefinitely, which would mean that the greatest weapons system the world had ever known—the Royal Navy—would not be used to starve Germany into submission.

Dennis Showalter: I don't believe the Germans had a grand design for hegemony. The Germans wanted to be the primary power on the continent, but there's a great difference between being a primary power and a hegemon. I think that Britain and Germany tried to avoid war; for example, they made an effort to establish a concert of Europe for the Balkans between 1912 and 1914 and couldn't do it in part because the British really weren't that concerned about the possibility of a general European war.

The Germans, I think, did hope that the British would remain neutral in the event of such a war. It was, after all, France and Russia that posed the major threat to the British Empire. And as for the primary German threat—the German navy—it was about the only adversary the British were convinced they could beat. The Royal Navy never had much serious doubt that they could take the Germans anytime, anywhere. Indeed, there's some indication in the archives that the salty types in particular welcomed the challenge to fight the German navy. So the Germans did hope for British neutrality, because they do not see themselves as fighting a war for hegemony. To some degree I think the German government saw itself as doing the job the British wouldn't do, of maintaining stability and order in Europe.

Robert Cowley: We have overlooked how much the ordinary European wanted to go to war. I think of George Steiner in his book *Bluebeard's Castle* comparing Europe in 1914 to a great pressure cooker that was about to explode. And I remember Michael Howard's point that the politicians were afraid of what would happen to them if they *didn't* go to war. They were afraid they'd be swept out of office.

PART 2

ARCHITECTURES OF WAR

From Verdun to the Maginot Line
Gerard J. Demaison

The purpose of this presentation is to explain how the events that took place at Verdun in 1916 influenced the conception, building, and use of the Maginot Line twenty-four years later. This is in keeping with an overriding theme of this conference, namely that the two world wars are best understood as two phases of a single "Thirty Years' War."

The Battle of Verdun lasted eleven months, from February 21 to December 18, 1916. Although it was later dubbed the longest and most intense artillery battle of all time, the actual size of the Verdun battlefield is surprisingly small, measuring on average only twenty-two kilometers long by six kilometers wide.

The town of Verdun was the hub of the so-called *Region Fortiflee de Verdun,* or Verdun Fortified Region, extending from Avocourt in the west to Saint-Mihiel in the southeast. Encircling the town were three concentric rings of forts built from the 1880s right up to the eve of the war, the best-armed and protected forts being situated in the outer ring, on the right bank of the Meuse facing northeast. This positioning was predicated on the expectation that an attack on the Fortified Region would come from the east, but such was not the way the battle initially unfolded. Instead, the German army attacked from the north on a six-mile front between Brabant and Ornes, advancing south through the thickly wooded hills and ravines that typified the region. The Germans chose the northerly approach for several reasons, one being that the woods and ravines could mask their movement preparatory to the battle. The northerly approach was also chosen because the French army's most numerous artillery piece, the 75mm field gun, fired its shells in a flat trajectory that could not sweep the hidden slopes and ravines beyond the hill crests where German forces were massing. Thus the German High Command was able to accumulate unhindered and largely undetected large numbers of troops, heavy artillery, and munitions in the army's staging areas.

Hindsight shows us that the German offensive at Verdun was inefficient, as demonstrated by the ratio of terrain captured to the duration of the battle, and to the number of casualties suffered and artillery shells fired. When the offensive finally ground to a halt in July 1916, it had advanced a mere eight kilometers (five miles) beyond its starting point, a paltry gain made at the cost of

340,000 casualties (of which 119,000, or 35 percent, were dead or missing in action), the expenditure of some 27 million artillery shells, and the creation of lasting morale problems in the ranks of the German army. The French defensive effort, followed by a counteroffensive which won back most of the battlefield in late 1916, was equally inefficient, in that it also achieved small territorial gains in exchange for 378,000 casualties (also with 35 percent, or 132,000, listed as dead or missing), and the expenditure of some 23 million artillery shells. Protracted artillery battles of this type and scale, occurring over such a limited area, would be unthinkable today because of aviation, which would disrupt logistic and supply efforts and make permanent heavy artillery positions untenable.

Three Forts

I should now like to turn to a brief discussion of the Verdun forts, in particular the three large forts facing north and east on the right bank of the Meuse—Douaumont, Vaux, and Moulainville. As we shall see, the performance of those three forts in 1916 was to have a tremendous impact on the designing of the Maginot Line. They were Verdun's sturdiest forts, having received, just before the war began, added protection in the form of two layers of reinforced concrete separated by a three-meter (nine-foot) layer of sand. (The other forts to the west and south of Verdun were obsolete structures built of stone masonry; disarmed in 1915, they served primarily as shelters and storage depots.) This triple-layer configuration was extremely resistant to large-caliber shells, so much so that these three forts were able to withstand eleven months of intense bombardment by heavy artillery and still remain operational at the end of the battle. (In contrast, the Belgian forts around Liège, which lacked such protection, were swiftly reduced in August 1914 by German siege guns.) It was the ability of these three forts to absorb so much punishment that proved to have a great influence on the design and construction of the Maginot Line. More deleterious to the future defense of France, however, was the effect this would have on the thinking of French military leaders, who would become convinced that a static defense system anchored on a number of heavily armored forts remained the most viable means of protecting the country from another German invasion.

A closer look at what happened to those three Verdun forts goes a long way toward explaining why the Maginot Line seemed, on the face of it, to be such a good idea. Fort Douaumont, for example, was hit by a total of 120,000 shells, including 1,200 shells of a caliber larger than 305 millimeters (twelve inches). At the battle's outset, of course, the fort was a target for German guns, but when the Germans captured Douaumont on February 25, 1916, and incorporated it into their line, it was subjected to seven months of incessant bombardment from French heavy batteries as well. When in October 1916 the French undertook to recapture the fort from the Germans, they hammered Douaumont with no less than ninety-two 400mm (16-inch) shells fired by a pair of railway guns located at Baleycourt, to the west of Verdun. The damage those two guns inflicted fell well below French expectations. Amazingly, despite the number of hits scored by both French and German guns, only five of Fort Douaumont's thirty casemates suffered damage sufficient to warrant their evacuation, and only three were actually pierced by shells. The lower levels of the fort were never penetrated. Neither of the fort's two artillery turrets (155mm and 75mm) received direct hits. An aerial view of Fort Douaumont today with its unscarred 155mm turret provides graphic evidence of the ineffectiveness of artillery bombardment. The same view reveals numerous craters in the ground around the fort, still in existence after almost eighty years, made by the French 400mm shells, each of which weighed about a ton and were packed with four hundred pounds of explosive. But the craters represent only superficial damage which left the interior of the fort as well as the gun turrets largely unscathed.

Fort Moulainville, situated south and a little east of Fort Douaumont and Fort Vaux, became the target of choice for two of the thirteen so-called Gamma Guns the Germans had in reserve. Better known as "Big Berthas" *(Dicke Berthas)*, these giant howitzers fired a 420mm (16.5-inch) shell. Previously used to smash the Belgian forts in August 1914, they scored 339 hits on Fort Moulainville (which is still the world record for most number of hits on a single military target by guns of that size) but nevertheless failed to put the fort out of action. The fort's entrance was demolished, the concrete exterior was severely scalloped by shell explosions, and three casemates were destroyed; but none of the turrets received direct hits, and although one of the turrets was immobilized by a glancing hit, the largest turret, housing a 155mm gun, continued to function until the end of the war. It is still standing today in its original condition, although it is heavily oxidized.

Fort Vaux also took a terrific pounding, as evidenced by its severely pockmarked surface, with each mark representing no fewer than three hits. The Germans captured the fort on June 7, 1916, and the French retook it four months later, in October. It was the only fort at Verdun to receive a direct hit on a turret, in this instance one housing a 75mm gun. The hit was scored on

February 26, 1915, by a German 305mm howitzer called a "Beta Gun." At the time the Germans were firing Beta Guns to test their effectiveness against the French forts when, by a miracle of luck, they managed to destroy Vaux's 75mm turret with just a few shots. (The remains of the shattered turret are still visible today on the fort's superstructure.) But this was an exceptional occurrence: the turret was only twenty feet wide, and the odds of scoring another lucky hit on such a small target from a distance of five miles (the range at which the Beta Guns were firing) were virtually nil, as evidenced by the Germans' failure to repeat their accomplishment.

The Role of the Forts

What was the role of the forts in the Battle of Verdun? The facts are as follows: the Germans captured Douaumont on February 25, 1916, just three days after launching their initial assault. So if Douaumont had played any important part in the battle, it would have done so as a German fort; yet it proved of little use to the attackers in the subsequent fighting, serving only as a shelter for troops and as a logistical base. The Germans captured Vaux later in the battle, on June 7, and it too proved of limited utility to them.

(The French recaptured Vaux on November 2, and it is interesting to note they did so without meeting any opposition, the intensity of their preliminary bombardment having forced the Germans to abandon the fort earlier that same day. Therefore the artillery bombardment against Vaux did succeed to the extent that it drove the Germans out. Even so, however, the fort, though its surfaces were thoroughly scarred by shell hits, remained essentially intact below ground. The survivability of Vaux's underground section made a strong impression on the French general staff, particularly with regard to the development of the Maginot Line.)

Now, in early March, the Germans had launched a series of flanking attacks on the left bank of the Meuse, in an area which encompassed the prominent ridges of Mort Homme and Hill 304. The stone masonry forts that were supposed to cover that approach to Verdun were incapable of withstanding the big-gun bombardments that had been directed against their right-bank counterparts. This failing was known early on to French military leaders, who in 1915 ordered the forts stripped of their guns so that the weapons could be put to better use elsewhere. As it happened, the Germans captured the crest lines of both Mort Homme and Hill 304 in May, but failed to advance any farther and achieve a breakthrough. Ultimately their southward progress was stopped not by the disarmed forts, but by some four hundred mobile artillery pieces, most of them 75s, which fired without letup and devastated German infantry as it attempted to push south across the open ground beyond the crest lines.

Official French military archives make clear that it was mobile artillery outside the forts, particularly the 75mm batteries which were always present in large numbers, that stopped the German onslaught at Verdun, and not the forts themselves. Instead of serving as strongpoints which provided artillery fire, the Verdun forts were for the most part used as shelters, observation posts, munition depots, infirmaries (the Germans used Douaumont for this purpose), or as collection stations where the French wounded were housed until nightfall, when they were transported down into the town of Verdun itself.

Statistical evidence of the minor role played by the Verdun forts is revealed in the archival record of the battle, as condensed in a seventeen-hundred-page doctoral thesis on the subject by Dr. Alain Denizot, who is regarded as the greatest modern expert on the history of the Verdun battle. According to the archives and Denizot's interpretation of the data therein, the forts had a combined total of only fourteen 155mm (six-inch) turreted guns in operation when the battle began in February 1916, and only seven such guns in operation from June through December of that year. Furthermore, throughout the battle, the same forts had no more than sixteen turreted 75mm guns in operation.

In all, therefore, the Verdun forts had about twenty-three turreted guns actively participating in the battle—a figure that is dwarfed by the mass of mobile artillery deployed by the French army in the Verdun sector, which at any given time during the fighting added up to well over fifteen hundred guns of all calibers.

By far the most effective antipersonnel gun in the French arsenal was the Model 1897 field gun, the so-called French 75. Only 312 such guns were in place at Verdun before the Germans attacked, but by June 1916, almost 1,200 were involved in the battle. By December the number of 75s at Verdun was down to just over one thousand. In August 1917, when Marshal Henri-Philippe Pétain launched the final French counteroffensive at Verdun, there were thirteen hundred 75s lined up on the battlefield. A battery of four 75s could fire eight hundred rounds in ten minutes, and eight thousand rounds in two hours! They fired shrapnel shells, each containing 350 lead balls, which were time-fused to burst in the air at the desired range, thus killing men crouching in shell holes and entrenchments as well as those caught out in the open. On the cratered and shell-torn Verdun battlefield, this airburst capability made the 75s much more effective than machine guns as antipersonnel weapons.

The French military archives also reveal that, between February 21 and September 30, 1916, the French fired over 23 million shells of all sizes in the Verdun sector. Of this number, the 75s account for fully 16 million rounds, or 71 percent, of the total; mobile, large-caliber, long-range guns, 22 percent, or 5.6 million; and the shorter-range guns—i.e., large-caliber mortars and howitzers—only 6 percent, or 1.4 million. In stunning contrast to these figures, ammunition consumption by the fixed fortress guns was insignificant: the 155mm turret at Fort Moulainville, for instance, fired only three thousand shells in the same period. (Note that Denizot was unable to locate enough data to compile a *detailed* tally of shell consumption from October through December.) Furthermore, it is estimated that all the turreted guns in the forts fired a combined total of only 36,000 shells, out of a total of over 25 million shells fired in 1916 by the French in the Verdun area. Thus, the archives provide irrefutable proof, based on shell consumption data, that the fixed guns in the forts had a negligible effect on the outcome of the Battle of Verdun. It was French mobile artillery, and particularly the 75mm batteries, that poured out over 95 percent of the steel, lead, and explosives expended in the battle, and thus inflicted the most damage on the enemy, thereby stopping the German offensive.

The Maginot Line

The Maginot Line was originally conceived in 1919 in response to Georges Clemenceau's stated concern over the potential for future German aggression against France. Marshal Pétain, in association with his followers in higher military circles, was instrumental in devising the strategic and tactical aims of the Maginot Line and in advising on its location and the technology that went into it. The French minister of finances in the 1920s, Paul Painlevé, was also a staunch supporter of the Maginot Line concept, but it is Pétain who, by virtue of his technical input and enthusiasm for the project, deserves to be called the "father" of the Maginot Line.

The conception of the Maginot Line reflected the defensive mentality of its proponents, especially Pétain. The latter was a highly professional military organizer and leader, a man sincerely respectful of his soldiers' lives, and a superb tactician. More than anyone else, he was responsible for the French victory at Verdun; moreover, he saved the French army from internal collapse during the mutinies in the spring of 1917. But, unfortunately for France, Pétain was neither a strategist of genius nor a visionary. In this he was not alone—in the 1920s, a blind conservatism with regard to strategy was a characteristic shared by the high commands of France's wartime allies. In particular, though, Pétain remained stuck in 1918 insofar as he continued to be an advocate of the defensive mode of thinking and its corollary, trench warfare. He viewed the tank as nothing more than a wire-crusher and machine gun-destroyer, and the airplane as, essentially, an observation platform for artillery spotting. He could not grasp the technological promise of mobile weapons for delivering massive amounts of firepower, much less imagine how such weapons might be employed in future conflicts. Instead, he chose to stay with what he knew and understood, namely the static fortress technologies and their associated weaponry which had been conceived in the late nineteenth century.

Built between 1929 and 1936, the Maginot Line was named after André Maginot, the French minister of war in 1930 and a decorated hero who had lost much of his mobility because of severe leg wounds sustained at Verdun in 1915. It was Maginot who secured funding for the line. He did not live to see its completion, however; always in poor health since the war, he died in 1932 at age fifty-five after a brief illness.

Upon completion, the Maginot Line protected some 150 kilometers of France's eastern frontier between the Belgian border and the Rhine. In the critical area between Montmédy and the Rhine on the northeast frontier with Germany, the line had fifty-eight forts equipped with a combined total of 152 retractable armored artillery turrets. The forts, which varied in size, were divided into two categories: thirty-five small forts (petit-ouvrages) with garrisons of 100–150 men, and twenty-two large forts (gros-ouvrages) with garrisons of 500–1,200 men. There were no large forts in the so-called Sarre Gap, which was to be defended by flooding; nor were there any large forts along the west bank of the Rhine River, where the defenses were limited to casemates and infantry bunkers which were built after 1936 and were totally inadequate for stopping a large-scale offensive.

The line did not extend west between the Belgian border and the English Channel because French politicians had deluded themselves into thinking that Belgium would remain neutral in any future conflict between France and Germany. The Belgians were no less deluded in this respect. They very much wanted to remain neutral and had signed a treaty with France which bound them to do so. Both parties to the signing believed the Germans would respect Belgian neutrality and thus avoid a repeat of 1914, when Germany's invasion of Belgium had provoked a declaration of war from Britain. Of course, as events were to demonstrate, Belgian neutrality was no more a deterrent to a German invasion in 1940 than it was in 1914. Georges Clemenceau, leader of the French government during much of the First World War, had predicted that this would be the case in the early 1920s. Told that France was once again counting on Belgian neutrality to keep the Germans out, the former premier (he was then in retirement) said, "You are mad. They're going to do it again." He was right; but, unfortunately for France, he was virtually alone in this belief.

In fairness to its proponents, it should be noted that the Maginot Line was not intended to contain a German invasion indefinitely. Rather, it was conceived as a barrier against a surprise attack which would hold up the enemy long enough to allow France to mobilize its forces and prepare for a counterstroke that would repel the invaders. It was thought that the Maginot Line could stop the enemy for as long as six months, a reasonable assumption given that the Germans were held in check at Verdun for the same length of time before being pushed back to their starting point.

The Maginot Line forts were located to the rear of the defended zone, behind a line of bunkers. The latter were essentially identical to the bunkers of the First World War except that they were now protected by antitank obstacles made of train rails, and many were armed with 25mm and 47mm antitank guns. The large forts were positioned to cover each other with artillery, so that enemy troops who gained a foothold on the roof of a fort could be eliminated by the guns of the fort's neighbors.

Typically, the heavy weapons of the large forts were situated in artillery blocks, which were distanced according to calculations dealing with the probabilities of sixteen-inch artillery fire and linked by tunnels to ammunition magazines and underground barracks. Each fort was quite self-sufficient, being totally powered by electricity—a significant improvement over the Verdun forts—and containing an independent water supply in the form of an artesian well, forced-air ventilation with filters that protected against toxic gas, and a sewerage system leading to the outside. Main armament was conceptually similar to that of the old Verdun forts insofar as it consisted chiefly of antipersonnel artillery (75mm guns and 135mm howitzers) mounted in retractable steel turrets with all-around fields of fire. The Maginot Line's turrets, however, were each equipped with two guns on paired mountings, whereas most of the Verdun turrets had only one 75mm or 155mm gun. In addition, the Maginot Line steel turrets were powered by electricity and hydraulics rather than by hand and, being newer, had superior optical systems for sighting.

The Maginot Line forts were also armed with numerous 75mm non-turreted guns, positioned to fire sideways from emplacements in flanking casemates. These casemates were identical to the "*Casemates de Bourges*" one can still observe and visit today in some of the Verdun forts, such as Froideterre and Douaumont.

In summary, the Maginot Line turrets and flanking casemates in the large forts were products of the Verdun experience, in that they were straightforward copies, albeit with substantial technical improvements, of their predecessors at Verdun.

In peacetime the Maginot Line forts were connected to the national power grid, purchasing electricity from the utility company like any civilian customer. In time of war, however, they were to produce electricity with their own self-contained power plants equipped with diesel engines—actually submarine engines—and transformers. Generation capacity ranged from between four hundred and one thousand kilowatt hours, depending on the size of the fort and its respective power plants. In addition to the gun turrets and ventilation systems, the power plants supplied the electricity needed to run little trains that linked the artillery blocks with the magazines and barracks. With their power plants and underground railways and multiple galleries, each large fort was, in effect, a miniature city.

Conclusion

Ultimately, all this expensive technology was of no avail against the German army of 1940. The Battle of Verdun had taught the German high command that frontal assault against a fortified position was not an efficient way to wage war. The Germans had learned the hard way that mobility combined with firepower was the key to success, and in applying this principle against the Maginot Line—using motorized units to outflank the French fortifications—they reinvented Napoleonic concepts of maneuver. Ironically, the French high command seemed to have forgotten those concepts: they were immobilized, both literally and figuratively, by the Maginot Line and the thinking that went into it. The fact that the line had not been built to cover the wooded hills of the Ardennes region on the Belgian border was the result not only of incorrect assumptions about Belgian neutrality, but also of the equally erroneous conviction held by French strategists—notably Pétain—that the Germans could not penetrate the region in force.

This conviction was not without foundation in the 1920s, when the Maginot Line was conceived—the tanks of that era were really incapable of negotiating the rough terrain of the Ardennes, and without tanks the prospects for a successful German offensive were virtually nil. By 1940, however, tank technology had improved to the extent where the Ardennes posed no obstacle to their passage. And so, as is well known, in May 1940 German panzer divisions got through the Ardennes with ease and, upon crossing the Meuse at Sedan, commenced an enveloping movement toward the English Channel that bypassed the Maginot Line at its northern terminus and led swiftly to the defeat of the bulk of the French and British field armies. Following the British evacuation at Dunkirk, the Germans turned south and came in behind the Maginot Line to finish off what remained of the opposition. It was only then that the Germans directly assaulted the line, mainly for the propaganda benefits to be gained by the capture of some of the forts. They brought up heavy artillery for the job but, predictably, as in 1916, failed to crack any of the forts on their target list. A venerable 420mm Skoda mortar left over from the First World War was used to bombard Forts Schoenenbourg and Four-à-Chaux, near Wissembourg, with disappointing results. Stuka dive bombers subsequently attacked the same forts with one thousand-pound bombs but failed to hit any of the gun turrets. More success was achieved, and much more damage inflicted, by firing 88mm flak guns against the highly visible, non-retracting observation bells and the thinly protected rear entrances of some of the forts. In the end, only one fort—La Ferté—fell to frontal assault, and it was a small one, located at the extreme left of the line on the Belgian border. The rest of the Maginot Line surrendered virtually intact after the armistice of June 22, having fought the campaign to an honorable conclusion but—and this is the point—without in any way affecting its outcome.

In conclusion, the Maginot Line was conceived as an analog to the Verdun experience, but it was a false analog based on the premise that the ability of Douaumont, Vaux, and Moulainville to withstand heavy shelling had been the critical factor that blocked the German onslaught. In other words, the Maginot Line was conceived without taking into account the fact that massed French mobile artillery, rather than the few gun turrets in the forts, had played the key role in defending Verdun. Moreover, there can be no doubt that the building of the Maginot Line was the result of a complete misperception by French military leaders of the potential impact of motorized warfare on the usefulness of fixed fortifications. (Again, it should be noted that France's former allies were no more astute in this regard; the British general staff, for instance, was just as resistant as the French top brass to the novel ideas of mobile, motorized warfare proposed by Basil Liddell Hart and Colonel Charles de Gaulle in the early 1930s.) Finally, the "Wall of France" (as the Maginot Line was known), besides creating a false sense of security attributable to the mistaken belief in the efficacy of fixed fortifications, was not cost effective. The Maginot Line cost five billion French francs in the 1930s. The return on the investment was a mere six hundred guns (including the smaller antitank guns in isolated forward bunkers) which were frozen in concrete. This meant that fewer guns were expected to cover 120 kilometers of front than were employed to stop the Germans along Verdun's 22-kilometer front in 1916. For the same amount of money, France could have purchased at least twenty thousand tanks, instead of making do in 1940 with four thousand machines of varying types and often negligible quality. Those twenty thousand tanks would have provided the mobile firepower needed to fight and win the kind of war the Germans were prepared to wage. One could even make the case that the Wehrmacht, which possessed only forty-five hundred first-line tanks in 1940, might never have attacked France if the latter's tank force was as large as it could have been in the absence of the Maginot Line.

I would like to close on a more colorful note concerning Fort Douaumont. Today the physical remains of the largest and most famous of the Verdun forts has a strong nostalgic appeal based on the importance of the Battle of Verdun to the subsequent history of Europe and the Western world. Many familiar historical figures passed through its underground corridors between 1914 and 1918, including Charles de Gaulle, Erwin Rommel, and other famous Allied politicians and military leaders of World War I. Verdun was to that war what Stalingrad was to the Second World War: a turning point where the tide of German conquest was decisively halted, casting doubt on notions of German invincibility. As I explained earlier, however, Fort Douaumont itself played only a minor tactical role in the Battle of Verdun. Its real significance lies in the enormous influence it had on the conception and construction of a defense system that was to a large degree responsible for the collapse of the French army, and France itself, in 1940. In the final analysis, France's downfall happened because grave errors of judgment were made by aging military leaders whose concepts were not sufficiently scrutinized and challenged by the civilian power structure and the media. Colonel Charles de Gaulle, in the 1930s, was the only French military voice to advocate, in his book *Vers une Armee de Metier*, the wholesale transformation of the French army into a mobile, armored, motorized force.

References

Denizot, Alain 1990. Verdun 1914–1918. *These pour le Doctorat d'Etat es-Lettres et Sciences Humaines*, under the direction of Prof. G. Pedroncini (Sorbonne), Universite Paris I.

Hohnadel, Alain, and Michel Truttman 1988. *Guide de la Ligne Maginot*. Editions Heimdal.

Q&A

Q. Were the Maginot forts intentionally left weak at the rear?

A. No. The 360mm turrets could traverse and defend the back of the forts as well. The rear entrances were also protected by other guns.

Q. Why were the German siege guns so effective against the forts at Liège in 1914 but not at Verdun?

A. At Verdun, the Germans had to contend with the special rein-forced, double-layer, concrete armor that was placed on Forts Douaumont, Moulainville, and Vaux between 1900 and 1913. The Belgian forts did not have this kind of protection, which was pretty tough. Also, the Belgian forts had bad luck—a Big Bertha shell went right down into one of the magazines.

Incidentally, the experience of the Belgian forts led Joffre to remove most of the guns and troops from the forts at Verdun. When the Germans captured Douaumont, it was garrisoned by only twenty-three men. The forts were given up for dead be-cause of what happened at Liège.

Q. Were the Maginot forts used as unemployment relief during the Depression to make jobs for French workers?

A. The answer is yes, but it was a political smokescreen, because a good half of the workers on the Maginot Line were foreigners, including Germans.

Q. Do you think Marshal Pétain will ever be buried at Verdun?

A. A very timely last question. I think eventually he will be buried at Verdun, but it will take another fifty years before this takes place. At least two generations must come and go before the French can put behind them the memory of his noxious deeds in the Second World War—a prerequisite to interment at Verdun.

Comment

Robert Cowley: Gerard Demaison's account of the Verdun and Maginot forts provides a perfect example of what happens in war when you don't improvise, when you simply take something that is large and ineffective and make it larger and more ineffective. I've been lucky enough to go to one of those Maginot forts, Hackenberg. Its size and complexity is breathtaking—it's this empty megastructure inside a mountain, a city in miniature.

Edward Coffman: Professor Demaison's paper on Verdun and the Maginot Line certainly speaks to the Thirty Years' War thesis. It also speaks to something else. In the military, there's a great emphasis on studying history for the lessons to be learned. But what can you learn from the past? Here's an example of learning the wrong lessons, just picking out parts of the past and learning them very well, doing a great deal more of the same thing—which was wrong to begin with.

Paul Fussell: One thing I learned from Gerard Demaison's wonderful performance on Verdun and the Maginot Line was the amazing resistance to artillery fire of these concrete works, especially those built on the sandwich principle with a layer of sand or earth between two immense concrete elements. What emerges from that understanding is a new appreciation of the weakness of artillery and its inability, despite publicity to the contrary, to do certain things. One can't escape the fleeting suspicion that weapons that cost a great deal of money and are heavy and difficult to manufacture, like airplanes and artillery pieces, get more credit for doing important things in war than weapons that are cheaper—human beings, pistols, bayonets, grenades—which aren't technologically fascinating, which don't have M and numbers, and that sort of thing. I wonder if anybody shares this interest in the kind of publicity which technological implements of war gather to themselves and the way publicity may deform our understanding of what actually happens in war.

Audience Member: But weren't the majority of First World War casualties caused by artillery fire?

Paul Fussell: Yes, I suppose they were.

Audience Member: They were 70 percent or more.

Audience Member: The majority of casualties in all wars since and including the Civil War, I believe, have been caused by artillery. That's certainly the case in World War I and World War II as well. If you leave out the nuclear weapon, and I think even counting that, you still have more casualties caused by artillery.

Audience Member: Gerard Demaison told us that the French and Germans fired a combined total of about 50 million shells which inflicted over seven hundred thousand casualties. That means it took an average of seventy or seventy-one shells to produce one casualty. It seems like it would almost be cheaper to take the money it cost to manufacture the shells and guns to bribe the other side to quit fighting.

Robert Cowley: I would think the classic example of overestimating the worth of a large weapon is the battleship. There's a wonderful book that came out several years ago on how inefficient the battleship is. It talks about the cult of the battleship, and how battleship people kept supporting these behemoths even though they weren't very effective. In World War II it worked to our advantage that all those battleships got sunk at Pearl Harbor. As a result we had to rely on something that worked; namely, the aircraft carrier.

Donald Abenheim: Well, our battleships were effective at doing something that they weren't created for. Maybe they didn't sink other battleships the way some people predicted, but they proved very effective in providing fire support for amphibious operations. Similarly, the B-52 was designed to drop hydrogen bombs on the Soviet Union; but in the Vietnam War and the Gulf War they were used for close air support. The unintended consequences of weapons are constant.

Audience Member: On the subject of the effectiveness of large, sophisticated weapons—without their big siege guns, the Germans could not have cracked the Belgian forts as soon as they did. At Verdun, the German guns literally blew away many of the defenders in the initial assault. And when the French turned their big guns on the German-occupied forts . . . I think a shell went into the bakery of one of the forts and exploded, and the Germans decided, "We can't stay here any longer." So they left.

I would also mention a large white elephant called the aircraft carrier. In the mid-1960s, I believe, the British, in the interests of economy, decommissioned their only remaining large carriers to save money. In my opinion, if they had kept the carriers in service, the Falklands War would not have occurred. And now the British are stuck down there with a garrison of two or three thousand troops. If economics were the main consideration, some of the large "white elephants" would in the long run be more cost effective than maintaining a large garrison on the island.

Audience Member: In World War II, the Germans devised a gun with a caliber of one meter. Its purpose was to penetrate and destroy the nerve centers of the Maginot Line. It was not ready in 1940. The Germans used it at the forts at Sebastopol, where one of its shells reached a Russian powder magazine at an incredible depth and blew it out.

Audience Member: What was the strategic importance of the forts at Verdun?

Gerard Demaison: The strategic importance of those forts after the Gamma Guns crushed the Belgian forts was thought to be nil. Joffre actually ordered the Verdun forts to be disarmed, and the guns in the flanking casements were removed. The guns in the turrets were not moved out because it was too difficult to do so.

Audience Member: Vis-à-vis the Eastern Front, many of you are familiar with Norman Stone's book *The Eastern Front* in which he makes an excellent case for the obsolescence and the "white elephant" character of the forts in that theater. He discusses the ring of forts around the Warsaw and the great effort in arming them, and concludes that their value was precisely zero. So the notion that the forts were strategically valueless was applicable to the Eastern Front as well as the Western Front.

Donald Abenheim: Speaking of strategy . . . the forts that had stood in the German invasion path in the Franco-Prussian War were upgraded after 1871, thus rendering impracticable the strategic-operational concepts the Germans had formulated for that conflict. The fortifications forced you to go someplace else, and that someplace else, of course, became the Schlieffen Plan. So the forts at Verdun were effective in the sense that, before 1914, they made the Germans think they couldn't win by going in that direction.

Gerard Demaison: Before the war, the forts were definitely a strategic threat. But not after the Gamma Gun was used. So we're both right.

Edward Coffman: I think what we're dealing with here is a classic example of a deterrent that might work for five years, ten years, or fifteen years, but twenty years down the pike is obsolete and won't work.

Robert Cowley: I think I should make one other point . . . that in 1914 the Germans came very close to taking those forts from the rear. They didn't because of the Battle of the Marne, but it was a very near thing.

34

An observation cupola on the Maginot Line shows the devastating effects of 88mm flak shells fired at point-blank range.

Gerard Demaison

Retractable twin-75mm turret on Block 8 of the Maginot Line's Fort Simserhof.

Gerard Demaison

155mm turret at Fort Douaumont, in retracted position.

Gerard Demaison

Fort Douaumont observation post (foreground) and machine-gun cupola.

Gerard Demaison

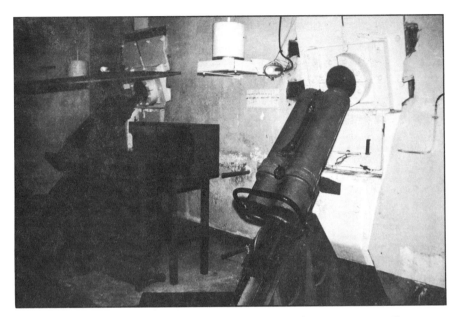

A pair of breech-loading 81mm mortars in the casemate of a *gros ouvrage* on the Maginot Line.

Gerard Demaison

German artillery men prepare to fire a 420mm "Big Bertha" howitzer at Verdun.

Gerard Demaison

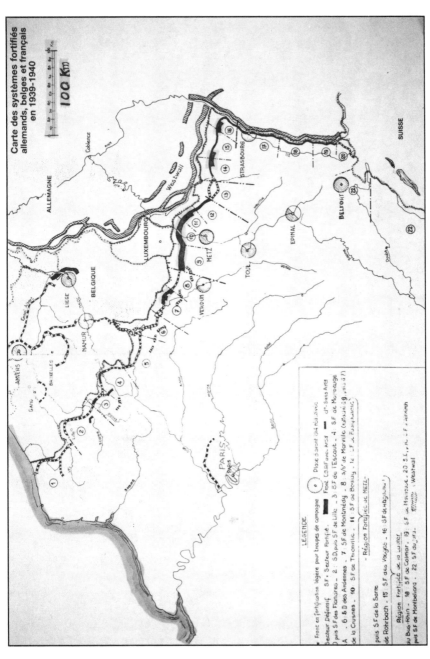

Map of the Maginot Line.

Gerard Demaison

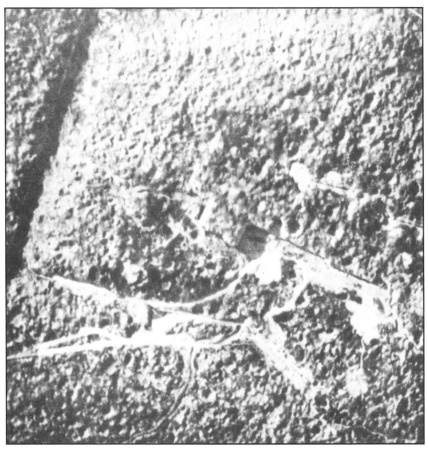

Aerial view of Fort Douaumont in 1918, after two years of shelling.

Gerard Demaison

Entrance to Fort Moulainville in 1918, with twin-75mm turret in foreground.

Gerard Demaison

Schematic of a typical Maginot Line *gros ouvrage*.

Gerard Demaison

The German Coastal Defenses in Flanders, 1914–1918
Aleks A. M. Deseyne

1. The German Naval Corps in Flanders

Formally constituted on August 23, 1914—just three weeks after the invasion of Belgium—the German Naval Corps (*Marinekorps*) was the creation of the German secretary of state, Grand Admiral Alfred von Tirpitz, who envisioned using it for the occupation of the Belgian coast in order to make the best possible use of German navy reserves on the Western Front. Previously these troops had contributed little to the war effort: most of those trained for sea duty were left ashore with nothing to do, there being neither space nor use for them aboard the ships of the German fleet; while the reservists who manned the coastal batteries on the North Sea and Baltic Sea were idled by the persistent lack of any Allied naval activity in their respective areas. There was, nevertheless, strong opposition to the idea of a naval corps, but von Tirpitz got his way and, on August 29, the high command agreed to the raising of the corps' first formation, to be designated the 1st Naval Division. Commanded by Admiral Ludwig von Schröder, the division consisted of nearly twenty thousand men of uneven quality: there were two naval infantry regiments raised from *Seebataillonen*, composed of elite troops; but there were also five *Matrosen Regimenten*, which were used for guard duty as they were usually composed of insufficiently trained troops, for the most part sailors who had never seen any infantry service. The naval artillery men, of course, were already familiar with the naval guns that were to be installed on the Belgian coast.

The first contingent of the division to go to the Western Front departed Wilhelmshaven on August 31, 1914. In early September the entire division was transferred to Brussels for a brief round of training. The first action involving the division took place on September 9 on the Dijle canal against Belgian forces. Additionally, division troops participated in the siege of Antwerp in the Walem sector as part of General von Beseler's III Reserve Corps, and were among the German forces that entered the city on October 11.

On October 21 the 1st Naval Division occupied Bruges, Zeebrugge, and Ostend, and Admiral von Schröder's headquarters was established at Bruges. On November 15 the division was united

40

with the recently organized 2nd Naval Division and the two became the Naval Corps under von Schröder's overall command. The
2nd Naval Division, commanded by Vice Admiral Schultz, would
be used mainly on the land front between Nieuport and Diksmuide.
It would also see action around Ypres after April 1915, on the
Somme in the summer of 1916, and in the Battle of the Third Ypres
(Passchendaele) in 1917. The 1st Naval Division, now commanded
by Vice Admiral Jacobsen, was put in charge of the coastal defense
between Middelkerke and the Dutch border.

2. General Ideas About the German Coastal Defenses in Flanders

Beginning in November 1914, field artillery guns and captured
Belgian fortress guns were installed in the dunes and on the sea
wall around the harbors of Ostend and Zeebrugge. This signaled
the birth of an impressive coastal defense system which would be
developed and improved extensively over the next four years.

In its early days the corps was chiefly responsible for defending the coastal area, which was regarded as a continuation of the
Western Front line that ran from the Swiss border to Nieuport. To
forestall Allied landings, a series of batteries were installed on top
of or behind the dunes of the coastal strip. In between the gun
emplacements were trenches and small infantry posts equipped
with machine guns and fortified with barbed wire.

The ongoing development and intensification of submarine
warfare by the Germans, however, meant that the naval corps would
increasingly be used to protect U-boat bases and port facilities from
attack by Allied warships. In due course this became the primary
mission of the corps. In particular danger were the Zeebrugge and
Ostend harbors, which offered the Allies a wealth of targets that
included U-boat and seaplane berths, lock gates and harbor entrances, docks and shipyards, and the mole at Zeebrugge. Accordingly, the bulk of the 1st Naval Division was deployed in the vicinity of the two harbors, with the heavier batteries installed just inland to fend off raids by enemy surface forces.

In June 1917 Admiral von Schröder issued a memorandum in
which he stated that the main objective of hostile enterprises against
the Flanders coast would be to paralyze Germany's ability to wage
submarine warfare. This would be accomplished by the destruction of Zeebrugge and Ostend by sea bombardment, with the main
targets to be the locks at Zeebrugge and secondary targets to be
harbor and dock facilities, batteries, and aerodromes. Raids by landing parties with the same objective might also be made, and there

might be a landing of large masses of troops for the capture of the coast, probably accompanied by simultaneous attack on the land front, and possibly also from Holland.

3. Heavy Batteries Along the Belgian Coast

The German coastal defense system consisted of a number of batteries situated along the entire coastal area, and which were capable of providing protective fire for the land front near Lombardzijde-Nieuport, the harbors of Ostend and Zeebrugge, and the estuary of the Scheldt River. Depending on their respective missions, the batteries could be divided into two main categories: batteries for use in long-range bombardments, and batteries to prevent amphibious landings.

The first group of batteries was situated inland and intended for indirect fire only. In this category were the Deutschland, Pommern, Kaiser Wilhelm II, Tirpitz, and Oldenburg batteries, all in fixed emplacements; and the Braunschweig, Hessen, Hannover, Preussen, Schlesien, and Sachsen batteries, with guns mounted on traveling carriages. The battery crews, who could not see their targets, received firing coordinates from advanced observation posts situated all along the coast. Some heavy batteries had three or four observation posts sited many kilometers apart. Target coordinates were usually calculated with the use of sophisticated equipment, such as position finders which could take the bearings of an enemy warship and mechanically correlate these figures with those sent in from a laterally placed observation post. The gun crews also received information from observation aircraft, whose crew observed the fall of shot and relayed the results to the batteries so that the necessary corrections could be made.

The guns of the secondary armament were installed on dunes near the sea and sited for direct fire against amphibious landings. All other coast batteries belonged to this category, which also included batteries responsible for the close defense of the harbors.

4. History of the German Coastal Defenses in Flanders

The Naval Corps started construction of heavy battery emplacements in November 1914. Initially, coastal batteries equipped with outmoded guns were transferred with their crews from positions on the German coast (Wilhelmshaven and Kiel) to Flanders. For example, the Hindenburg battery, originally located at Fort Heppen near Wilhelmshaven and equipped with 28cm guns dating from 1886, was transferred to Ostend, where its guns were installed exactly as they had been in their former positions. Similarly, Battery Groden, also located near Wilhelmshaven, moved to Blankenberge; however, as this battery was equipped with 21cm howitzers dating from 1892, it was of no use whatsoever for coastal defense purposes.

Eventually the Naval Corps obtained newer and better guns from dismantled German warships, whose turrets were removed and sent intact to Flanders. Not all guns taken from warships were mounted in turrets, however; for example, the Beseler battery near Ostend was equipped with 15cm guns protected by small armored shields. During the war, the shields on such guns were enlarged, thereby providing the crew with more protection from Allied bombardments.

In 1915 installation of nearly all batteries on the crest of the dunes was completed. After that, however, the new heavy batteries were located at widely scattered positions farther inland. The first to be installed was Battery Tirpitz near Ostend, which was tasked not only with the defense of Ostend harbor but also with firing on enemy positions on the Yser front.

In 1916 Germany's military leadership seriously considered the possibility of Holland renouncing its neutrality and siding with the Allies, thus opening the way for an Allied attack on the German rear via the Scheldt estuary. To prevent a landing in this area, a new heavy battery, Kaiser Wilhelm II, was installed near Knocke. Equipped with four 30.5cm guns, this battery could reach Zeebrugge as well as the Dutch border and the River Scheldt. The battery was complemented by the construction of a defense line extending from Knocke to Antwerp and fortified with well-camouflaged pillboxes, most of which are still in good condition after the passage of nearly eighty years.

The year 1917 saw the installation of more heavy batteries, the most important being the Deutschland battery at Bredene near Ostend. This battery had four recently manufactured guns of 38cm, making it the heaviest battery on the Flemish coast. Deutschland could reach the Ypres Salient in Belgium and parts of extreme northeastern France as well as the Dutch border, and, by firing at maximum range, could engage British monitors attacking German positions on the Western Front near the coast.

An interesting feature of this battery was its huge concrete gun emplacements, which were constructed by German companies using Belgian forced laborers (wearing white straps on their jackets and trousers to mark them as such and thus hinder escape attempts) and more than seven hundred Russian prisoners. Upon completion, the emplacements were sunk into the ground and the guns were installed. Each gun arrived in several parts. First, the carriage was fixed into the concrete bedding, then the barrel was mounted on the carriage, and, finally, the heavy counterweight was installed, thus enabling maximum elevation.

In 1917 obsolete guns such as those equipping the Friedrichsort battery near Heist were replaced by new 17cm guns. That same year, Antwerp battery near Ostend was abandoned and a new battery, usually called "Oldenburg" but sometimes "New Antwerp," was built to replace it. More heavy batteries, equipped with 28cm guns mounted on railway carriages or 17cm guns on wheel carriages, were installed in the autumn and winter of that year. Both types could be positioned at several points along the coast, well back from the shore but close to the fixed heavy batteries; movement from one position to another and installation could be accomplished in one hour. The positions were poorly constructed, as evidenced by the open-air configuration of Battery Preussen; also, the batteries could avail themselves of alternative emplacements (*Ausweichstellung*). Intended to supplant such heavy batteries as Tirpitz, Deutschland, and Wilhelm II as the latter's guns became worn out, the mobile batteries often had their guns removed for use in special batteries (*Sonderbatterie*) on other sectors of the front (for example, the Ypres Salient).

Finally, just a few months before the war ended, the Germans installed several light batteries at Zeebrugge and Ostend in response to prior British attempts to close the ports. These included Lübeck battery at the entrance of the Zeebrugge mole, and Gneisenau II battery near the Palace Hotel, facing the Ostend harbor entrances.

5. General Aspects of a German Battery

The standard coastal battery consisted of four naval guns, which were taken from dismantled warships or arsenals and either housed in armored turrets or installed on open mounts with armored shields. Both the turrets and the open mounts rested on reinforced concrete platforms in deeply excavated pits equipped with pumps to remove the rain water that collected there. The platforms for the heavy pieces were set on concrete pillars, and the guns had to be redirected every day in order to avoid putting too much weight for too long on any one section of the platform's surface. (The pressure their weight exerted would otherwise have caused the pillars in the affected section to sink lower than the others, resulting in a tilted platform which would have rendered the guns inoperable.) Initially the guns were protected by concrete parapets, but toward the end of the war, when batteries with guns on traveling carriages were brought into use, these were supplanted by earthen walls.

In the small batteries the ammunition stores were placed between or under the guns and contained about two hundred rounds. The rounds were transported to the guns by hand or a small lift; for security reasons, no more than twenty rounds were stocked near each individual weapon. The bulk of the ammunition was stowed in magazines which were situated well to the rear of the battery and protected by a concrete roof and a layer of sand or earth. Some of the magazines, known as "elephant shelters," were covered by one meter of concrete. Depending on the magazine, however, the combined thickness of the concrete and earth or sand layer could measure anywhere from sixty centimeters to nearly three meters.

The heavy batteries had their ammunition stowed in bunkers located near the guns. Batteries with guns on traveling carriages had very limited accommodation for ammunition; in addition, their stores were poorly built and offered negligible protection from the elements. Shells and charges were usually stored separately except in the case of fixed ammunition and ammunition for star shell guns. Charges were kept in silk or cotton bags placed in brass cases. The brass cases were not stored loose but rather in sturdy zinc cylinders, with up to five cases in each cylinder. Shells for the heavy batteries (21cm and larger) had protectors for the driving bands which consisted of long strips of canvas lined on the inside with leather or felt. Fuses, exploders, and friction tubes were usually packed in finished metal boxes with wood linings.

In most instances, ammunition was transported to the coastal zone by railway. The ammunition was then brought to the battery magazines via narrow gauge railways that linked up to the local prewar tram system. Heavy batteries were equipped with internal overhead carriers and special trolleys to bring the shells to the gun emplacements.

The batteries had one or more observation posts which were usually situated on the dune tops, but sometimes in conveniently located hotels and villas as well. (The Wilhelm II battery at Knocke had its own steel watchtower.) Each battery also had a command post from which orders to fire were issued to the gun crews, sometimes by telephone, but usually by ringing a bell. The command posts for the heavy batteries communicated firing instructions to the gun crews by means of large panels on which target coordinates and other necessary information were written.

The bunkers for the observation and command posts were usually built so as to blend in with the dunes, and were revealed only by observation slits which provided them with a 180-degree viewing arc toward the sea. Telemeters to measure target distance were set up on top of the posts and linked by a speaking tube to the crews inside. When not in use, these devices could be stored in a specially made box, although in one instance it could be lowered into the bunker by means of a hydraulic elevator system. The observation bunkers were usually provided with drawings which depicted enemy vessels in profile for identification purposes. Heavy batteries also had observation aircraft at their disposal to observe enemy vessels and report the fall of shot. In addition, most of the batteries had been given a number of predetermined coordinates for barrage fire *(Sperrfeuer)*. This information was painted on the inside of the gun shields or on the platform parapets.

The construction of the battery emplacements with their command and observation posts was usually carried out by companies of the 124th *Armierungsbataillon*, which was attached to the Naval Corps. However, some works were constructed by German building contractors (the Irene battery, for example, was built by Schuster of Dortmund) using German workers; at Bredene and Knocke, press-ganged Belgian laborers and Russian prisoners *(Russenkommando)* were used as well.

Generally the batteries were also equipped with searchlights capable of illuminating targets up to a distance of forty-five hundred meters. The searchlights varied in size (with diameters of 35, 60, 90, 120, or 150 centimeters) and were concealed in small shelters during the day. The larger searchlights were mounted on lorries and could easily be driven to any destination. All were powered by Siemens-Schuckert generators, which were set up near each light.

In addition to searchlights, star shells could be fired by all 8.8cm, 10.5cm and 15cm guns, and also by special 10.5cm guns (10.5cm B.L. L/35) and 15cm howitzers (15cm How. L/14) which were used solely for illumination. The guns were fired in barrage so as to fully illuminate a large area. The barrage was launched on receipt of a code word, with the shells set to explode at an altitude of five hundred meters. A six-shell salvo was sufficient to obtain light for two minutes, which was usually time enough to spot any activity in a given area.

Many measures were used to conceal the batteries from enemy observation, including wire netting interwoven with twigs, brushwood, or small bundles of reeds, and faggots or panels with interlaced reed. Construction sites of new batteries were fully covered with camouflage netting. Vegetation was planted in order to conceal any traces of building activities. Gun shields were painted over with realistic illustrations which mimicked their surroundings. The camouflage of the Oldenburg battery, which gave it the appearance of houses (with brushwood roofs and chimneys placed on top of the bunkers, and *faux* doors and windows painted on the sides) was considered a textbook case by the Allies.

From 1917 the Germans made extensive use of smoke to conceal the batteries from would-be attackers and to confound the crew of British observation planes during bombardments. The use of smoke, which entailed the spreading of an artificial mist known as *Rauchverschleierung*, was usually produced from two types of pots: round drums in which acid was poured on lime, producing a chemical reaction that created the mist; and square iron pans containing a creosote substance which produced black smoke when burned. Both kinds were used simultaneously in order to obtain natural mist colors.

Elsewhere, in a measure aimed at deceiving the crew of British observation planes, the Germans installed fake batteries which usually consisted of wood poles to simulate guns. Obsolete guns were installed for the same purpose. For example, four Warendorff guns which were manufactured in Liège in 1865 were set up west of the Aachen battery (located near Raversijde) and east of the Block battery near Blankenberge.

Harbors and batteries were also defended by 8.8cm antiaircraft guns. The first pieces of Grossherzon battery arrived in Ostend at the end of October 1914 and were installed at the harbor near the Homardieres. Initially each unit had its own antiaircraft group, trained at the Blankenberge *Flakschule*. Batteries under construction were also provided with their own antiaircraft guns. Eventually, however, the growing frequency of Allied air attacks (particularly from the summer of 1917) forced the Germans to find a more effective way of combating this menace. They did so by consolidating their antiaircraft guns into three groups, *Flakgruppe Brugge*, *Flakgruppe Kuste*, and *Flakgruppe West*. There was also a mobile antiaircraft group (*Bayer Flugabwehr MG-Abt* at Stalhille) which could be moved as needed to any threatened sector. Such movement was usually accomplished by railway. Around Bruges as well, there was a large number of antiaircraft guns emplaced to protect U-boat berths and workshops.

Officers' and men's quarters were built in the dunes using wooden beams for support and steel plates covered by a thick layer of sand for protection. However, as the war went on and British bombardments became more frequent, these quarters were reinforced with concrete. Just as they did everywhere on the Western Front, the Germans worked to make their accommodations reasonably pleasant, planting flower beds and vegetable gardens and decorating many battery entrances with deactivated British sea mines or artillery shells.

Except during British bombardments from the sea, life was quiet in the coastal area, and probably the artillery men did not in the least fancy changing places with their comrades in the *Matrosen Regimenten* on the Yser Front, where losses were more severe. The only heavy action in the coastal area occurred on April 23, 1918, when the British navy undertook to block the harbors at Zeebrugge and Ostend by deliberately sinking derelict warships in the harbor channels. At Zeebrugge the British were able to create a partial block with HMS *Thetis, Intrepid,* and *Iphigenia,* but at Ostend the operation failed entirely when the defending German batteries sank HMS *Sirius* and *Brilliant* before these vessels could be maneuvered into the desired position. During a second raid on Ostend (May 10, 1918), the HMS *Vindictive* was sunk in the harbor entrance, but its positioning was such that it did not prevent German ships from going in and out.

6. The End of the Naval Corps

September 28, 1918, was the start of the Allied Liberation Offensive in Flanders. On the next day a telegram from Imperial Headquarters at Spa informed Admiral von Schröder that the evacuation of the coast was to be taken into consideration. On October 14, on the advice of the IV *Armeekommando,* the order arrived to give up the Yser Front. Evacuation followed on October 15. That same night a few ships that had not already absconded to German harbors dropped a number of sea mines off the coast, after which the vessels were sunk. On October 16, von Schröder issued his last corps order, which ended with these words: "You have been an honor to your colors to the last day." On the belfry of Bruges, the imperial flag was lowered after four years.

All the pieces of the coastal defense system were then destroyed by their crews. The Germans also inflicted heavy damage on the harbors of Ostend and Bruges as well as the locks of Zeebrugge, and blew up bridges and railway viaducts in the path of the Allied advance. The Naval Corps withdrew and established its headquarters in Eeklo. On November 6, 1918, the headquarters were re-established at St. Nicholas and von Schröder was ordered to Kiel to suppress the riots that had broken out in the town. The order was almost immediately canceled by the new German chancellor, Max von

Baden, who did not trust the admiral. The Naval Corps was in Lokeren when it laid down its arms on November 11, 1918. In accordance with the terms set forth in the Armistice agreement, the troops then retreated in good order to Germany via Antwerp and Hasselt. On November 20, the Naval Corps reached the German border and Admiral von Schröder reviewed his troops for the last time. Finally, the corps was disbanded at Wilhelmshaven on December 6, 1918.

7. The German Coastal Batteries Between the Two World Wars

Most of the Naval Corps' guns, having been destroyed by their crews in mid-October of 1918, were left behind by the Germans when the latter withdrew to the east in the final weeks of the war. The wrecked guns fell into the hands of advancing Allied troops, who posted guards at the battery positions to prevent theft and accidents involving the large quantities of ammunition then stockpiled in the immediate vicinity.

The Allies subsequently showed great interest in the German defense system. Engineers made reports, British and French artillery officers came to examine the pieces, and the United States government dispatched a military mission to do likewise. The main purpose in all this, of course, was to learn as much as possible about this unequaled masterpiece of military fortress construction. The information thus acquired formed the basis of study for a number of military course offerings; for instance, prior to 1940, the course "Coastal Defense" at the Brussels Royal Military School was based on the aforesaid reports. The ammunition left behind by the Germans was accurately analyzed as well. Many dignitaries visited the battery positions, among them Belgium's King Albert, King George V of England, and President Poincaré of France. In 1919 the British Admiralty obtained permission to carry off four 8.8cm guns from the Zeebrugge mole as a souvenir of their attack on that place. A number of towns (among them Dunkirk) obtained as trophies a few shells and cartridges of the heavy 38cm batteries.

In the aftermath of the war the defense system soon fell into decay, and the Belgian government, in an effort to preserve the batteries as historical sites, offered one or more of them to each town on the coast. But the towns showed little or no interest in the batteries, and they continued to deteriorate. In due course, most of the system's equipment was scrapped and auctioned off at Bruges on May 3, 1923. The auction catalogue notes that in the five years that had elapsed since the end of the war, a number of guns had already been sold, while others had silted up, fallen down, or simply disappeared outright.

In the meantime private organizations had taken steps to turn these vestiges of the Great War into tourist attractions. A leader in the initiatives to do so was the Belgian Colonel Stinglhamber, founder of the Zeebrugge Museum. Presumably that is the reason, made evident in the terms of the 1923 auction, that the Wilhelm II battery at Knocke, Freya battery at Heist, Lübeck battery at Zeebrugge, Deutschland battery at Bredene, and Tirpitz battery at Ostend were not put up for sale.

In the event, the coastal batteries proved extremely popular with tourists. Postcards of the batteries sold easily, and full busloads visited them in guided tours. War museums were established in the former ammunition bunkers near the Wilhelm II battery and in a large bunker (renamed "Abri de l'Amirauté") at Middelkerke. As the years went by, however, public interest in the batteries gradually waned, leading to their eventual dismantlement. This process was essentially completed in the late 1930s when the last pieces of the Deutschland battery were scrapped, although the 1939 mobilization would see the old guns of the Wilhelm II battery removed and replaced with updated pieces manned by Belgian troops.

The construction of the Atlantic Wall during World War II eradicated nearly every trace of the previous war's coastal defense system. It was not until 1983, after the death of Prince Charles of Belgium, that a large, well-preserved complex dating from both world wars was discovered at his Raversijde estate near Ostend. After some research it was determined that this was the Aachen battery, constructed in 1915.

8. Aachen Battery

The battery consisted of four 15cm naval guns (15cm S. K. L/40), manufactured by Krupp in 1901. The guns had a maximum range of 18,700 meters and were mounted in almost square concrete gun pits on the forward edge of the crest of the dunes. Until 1987 these emplacements were filled with sand and covered with vegetation. In the process of cleaning up the battery, two of the emplacements were emptied and revealed to be in good condition, with gun pits that have more or less preserved their original appearance. The entrances to the other two gun positions were bricked up during the Second World War. In all four positions, the guns were mounted on a central pivot which was anchored to the concrete platforms by heavy bolts, the traces of which can still be seen. The turret's front shield armor had a maximum thickness of ten centimeters, and was inscribed on its inside surface (facing the gunners) with coordinates for barrage fire on Ostend's harbor entrance (the *Hafensperre*). Each piece, armoring included, weighed forty tons.

The battery had two ammunition stores, both protected by double steel doors, which were situated beneath the gun positions. One store contained shells (between 150 and 200 pieces); the other, cartridges (174 pieces in zinc cylinders, 200 if stored loose). The ammunition was conveyed to the emplacements via a double narrow gauge railway and transferred from the railway cars into the stores through a small round aperture at track level—an expedient that spared the men from having to hand-carry the ammunition down the narrow staircase leading from the gun pit to the stores. The ammunition was then hoisted from the stores to the guns by means of a small lift.

The walls of the ammunition stores are still inscribed with a kind of inventory of the ammunition they once contained. Other inscriptions serve to warn against the danger of explosion: *Rauchen verboten--Kein offenes Licht benützen* (No smoking—do not use an open light).

The narrow gauge railway connected the gun positions to the battery's two main ammunition stores, situated to the rear, which the Germans blew up in October 1918. The railway followed the course of an existing sunken path which led to the king's chalet. In addition to laying a double set of tracks on the path, the Germans covered the path's walls with wood in order to prevent it from silting up.

As with most of the batteries, Aachen was provided with several observation and command posts. The bunker to the left of the battery had a telemeter position on top and an observation slit which could be sealed with iron shutters. When first built, this bunker offered only minimal protection against bombardment, which was announced by the clanging of a brass ship's bell, installed in 1915. However, inasmuch as it contained precious optical equipment for heavy batteries of the Freya type (21cm and larger), its roof was subsequently armored with a concrete block set atop a layer of sand to absorb the shock of exploding shells.

From 1917 this bunker also served as *Hauptstand West* (Command Post West) for the Deutschland battery at Bredene. The bunker saw further service in the Second World War, as attested to by the remains of a brick antiaircraft emplacement on the rooftop (which replaced the First World War telemeter position) and various 1940s-vintage graffiti and inscriptions inside.

The observation bunker to the right is now very hard to identify as such. Only the substructure is from World War I. An antiaircraft gun platform and an observation room which is oriented to the sea were added during the Second World War, when the original observation slit was bricked up. There was a telemeter position on the roof. Troops inside the bunker could operate a searchlight located nearby which had a range of forty-five hundred meters and was put

away during the day in a small shelter. Illumination was also provided by star shells which could be fired by two of the battery's guns.

The First World War crew quarters were dug into the rear slope
of the dunes and built of heavy timbers covered with iron plates
and a layer of sand on top. Usually the men slept in hammocks, as
aboard ships. The presence of ammunition precluded the use of
candles, hence the quarters were wired for electric lights.

Along the Duinenstraat, near the small bridge linking the two
parts of the Royal Domain, there was a guard room. There was also
a first aid station, which was a simple wooden structure with a
treatment room, a twenty-bed ward, and accommodation for the
medical officer. In 1916, in response to the British bombardments,
the aid station was transferred to the officers' quarters, which were
more solidly built (they could withstand the impact of 21cm shells)
and could house forty men. A new reinforced concrete first aid station, much similar to that of the Beseler battery, was built in 1917
between the Aachen and the Antwerp batteries.

Nothing of the wooden constructions has been preserved. The
wood was removed shortly after the war by the local populace, which
also made off with the electrical wiring, switchboards, lighting fix-
tures, and furnishings.

From 1916, frequent British bombardments required that each
battery be equipped with at least one bombproof shelter. Aachen's
shelter has been well preserved. It is a construction of the
schutzsicherer Wellblechunterstand type and was built with sheets
of corrugated iron covered with concrete and sand. The inside was
furnished with simple benches where the soldiers could sit while
waiting for the bombardments to end. The bunker also had an escape passage leading to the sunken path behind the battery.

Only one-fifth of the troops were present at or near the guns
when the batteries were being fired. Of the remaining troops, half
were employed to bring up ammunition and half to perform duties
involving first aid, observation, searchlights, antiaircraft, and close
defense of the battery. When the guns were silent, as they were
most of the time, life was quiet on the Aachen battery. The troops
grew flowers, and vegetables to supplement their rations.

The battery had three wells, one of which was named "Barbara Brunnen" after the patron saint of artillery men. A fountain
fed by the wells is still in place at the site of the latter, but with the
German name removed. Two metal light towers, erected in 1894 in
the dunes to the west of the Royal Domain, were still standing in
1914 when the war began, but the Germans pulled them down in
the spring of 1915 because they provided a target for enemy warships. The remains of the towers were discovered by advancing

Allied forces during their Liberation Offensive in October 1918. British officers erroneously believed them to be sabotaged German "observation towers" of the Aachen battery. Neither of the towers was rebuilt after the war. In 1930 Prince Charles acquired the lands where they stood, and the last remains were removed in 1931. The battery has been restored, and has been open to the public since 1993 as part of the Atlantic Wall Museum.

Q&A

Q. *Did the Deutschland battery play any role in the destruction of Ypres or the battle of Passchendaele?*

A. No. Although this battery could reach the whole Ypres front, it never fired on it.

Q. *How were the large guns traversed? Mechanically or manually?*

A. With electric motors. Even the small guns were traversed by motors. But they could also be moved by hand in case there was a loss of electrical power.

Q. *Did the Germans use the coastal defenses in the Second World War?*

A. There was hardly anything left of the defenses in 1940, except on the estate of Prince Charles. But the gun emplacements there were not used because the type of gun they were designed for was not available.

Q. *Were any German surface ships based at Ostend?*

A. No large ships—just torpedo boats. There were U-boats based at Bruges. They reached the sea via canals that led to Zeebrugge and Ostend.

Grand Admiral Alfred von Tirpitz, commander in chief of the Imperial German Navy during the Great War.
Aleks Deseyne

The four turrets of Hindenburg battery, equipped with 28cm guns, with the spires of Ostend in the background.

Aleks Deseyne

German naval artillery men pose atop—and inside—the gun of an unidentified battery on the Flemish coast.

Aleks Deseyne

A barrel for one of Deutschland battery's guns is lowered onto a flatcar for transport to Bredene.

Aleks Deseyne

Telescope observatory for Kaiser Wilhelm II battery near Knocke, as it appeared in World War II.

Aleks Deseyne

A 17cm gun belonging to Oldenburg battery protrudes from the *faux* house built to conceal it.

Aleks Deseyne

Derelict British warships sunk at the mouth of the Bruges Canal at Zeebrugge to block U-boats transiting into the North Sea. The ship in the foreground burns from hits by German coastal defense batteries; note the shell hole in the funnel.

Aleks Deseyne

A German coastal defense gun spiked to deny its use to advancing Allied troops, October 1918.

Aleks Deseyne

Mannequins are the only occupants in the restored interior of a World War I-vintage personnel bunker at Aachen battery.

Aleks Deseyne

Belgian soldiers stand guard at the barracks of Aachen battery in the winter of 1918.

Aleks Deseyne

"Barbara Brunnen" fountain, named after the patron saint of artillery men, was fed by one of three fresh-water wells at Aachen battery.

Aleks Deseyne

PART 3

THE OTHER SIDE

The German Soldier of World War I: Myths and Realities

Dennis E. Showalter

The German army of World War I is one of military history's principal remaining enigmas. Contemporaries and scholars alike regard it as master of the battlefield in every theater where it appeared in force. The sharpest critics of the army's performance at policy and strategic levels concede its operational and tactical virtuosity.[1] Attempts, usually German, to depict the kaiser's army as stepping off on the wrong foot in its human and institutional dynamics, as being less effective as a military instrument in fact than in legend, ultimately remain unconvincing—not least because of the present-mindedness that tends to shape their authors's arguments.[2]

In this story, however, the German soldier remains the invisible man—a sharp contrast to his World War II successor. The men in the coal-scuttle helmets who bore the burden of the trenches have been essentially defined by their enemies, particularly in the English-speaking world. Germans are "others" in the wartime memoirs of Sassoon, Graves, Guy Chapman, and their counterparts. For scholars like John Terraine and Tim Travers the German soldier is similarly objectified: an impersonal opposition to be overcome by fresh combinations of tactics, training, and morale. For casual students of World War I the image of the German fighting man at war is most likely to be built around the doomed youths of Erich Maria Remarque, particularly the cinematic images culminating in the doomed Paul Bäumer's final, futile reach for that famous butterfly.

This limited perspective is not the product of moral revulsion. The German army of World War I bore no significant resemblance to its National Socialist successor in respect to its behavior. Apart from brutally heavy-handed treatment of suspected *franc-tireurs* during the initial sweep through Belgium and northern France, the kaiser's army fought by recognized rules and conventions about as well as did its enemies.[3] Germans, like all the combatants, committed a significant number of battlefield atrocities. These, however, were part of the "filth of war" as opposed to systematic policy, and were subject to heavy penalties if officially discovered. Wartime propaganda tales such as the Canadian allegedly crucified with bayonets lost credibility even during the fighting. The major arguable blot on the army's record, the large-scale introduction of poison gas, was a high-level policy decision—one, moreover, that anticipated the Allies as opposed to forcing their hands.[4]

The German soldier of World War I has also been obscured by academic and cultural barriers erected by the Germans themselves. During the Weimar years fiction and memoirs alike were polarized between deniers and affirmers of the war experience. In either case the soldier became an archetype: the doomed defender of his homeland and culture or the nameless victim of capitalists and militarists.[5] The Nazi regime tolerated only one school of expression on the subject: a heroic vitalism with no more than the remotest relationship to reality. After 1945 the Great War was overshadowed in German memory by a far more comprehensive tragedy. Even in direct terms the discrepancy between the two conflicts becomes clear upon examining the rolls of honor in any parish church or town hall. The list of names from 1914 to 1918 will almost always be a good bit shorter than that from 1939 to 1945. In this respect Germany resembles the U.S. more than France or Britain, where the human costs of World War I left far deeper scars than those of the later conflict.

I.

This essay is a beginning exercise in recovery. It proposes to offer the hint of an explanation of what made the German soldier of the First World War fight when, as John Keegan argues, common sense insists on the wisdom of flight. That story cannot begin with the first rounds fired from the guns of August. The men who donned their country's field grey were not, unlike their British counterparts or the Americans in 1917, entering a system of improvisation. Nor were they embarking on quite the same kind of a "great adventure." Since the German Empire's foundation in 1871, the army had been a primary instrument of structural integration in a state otherwise conspicuously lacking equivalent symbols. On the most basic level the army certified males as adults. The drastic changes in German society since the 1780s had invalidated many traditional male rites of passage. For women, menstruation and marriage remained the keys to adult status. Males had no equivalent ways of defining themselves as men in a fashion that was generally acceptable. The peasant youth waiting to inherit a farm, the unskilled laborer living with parents and contributing his paycheck each week, the freshly-minted *Abiturent* (graduate), the last-hired clerk in a department store—all faced a similar problem. Their own in-group might have rituals that separated the men from the boys. These rituals, however, were likely to be meaningless or irrelevant to anyone else.[6]

Universal military service altered this pattern. Germany's rapid population growth combined with the reluctance of conservative administrators to enlarge the army, and the dislike of liberals and socialists for large military budgets, to limit the actual proportion of men drafted for a full term. Nevertheless every man who reached the age of twenty underwent the same process of examination and evaluation. While it was possible for individuals to pull strings and get themselves declared medically unfit or eligible for call-up only on general mobilization, the images of universal obligation and universal service were nevertheless successfully sustained.

Official and unofficial loopholes, deferments, or exemptions for hardship cases and certain medical problems, lessened the burden of the system just enough to retard efforts at evading or rejecting it. And once completed, military service came increasingly to be a gateway to the adult world. Marriage, permanent employment, a place at the men's table in the local gasthaus—all were associated, directly or indirectly, with a certificate of demobilization.

Nor was active duty in the Imperial German Army necessarily brutalizing or dehumanizing. It could even be relatively pleasant. German standards of comfort were still Spartan enough that army beds, army food, and army work days did not represent the kind of steep decline in life style that has shocked so many contemporary conscripts from the affluent West, and arguably contributed far more to protests against military service than abstract principles of brotherhood and pacifism. Not a few soldiers found their life in the ranks an improvement over their lot as civilians. This frequently repeated boast of army spokesmen said more about the living conditions of the German laborer than about the German army as a welfare institution. It was nevertheless not the pure invention of military propagandists.[7]

More than simple physical factors were involved in this process. Once in uniform the German recruit found himself part of an institution whose challenges and rewards could salve the wounds inflicted by modernization. The myths of modern liberalism and traditional society asserted a direct and perceptible connection between endeavor and achievement. A real man made his way through his own efforts, individually or in a group context. This contradiction is more apparent to contemporary sociologists than it was in practice in the home towns and villages of Biedermeyer Germany. From the mid-nineteenth century, however, industrialization, agribusiness, and integration into an international economy, diminished to the vanishing point any links between those myths and everyday reality. The watchword was still "work till you drop"— but for no tangible purpose. The alienation of labor in mines and factories was paralleled by the resentments of clerks, postmen, and the rest of an emerging white-collar world, by the frustrations of independent peasants whose economic position was visibly declining—even by the anger of farm workers undercut by seasonal competition from the Russian Empire. The prizes, tangible and intangible, of the new Germany seemed either completely out of reach, or bestowed by criteria incomprehensible to the average man. Now hard work pitted a man either against machines which wore him down and broke his spirit directly, or against a system impossible to comprehend, much less master.

The army was different. It was ultimately designed to promote success instead of failure. No military system, particularly one based on conscription, can function if it sets standards impossible to reach. The demands of the parallel bars, the rifle range, the drill ground, might be high but they could be met—and not only by a chosen, exceptional few. One reason why so many Germans spoke so favorably of their military service is that they experienced there the kind of triumphs, visible and recognized, that would be denied them the rest of their working lives in an industrial society. A cigar or a mark piece from the captain for duty well done, a chance to win one of the kaiser's medals, perhaps even promotion to *Gefreiter* (private first class) towards the end of one's second or third year on active duty—these might seem trifles to the opulent bourgeoisie of the late twentieth century. But such trifles, and the implications behind them, can often do more to motivate behavior and develop attitudes than the most high-flown of abstract rhetoric, whether on the glory of patriotism or the evil of militarism.

This point does not exonerate the German military establishment of treating its draftees harshly. A familiar joke begins with a recruit asked by his regimental commander, "Who are the father and the mother of your company?" He gave the expected answer: "The captain and the *Feldwebel*" [first sergeant]. When asked what he would like to become in the service, he promptly answered "An orphan!" The army was no easy rite of passage. But an easy rite of passage is a contradiction in terms. In Western societies since at least the Renaissance, if not the Age of Pericles, males in particular have been conditioned against accepting the verdict of Lewis Carroll's Caucus Race: everyone has won and all must receive prizes. The fathers, uncles, and older brothers of Imperial Germany may have enjoyed telling horror stories about their time "with the Prussians." They did not significantly discourage the new generations of conscripts.[8] Nor for that matter were men in their second or third years of service likely to be sympathetic to freshly-shorn recruits undergoing their initial weeks of torment.

While it might be possible to apply Erich Fromm's concept of a sado-masochistic German bourgeoisie to the workers and peasants who made up the bulk of the army's rank and file, it seems more reasonable to conclude that on the whole the everyday routine of peacetime service between 1871 and 1914 was not regarded as an unbearable strain on the average man in his early twenties. Exceptions were seen as just that: exceptions. If company offices were not crowded with men anxious to make the army their career, neither were guardhouses filled with rebellious conscripts. The average German soldier of the Empire was willing enough to put in his time.

II.

The guns of August created new archetypes. The dominant image of the German soldier during the Great War's first eighteen months is of the volunteers—the teenagers who flocked to the colors in August 1914 marched away with flowers in their buttonholes, and died in the mud of Flanders with the *Deutschlandlied*, the German national anthem, on their lips. Recent revisions of the myth concentrate on debunking. They describe enthusiasm sacrificed to incompetence, giving way to disillusion and despair as the grim realities of modern war and Imperial Germany's class system crushed the spirit of young men deluded by prewar patrioteering.[9]

Reality is a good deal more complex. A more accurate model of the German soldier at the beginning of the war involves men of all ages pitchforked into a system that failed to meet both their expectations and its standards. As the first section of this essay shows, the pre-World War German army was generally accepted as competent by definition. The popularity of military service also depended heavily on the absence of wars and rumors of wars. Much of the popular militarism characteristic of the Second Reich was based on attitudes and posturing. The rite of passage was important; killing the kaiser's enemies was definitely a secondary factor.[10]

This point was apparent to anyone who cared to look below the surface of public behavior in August 1914. Enthusiasm for the war did exist, and permeated classes and regions long held under suspicion by the government. Working class neighborhoods in Berlin and Polish villages in Silesia alike sported national flags. Corps districts discreetly pigeonholed contingency plans for the roundup of Social Democrats and other prospective dissidents. In industrial cities like Hamburg, initial concern that this was just another bourgeois war was papered over by the perceived necessity for defending the gains made by German Marxists from the peasant hordes of Tsarist Russia.

Yet at the same time Germans of all castes and classes kept a wary eye on the course of everyday events. In Düsseldorf there was a brief run on the banks. From the Rhineland to East Prussia, panics broke out at rumors of spies, airships, or Cossacks. If young men rushed from regiment to regiment eager to enlist, other young men prepared petitions describing their indispensability to family farms or businesses. The people of Germany supported war—but war of a specific kind: a defensive conflict against a coalition of implacable enemies, to be decided by a series of quick, decisive victories.[11]

The process of awakening to reality began in the depots and barracks. The army was well able to feed, arm, and equip the first-line reservists who filled out the active regiments and formed the reserve divisions and corps provided for in prewar mobilization plans. There remained, however, steadily increasing numbers of older men called to the colors to what seemed no purpose. Many of these belonged to the Ersatz Reserve. These were men called up and found fit for service during peacetime but never actually inducted, whether for medical, social, or political reasons, or simply because they were not needed. The Ersatz Reserve, in short, was a safety valve, operating in practice much like the Selective Service System in the U.S. during the 1950s and '60s. Now that valve was shut, and not everyone was happy at its closing. As for the "war volunteers," while their actual number was far less than postwar mythology depicted, most of them were idealistic and literate. Such men are likely to find their first days in uniform a shock anywhere, at any time. The War Ministry's decision of August 1914 to create new army corps from this particular manpower pool was correspondingly one of the war's great mistakes.

The new formations lacked everything from maps to lieutenants. Most of their officers and NCOs had been long retired and were correspondingly unfamiliar with recent innovations in weapons and tactics. Accurate information about conditions at the front was scarce: most returning veterans went directly to hospitals or asylums. Apart from ignorance, shortages of everything reduced many of the new units to keeping their men busy with saluting drill and exercises in foot care and oral hygiene—not so much from peacetime pedantry as for lack of any reasonable alternatives. Rations were slim. Meals too often tasted as if the cooks had taken special army courses in how to ruin them.[12]

These circumstances were more significant for the German soldier than either his French or British counterpart. France, with its smaller manpower pool, had a pre-existing place for every reasonably able-bodied male. Fewer improvisations made for fewer egregious inefficiencies. As for the British New Armies, the absence of anything like a prewar military culture meant the new recruits had no expectations of what army life was supposed to be and were correspondingly flexible.[13] Germans, on the contrary, had such expectations. They were *not* being fulfilled.

Success at the sharp end would have transformed the problems of depots and training grounds into the stuff of fond reminiscence at postwar reunions. Such success, however, proved both elusive and dearly bought. On the Western Front both active and first-line reserve formations endured from the beginning hard marches and short rations. As supply systems stretched, then broke, whatever alcohol the quartermasters could requisition or the troops could pilfer was used as a stimulant, to keep the men marching. German troops supplemented their rations by field expedients that included large amounts of half-ripe fruit. The results were all too predictable. The German army stumbled towards the Marne hung over, with its trousers around its ankles.[14]

When the bullets started flying the results were no more glorious. Against automatic machine guns, rapid-firing rifles, and long-range artillery the German infantryman had the speed of his two feet and the protection of a fraction of an inch of cloth. Nor did the regimental officers' field performance inspire the respect their behavior in garrison had demanded. Erwin Rommel was a professional soldier. Walter Bloem was a novelist with a reserve commission. They served in corps with reputations among the highest in the army: XIII Württemberg and III Brandenburg, respectively. Yet *Infantry Attacks* by Rommel and Bloem's *The Advance from Mons* are classic illustrations of Clausewitz's aphorism that war is the province of confusion—or in more contemporary terms, the natural home of FUBAR-X (politely translated as "fouled up beyond all repair—by experts").[15]

If first-class regular units faced such problems, reserve units' battles with fog and friction were exponentially greater. The Hessians of XVIII Reserve Corps may have won the Battle of Neufchateau against half their number of French colonial troops on August 22, 1914, but the survivors of the frontline battalions hardly seem to have been uplifted by a sense of victory. The discrediting of prewar training and tactics reached its first peak at Ypres when not only newly raised formations, but elite regiments of the Prussian Guard, were shot to pieces by handfuls of British troops, themselves the exhausted survivors of once-proud battalions.[16]

The morale of Germany's infantrymen was tested further in the first months of 1915. A few local operations achieved useful results. The attack of III Corps at Soissons in January 1915, orchestrated by its chief of staff Hans von Seeckt, is probably the

best and best-known example.[17] But the French spring offensives in
Artois and Champagne were met with what could only be described
as a comprehensive lack of tactical imagination. Prewar German army
doctrines paid little attention to defensive operations as such. Loss
of ground was seen as damaging to both the propaganda war and to
unit morale. As a result thousands of men were expended "holding
what there was to hold," or counterattacking to retake lost positions
representing nothing more than map coordinates.[18]

The effect of these sacrifices on frontline morale was exacerbated by the close-up, in-your-face nature of the fighting at places
like Notre Dame de Lorette—brutality untempered as a rule by anything remotely resembling artifice or finesse.[19] Too many regular officers had become casualties. Their replacements were too often
exercising responsibilities beyond their current capacities. The army's
prewar reluctance to expand its corps of regular officers paid bitter
dividends as the war approached its second year. Men who in August 1914 were lieutenants learning how to lead platoons were now
captains in charge of battalions. It was scarcely remarkable that the
zeal of 1914 was turning to skepticism a year later among the men
whose blood paid their superiors' tuition in their craft.

Three factors began turning the situation around. The first
was that however badly the Germans were commanded, the Allies
were in worse shape. The French were grappling with problems of
offensive warfare on a scale that would not be solved until 1918.
The British simply had it all to learn after the fighting of 1914 virtually destroyed their regular army. The defining events in this
latter context was the attack of the 21st and 24th British Divisions
on the second day of the Battle of Loos: September 26, 1915. Elements of two German regiments shot down over eight thousand
English greenhorns in a few minutes until in some places, disgusted with the killing, the riflemen and machine gunners ceased
fire on their own initiative.[20]

This and similar experiences all along the front helped re-
build relative confidence in one's own system. The German High
Command cooperated in the process by increasingly recognizing
that this war was not 1870 written large. As 1915 progressed it
was increasingly apparent that Germany possessed neither the will
nor the means to overrun France physically. While the concept of
elastic defense was still embryonic, senior officers no longer felt
compelled to retain possession of every terrain feature. Killing
Frenchmen and Tommies was becoming more important.[21]

The third morale-booster that made its appearance in 1915 was
stormtroop tactics. These too were in their infancy, representing local responses to specific circumstances rather than any army-wide

policies. They did, however, offer the promise of inflicting disproportionate losses on selected enemy positions. Even more significantly,
carefully prepared, in-and-out raids provided at least the beginnings
of an opportunity to be a warrior rather than a piece of machine gun
fodder. This was not exactly the kind of war the men of 1914 had
expected when they joined the colors. It was, however, a closer ap-
proximation than most of what they had so far experienced.[22]

III.

The war's third period, from the Verdun offensive of 1916
through the Flanders campaign of 1917, marked another shift in
the *mentalité* of Germany's soldiers. This reflected domestic circumstances as well as battlefield conditions. Initial expectations
of a short war waged in the context of a frontloaded military system
resulted in unconcern for the problems of maintaining a labor force
on the home front. The war would be fought with the resources on
hand; the crops could be brought in by women, children, and old
men; and everyone would be home for Christmas. As hopes for a
quick victory disappeared, the War Ministry began organizing a
system of exemptions keeping not only skilled workers but some
strong backs as well for an economy rapidly approaching its limits.
By early 1916, 1.2 million exempted workers were employed in
industry—not a few of whom had been recalled from the front. This
process continued for the rest of the war. At the most basic level it
created opportunities for an honorable way out of a technowar
whose nature challenged the limits of human imagination. It encouraged doing everything in one's power to avoid being sent back.
It also generated resentment among the unskilled and the unlucky
who remained with their units.[23]

Apart from the men released or exempted as necessary to the
war effort, German soldiers received regular leave. Its psychological impact was more likely to resemble that of GIs returning from
Vietnam in 1969 than of *Landser* coming home from the Russian
Front in 1944. The latter experience usually involved a period of
travel time long enough to allow for decompression. The former
could and often did involve leaving a fire base in the Central Highlands one morning and getting off an airplane in the United States
in a few days. Germans on furlough from the Western Front, with
its excellent railway connections to the Fatherland, might similarly find themselves home in a matter of hours—with corresponding emotional shocks. Casualties too were likely to be returned
whenever possible to hospitals, asylums, and convalescent homes
in Germany, if for no better reason than to make room for the next

intake of broken minds and bodies. Disabled men were discharged, with the prospect of recall to service should their condition improve—hardly an incentive to rapid recovery.[24]

These *Soldatenwanderungen* have been accurately described as challenging the postwar nationalist myth of a "front generation" bonded by the comradeship of four uninterrupted years in the trenches.[25] They also facilitated direst exchanges of information about conditions at home and conditions at the front—information that seldom redounded to the credit of Germany's ruling establishment. Disabled veterans, for example, tended to be regarded as a public embarrassment, challenging traditional images of what war ought to be. This was particularly true for the *grandes mutilés* produced by the combination of modern high explosives and modern medical techniques. A discreet caste or sling was one thing, a limbless torso quite another for the good burghers of Mainz or Berlin.[26] Soldiers back from the front were also increasingly exposed to the visible consequences of a rationing system that allowed people with money to purchase luxury items virtually at will.[27] Examples could be multiplied to make the same point. Personal experience was more likely to exacerbate than improve emotional ties men in uniform felt to the government and the society that sent them off to war. But neither did that experience generate automatic bonding with everyone else in uniform. "Trench comradeship" was challenged, and often overcome, by self-interest.

In the war zones, similar tensions developed between men assigned to frontline units and those in the rear echelons. The very concept of "rear echelon" was in a sense new to a German army that, expecting to win its war in six weeks, had initially put most of its men into combat-arms formations and made no systematic plans for controlling occupied territory on a long-term basis. Improvisation always favors opportunists. Few rifle companies did not have someone luckier, less scrupulous, or more egocentric than his former comrades, who had wangled a job sorting mail or guarding a supply dump in a French or Belgian village.

Far from being out of sight, out of mind, these *Etappenhengsten* (loosely translated as "rear-echelon heroes") were all too visible to any frontline division temporarily rotated for retraining, reinforcements, and recreation. As early as 1916 cynics and idealists alike spoke of two armies: one in the trenches, the other fighting its war in the bars and brothels of the occupied zone.[28]

Growing internal divisions were facilitated as well by changes in the army's demographics. The prewar conscription system's inability to absorb all the potential recruits meant that in 1914 large numbers of men in their early twenties were called up, but by necessity assigned to the depots for training while relatively older trained reservists took the field. As casualties increased—monthly losses during the war averaged about 130,000—the replacements tended to be younger men. Their elders were more likely to have skills useful in the wartime economy. The physical and emotional demands of trench warfare favored youth. The existence of whole classes of eighteen- and nineteen-year-olds invited "anticipating" call-ups as opposed to combing out the older-age groups, with the accompanying morale problems this entailed.

In the war's last two years, up to a quarter of the German army was twenty years old or younger. The results prefigured in some ways the U.S. Army's experience in Vietnam. Rifle companies contained fewer and fewer men with established civilian lives. The generational rebellion characteristic of the prewar youth movement manifested itself not only in the heroic vitalism of the storm troopers, but more generally in a growing gap between the young-adult rank and file and the older men of the noncommissioned officer corps, who played such an important role bridging the social and professional gaps between officers and enlisted men in the kaiser's army.

Military demographics shifted in another crucial way as well. Prewar recruitment favored conscripts from small towns and rural areas. The political aspects of this policy, the effort to limit the number of actual or potential Social Democrats in uniform and with military training, existed but must not be overstated. It was an article of faith everywhere in Europe that men from the countryside were better suited physically and psychologically to the conditions of modern war than the allegedly less physically developed, more highly strung townsmen. The German army, moreover, was recruited territorially, and the boundaries of its corps districts failed in general to keep pace with the major rapid population shuffles at the century's turn.

The overall result was that rural areas were disproportionately represented in the army that took the field in 1914, and bore a correspondingly high proportion of the initial casualties. The negative effects on morale appeared in the steadily declining effectiveness of many divisions recruited in rural Germany. The process was exacerbated by the increasing need to replace losses in these formations from any and all available sources.[29]

Structurally, then, the German army that entered the war's middle years was not well adapted to maximize the positive aspects of the frontline experiences discussed in Part II of this paper. Experience only made the situation worse. The attack on Verdun, which began in February 1916, was originally planned as a limited operation designed to draw the numerically weaker French into a killing ground. Within weeks the vanity of senior officers and the force of circumstances had sucked the Germans into an attritional battle whose numbers increasingly came up on the wrong side of the balance sheet.[30] The Anglo-French offensive on the Somme, which began on July 1, 1916, and mercifully expired four months later in the swamps along the Ancre River, cost the Germans a half million more casualties. The dead and mutilated were merely the tip of an iceberg. The losses in both sectors included disproportionate numbers of the regular officers and NCOs who were the soul as well as the heart of a conscript army that had never quite become a citizen force in the sense of its French counterpart. Losses were also heavy among the peacetime-trained reserve officers whose civilian skills were often valuable in administration, and whose concepts of leadership often proved better suited to units composed of a broader age group than the twenty- and twenty-one-year-old conscripts of the prewar army.

Not all the losses among the army's cadres were to death or wounds. By the end of 1916 an increasing number of the regular officers who survived had been promoted above the battalion level. As for the NCOs, in another situation prefiguring Vietnam, many of them had seen enough combat to calculate the point at which their luck would expire or their nerves collapse. The men who had enthusiastically led squads and platoons from the front in August 1914 were by December 1916 not exactly disappointed when transferred to staff and administrative jobs. By 1918, for example, two-thirds of the staffs of active army corps headquarters or their equivalents were composed of regular officers. Apart from the competence of their replacements, the result was often a sense of abandonment among enlisted men who had begun the war as civilians and expected to be led by professionals, or reasonable facsimiles thereof.[31]

It would be an error to describe the German army as on the verge of breaking at the end of 1916. The Somme in particular seems to have generated a certain pride in being able to endure under days and weeks of bombardment, inflict ruinous casualties, and maintain the front line. Admittedly the regimental histories stressing these points are best read with a good shaker of salt; postwar pieties tended to obscure frontline memories. Nevertheless by the turn of the year a new self-image seemed to be emerging. Instead of being an occupier and attacker, the German soldier saw—or was encouraged to see—himself as *defending* his country, home, and family even if he was doing so on someone else's territory.[32]

This altered consciousness may have reinforced the development in the war's final years of the German army's first distinctive archetype in a century. During the Wars of Liberation against

Napoleon, Prussia's military mythology had glorified the patriotic volunteer. Since the Wars of Unification, however, Germany's soldiers had been faceless, without even the distinctive nicknames of their Allied counterparts: Tommies and *poilus*. Now the idealists of Langemarck and the trench fodder of Verdun were increasingly perceived as fusing into a new kind of warrior. Combining the *mentalités* of fighter and technician, he had assimilated and risen above the pressures of the modern battlefield. A man of controlled willpower, cool and hardened, he understood war as the ultimate manifestation of industrial life. He found personal fulfillment through his mastery of war's moral, physical, and technical demands.

This image of the front soldier, the man who had become a fighting machine, was epitomized in the writings of Ernst Jünger and the sketches of Otto Dix: the man of asphalt, a cigarette butt in his mouth, a grenade thrust into his belt, cradling one of the new submachine guns with the ease of familiarity. His home was the front line; his family the half-dozen men of his squad. To the horror of war's destruction he balanced the pleasure of war's sacrifice—the more meaningless the better.[33]

While this model was certainly no artificial creation, its existence had more to do with postwar myth than wartime reality.[34] The German soldier of the Western Front defied easy categorization—or indeed any categorization at all. By the last month of 1916 the German High Command had accepted, however unwillingly, that the war had become an industrial war and the army a labor force—not least because by then not only the cadres but the active infantry, the men actually with the colors at the outbreak of war, had been bled white. What remained was a mélange of peacetime reservists with families and wartime conscripts without futures.

Two approaches to the problem were possible. One involved developing Germany's capacity to wage a war of machines and material. At all levels this proved a failure. The Hindenburg Program for total economic mobilization proved instead that, to paraphrase R. H. Tawney, a general with a factory is like a monkey with a watch. The General Staff's and the War Ministry's cavalier indifference to the realities of German human and material resources generated a spectrum of negative results uncompensated by any temporary increases in production. Nor could German factories and German designers keep up in such crucial fields as motor transport, armored fighting vehicles, and aircraft. German fighter pilots in particular spent most of 1917 and 1918 flying planes significantly inferior to the latest allied designs.[35]

In tactical and operational contexts the Germans were more successful. The concept of defense in depth systematically developed at General Staff levels after the Somme had its counterpart in the increasingly refined stormtroop tactics that grew out of the grassroots trench experience. Now the frontline infantry was trained to "resist, bend, and snap back," mounting counterattacks at every stage—counterattacks using now the techniques of fire and movement by mutually supporting small groups developed and employed by the Assault Battalions. By 1917 there were sixteen such battalions, and they played a role unique in modern military history. Elite forces—rangers, commandos, *arditi,* paratroopers—are as a general rule conceived as shock troops to be used in desperate missions, then withdrawn to refit and reorganize. Germany's Assault Battalions were arguably more important as school troops than combat units. Their essential mission, one absorbing more time than actual fighting, was to show the rest of the army how to do it.

The new doctrines and tactics proved their worth time and again in defense during the Nivelle Offensive and the Passchendaele campaign of 1917. At the same time German planners began adapting them for the offensive. The combination of infiltration tactics with brief, intense bombardments conducted by guns which no longer needed to fire preregistering rounds, is well known. Tested successfully at Riga on the Eastern Front in September 1917, Caporetto in October, and Cambrai in November, they achieved their apogee in the great offenses of March 1918.[36]

The frontline soldiers had the initial misgivings of veterans, but on the whole embraced the new techniques with increasing enthusiasm as they produced results. Beneath the surface, however, alienation from the system continued to expand. The process began in the depots and training centers in Germany itself. As scholars from the former GDR have demonstrated, antiwar propaganda, Marxist and humanitarian, had an increasing impact on increasingly reluctant warriors. Whether asked by principled revolutionaries or by men with principled objections to spilling blood—their own as well as others'—the question "is this *really* necessary?" became increasingly difficult even for patriots to answer with a wholehearted "yes."[37]

The late-wartime conscript was even less likely than his midwar predecessors to be well-commanded. The army consistently refused to expand its permanent officer corps in proportion to its increased size. The number did no more than double during the war, to around forty-six thousand. The major increase came in the reserves. Regiments were allowed to nominate enlisted men with combat experience for officer training courses whose standards were extremely high. Candidates who passed were reassigned to the front, usually as platoon sergeants and often to their old regiments. If they performed their new responsibilities well they were commissioned. By 1918 there were over 225,000 reserve officers in the kaiser's army.

Most of them came, however, from the same social classes that had supplied the prewar reserve officer corps. Logic and experience alike suggested that drawing deeper from the same pool diminished overall quality—a point increasingly noticeable under frontline conditions that highlighted personal and professional shortcomings. In human terms it is worth mentioning that given the life expectancy of a junior officer in a frontline battalion, not a few of the commissioned youngsters, regular or reserve, fell prey to a *gaudeamus igitur* mentality, taking whatever pleasures they could find out of the line however bravely they might act in the forward trenches. The ranks of *Offizierstellvertreter* (deputy officer) and *Feldwebel Leutnant* (sergeant-lieutenant) given to men whose social origins or educational background rendered them unsuitable for a "real" commission created a further gap, particularly in the frontline units where most of these military hermaphrodites were to be found. Nor could an NCO corps by now drawn heavily from "hostilities only" rank and file bridge the gap in prewar fashion— not least because too many of its best men were strained to their limits commanding platoons owing to a shortage of officers.[38]

The result of these changes was, surprisingly, *not* a greater emphasis on official authority. For all the horror stories about Prussian discipline, only forty-eight German soldiers were executed during the war.[39] Minor offenders were sometimes tied up in the open in lieu of confinement in a guardhouse, but the German army had no counterpart to Britain's notorious Field Punishment Number One. What happened instead was a gradual evolution towards command by consensus, with force or personality outweighing grades and ranks, and group agreement ultimately determining group behavior. Such a pattern is common to elite units in all armies, and in those contexts can contribute significantly to small-unit fighting power. Among warriors for the working day, results are often less felicitous. By the end of 1917 the German soldier found himself increasingly tempted to ask just who was minding the store in his particular company. The usually ambiguous answer eroded confidence. That erosion was further facilitated by material shortages. That officers enjoyed certain privileges—better food, better quarters, easier access to alcohol, tobacco, and women—was tolerable as long as the army's rank and file were reasonably well fed and could enjoy a regular cigar, mug of beer, and shot of schnapps. As life's good things from bread to toilet paper grew scarcer and coarser, the inequalities of a caste/class society once taken for granted became less and less bearable—particularly since the ones enjoying the privileges apparently did less and less to earn them. The words "grievance" and "injustice" appeared in an increasing number of letters home—and in barracks gossip and on latrine walls as well.[40]

The High Command's decision to prepare for the 1918 offensive by dividing the army into two tiers was a final major signpost of crisis. About 70 of the army's 240-odd divisions were designated "attack" formations and given first priority on replacements, equipment, and supplies, including food and medical supplies. The remaining units were regarded as "position troops" useful at best for consolidating gains, most likely to spend the rest of the war holding trenches. The results were negative in both directions. On one hand the "position divisions" were by this time undisturbed at their loss of status except for a few fire-eating officers still dreaming of the *Pour le Mérite.* But their already short rations grew even shorter. Their replacements, when they were provided, included increasing numbers of the partially disabled and the more or less disaffected. As for the attack divisions, there were too many of them relative to the rest of the army to create a solid sense of special status—an elite of 30 percent is a contradiction in terms. The extra rations were welcome and the special training accepted as facilitating survival and success. Nevertheless the process as a whole also generated a definite sense of being fattened for slaughter.[41]

To speak of disaffection in the spring of 1918 would be an exaggeration. The German soldier fought as bravely and effectively in March and April as at any time during the war. Confidence was initially high enough that regimental officers spoke of a spirit reminiscent of 1914. To speak of an underlying skepticism, however, is fully appropriate. Many observers noted the tactical contretemps generated as assault units looted British dumps and dugouts of items they had not seen in months, if not years.

The long-term impact on morale as the *Frontschweine* realized just how well-supplied their opponents were was exacerbated by the bogging-down of Ludendorff's shortsighted and ill-planned operations. By the time of the great Allied counterattacks in July and August, the German army's frontline units were burned out. Between July and November almost a million men were lost: dead, wounded, missing, and an increasing number of sick no longer able to force exhausted bodies through the motions. The battle casualties included a disproportionate number of true believers, officers and men willing for whatever reasons to risk themselves in one last try. Companies and battalions were reduced to handfuls. One regiment could count only 200 men, while another could muster only 120, organized in four companies instead of the regulation twelve. These were by no means exceptions, and units with such low strengths fell far below the critical mass necessary to sustain cohesion as a fighting force as opposed to bands or survivors.

The result was what Wilhelm Deist perceptively describes as a "camouflaged strike." More and more men began looking out for Number One—not by such drastic acts as deserting, but by reporting sick at every opportunity, hanging back when volunteers were wanted, or simply becoming "lost" for a few hours or days. A system already strained to its limits could not punish everyone found behind the lines with no more authority than a plausible excuse. Probably, indeed, the will to enforce more than the minimum forms of discipline had by now evaporated—less from fear of a bullet in the back than a sense that it no longer mattered.[42]

Deist correctly argues that this "strike" had revolutionary consequences only in that it destroyed the imperial system's ultimate guarantor, the army. For the most part the soldiers were homesick revolutionaries, whose desires could probably be expressed by a joke familiar to American GIs in World War II. A suitably edited version runs, "When I get home, I'm going to do three things. First I'll have a beer. Then I'll make love to my wife. Then I'll take off my pack." Such a mind set may not make revolutions. It can end wars. By November 1918 the High Command could count no more than a dozen or so of its divisions as operational: able and willing to fight. Far from being stabbed in the back, the Imperial German Army ended its existence with a sigh of relief.

V.

The postwar behavior of the kaiser's veterans suggests strongly that the "front generation" and its "trench comradeship" had been, if not quite a myth, an instrumental phenomenon created by the specific conditions of the Great War. It was as much negative as positive. Primary-group identity under the completely unfamiliar conditions of the Western Front was arguably even more necessary for emotional and physical survival than during World War II, when participants more or less knew what to expect. The returning soldiers quickly began redefining themselves in civilian terms—a process facilitated by the Weimar Republic's relatively generous psychological and financial treatment of the men who survived the trenches.[43] The "front experience" was in good part a postwar phenomenon, stoked by right-wing propaganda as memories blurred into myth. German veterans might refight the war over a beer, but in practical terms they tended to be significantly non-belligerent. The military forces that poisoned Weimar's politics in the 1920s drew heavily on those who had been too young for the real thing.[44] And the veterans who voted for Hitler after 1930 did so with the hope, when not the faith, that no one who himself had been "out there" would seek a repeat performance.

In more general terms the German army's rise and fall during World War I suggests an alternate approach to considering the cohesion and the fighting power of armed forces. Modern conscript armies are generally depicted as held together by varying combinations of patriotism, force, and ideology. Underlying all of these, however, is an implied contract between the soldier and the state. It may be the kind of contract depicted eloquently by F. Scott Fitzgerald in *Tender Is the Night:*

> See that little stream—we could walk to it in two minutes. It took the British a month to walk to it—a whole empire walking very slowly, dying in front and pushing forward behind. And another empire walked very slowly backward a few inches a day, leaving the dead like a million blocky rugs. No European will ever do that again in this generation. . . . This took religion and years of plenty and tremendous sureties and the exact relation that existed between the classes. . . . You had to have a whole-souled sentimental equipment going back further than you could remember.[45]

However implied, however deeply rooted, it remains a contract nevertheless. The demands a system proposes to make on the men who fight for it are no less real for being unwritten. So are the rewards promised to those who do their duty. When the nature or conduct of a particular conflict breaks that contract, soldiers respond with a suit for breach of promise. This phenomenon is generally linked with mercenaries, the Indian troops in Flanders during World War I, or the Prussian soldier who allegedly informed his king on the bloody field of Kolin: "Fritz, we've earned our fifty cents for today." Yet the Iraqi army in the Second Gulf War, the Italian army of 1941–42, the U.S. Army in the latter stages of Vietnam, all manifested behaviors similar to the kaiser's troops in 1917–18. On the other hand Robert E. Lee's Army of Northern Virginia, arguably in straits more dire than any of the others mentioned here, was a cohesive fighting force until the day of Appomattox. A comparative study of strikes and slowdowns in nineteenth- and twentieth-century armies might prove a welcome extension of one of the themes of this conference.[46]

Q&A

Q. What was the German army's policy on leave?

A. It was actually fairly good. You could get home maybe once a year, maybe even twice if you were lucky.

Q. How long was the average leave?

A. About ten days to two weeks. If your unit was deployed farther east, you would take a long time getting back. But a lot of the soldiers were deployed close to Germany, and they could make the trip fairly quickly. The railway network was efficient and you could deadhead home—you could ride the boxcars if you wanted to, and a lot of them did. We don't know enough about the impact of leave on German soldiers, but I think it was significant when they came back. They could see the problems in their own families. And rather than being alienated from the rear areas, as postwar right-wing mythology has it, the German soldiers, even the storm troopers, tended to identify closely with the people at home.

Q. Were self-inflicted wounds a problem?

A. I would say probably by 1916 or 1917, self-inflicted wounds had become a significant problem in the German army, as it was in all armies. I would also say that, much as was the case in Vietnam, SIWs were more likely to be defined as "accidents" . . . if you get my drift. If it was a light wound, they'd send the soldiers back to the battalion aid station or divisional field hospital, patch him up, and ship him back to the front as an object lesson. In other words, there's no easy way out unless you're really prepared to cripple yourself. But although SIWs were a problem, they don't show up in the records too often because the Germans didn't count light wounds the same way the British did.

Q. Are your comments about the German army applicable to the German navy?

A. The German navy's problem was simple boredom. How does that old song go? "We didn't sink the Bismarck and we didn't fight at all, we spent our time in Norfolk chasing after women while our ship was overhauled; living it up on grapefruit juice and sick-bay alcohol." Except there was no grapefruit juice or sick-bay alcohol for the grunts on the German warships. So I'd say the navy's mutiny in 1918 was a mutiny against boredom as much as anything else. Of course, it was also due to the sailors' reluctance to embark on the "death ride" that the captains and admirals were talking about. After four years in harbor, the average German sailor said, "Sir, I think you'd better go on the death ride by yourself."

Q. Certainly we know that Hitler amplified the stab-in-the-back theory. But I've always been interested to know whether it was perpetuated by the officer corps merely as a means of restoring the army to power; or did the officers really believe that the army was capable of further resistance in the autumn of 1918 and would have continued fighting had their government not accepted Allied terms for an armistice?

A. When the German soldiers came home they actually got victory parades. Nevertheless, the ordinary German soldier had very little doubt that the army had been beaten in the field. To some degree, particularly in the right-wing veterans' organizations—well, I don't mean any disrespect, gentlemen, when I say that, at the American Legion and VFW posts, the flak gets heavier and the snipers more accurate every time you tell stories about the war. And I think there was a fair amount of this going on in Germany after the war. But the thing that is very characteristic of German veterans in the 1920s and '30s was that they were not anxious for a repeat performance. The veterans who voted for Hitler did so largely out of the firm belief that he had been out there and "he won't send us back."

Q. Do you feel that you might have been too sympathetic to the German soldier? That you've placed too much emphasis on their innocence and essential naiveté?

A. I do not believe so. The whole Fritz Fischer thesis of a German conspiracy to take over Europe and the world is an academic construction. The ordinary German went to war in 1914 and stayed in the trenches and behaved as he did because he felt he was fighting a just war, a defensive war. If they were fighting it on the other man's territory they figured, well, after all, that's where you should fight a war isn't it?

I do think that, at the end of World War I, the German people as a whole, and certainly the German soldiers, felt neither guilt nor shame for what they had done. Their position was, "We fought a hard war. We bayoneted prisoners, we killed prisoners out of hand, but we lost our men that way, too. And if we launched unrestricted submarine warfare, the Allied blockade starved our women and children. We didn't start the war. We weren't able to finish the war, but we didn't start it either."

In the absence of shame and guilt, none of the intellectuals and the preachers and the pacifists in the world, and certainly none in the Weimar Republic, could convince the German people that World War I had been an unjust war or an offensive war.

Q. Who did they think started the war, then?

A. The French, the British, and the Russians. Remember, this attitude is typical of the First World War: "everybody started it except our country." Every nation believed it was fighting a defensive war.

Q. But German war plans ensured that Germany would initiate hostilities.

A. Every nation had some sort of plan for war. That was what you paid general staffs for. The Germans were just better at executing their plan. It reminds me of my Uncle Vic. He farmed with mules in the old days, and once he had a mule with colic and the veterinarian gave him a pill to give the animal. And the vet said, "Vic, all you've got to do is put the pill in a rubber hose and blow it down the mule's throat." A half hour later my uncle came staggering into the farmhouse saying, "Boys, that mule blew first."

The way the Germans saw it, they simply blew first, like my Uncle Vic's mule.

Comment

Paul Fussell: I greatly appreciated the comparisons Dennis made between the First World War and the Vietnam War. In either case, troops went home and came back to the front realizing the inevitable result of a long tour of duty and trying to mitigate its threat to them.

One thing that fascinated me—it is possible to imagine that the storm trooper of World War I, as Showalter described him, provided the model for the SS man of the next war and a paradigm for the ideal German male.

I was also interested in the way Dennis dealt with the issue of unit continuity and morale, emphasizing the relation between the post-Versailles German army to the pre-World War I army. That reminded me of the problem of rehabilitating the U.S. 1st Infantry Division between the wars, of restoring it to excellence with the nation facing involvement in the Second World War.

Another thing he focused on, and which we don't pay enough attention to, is the problem of reconstituting a fighting unit in wartime. Most people forget that in a war of any length, a unit is only its number; that is, the term "1st Division" comes to represent the number of a particular formation rather than the men who serve in it.

After a while combat takes its toll and the unit becomes populated entirely by different personnel. An example of this—just after World War II ended, when I was in Europe and about to be shipped home, I was in the 45th Infantry Division, which had been part of Patton's Third Army for a very long time. None of us could go home until we had been addressed by Patton because it was one of his favorite divisions. So we were all assembled, officers and NCOs, in this immensely hot field, and Patton drove up and addressed us for a boring half hour. He thought it was the 45th Division which he had first fought with in Sicily. It was not. It was the remains of something *called* the 45th Division. There was nobody there whom he had commanded in Sicily. And he thought that we were the same people, or he affected to think that. So the matter of reconstitution and the reality of division specifications, numbers, names and so on, is a question that needs to come up more when we discuss what happens to men and armies in war.

Dennis Showalter: The storm trooper does emerge as an ideal German male, but the storm trooper of the Nazis was not the storm trooper of the First World War. He was rather an idealized construct. It would be interesting to draw some parallels with, say, the United States military. For example, how does a Marine behave? A Marine knows how to behave because he's been brought up with stories of Marine heroes. How does a paratrooper behave? He's been brought up with tales of Ridgway's men. Such archetypes are present in any army, and indeed in any social system.

Tim Travers: Dennis Showalter's excellent paper reminds me of a story I read recently in a new book by Ben Greenhouse on the Battle of Vimy Ridge. He tells the story of two German soldiers who were lost on the battlefield . . . they were wandering around during the offensive and wondering how they were going to get out of it alive, and they went down into a dugout where they found four Canadian soldiers playing cards. The Canadians had "forgotten" about the offensive. They'd just gone into the dugout and started playing cards, and they invited the two Germans to join them. And you know, Vimy Ridge has the same sort of status for Canadians as Gallipoli does for Australians, so it's bad, really, for a Canadian like myself to read this. But it gives you a whole different sense of the battlefield.

Another point that comes to mind is the question of mutinies as it pertains to the British army. Why did the British army not mutiny in the First World War, or at least show signs of mutinous behavior? It has been said that the British army did not have such problems because the common soldiers were conditioned by the class structure of British society to defer to their officers. I don't think that's true. I think there was excellent rapport between junior officers and soldiers in the British army during the war and I think that went a very long way to help keep the army together.

Audience Member: In conjunction with the question of the German soldier in the Second World War, I confess I haven't read the novel *Cross of Iron,* but I have seen the movie. I thought it was a superb representation of what the Wehrmacht soldier in Russia could have been and was. It depicted the men of a small unit— their close camaraderie and their struggle to stay alive under the stewardship of this one dynamic sergeant, Steiner, who kept them together as a harmonious team. They had one Nazi in their midst whom they distrusted and disliked, but they fought as a unit to stay alive, almost like a brotherhood.

Dennis Showalter: The movie is an interesting symbiosis, because the author of *Cross of Iron,* Willi Heinrich, wrote from a postwar Marxist perspective. And Sam Peckinpah, of course, the classic gonzo-macho director, took the novel and sort of made it into a World War II equivalent of *The Wild Bunch.* The movie has little in common with the novel except the title and the names of some of the characters. But it is certain that Peckinpah was heavily influenced by what you might call the "Landser mystique" of World War II. *Cross of Iron* is a movie the German army, that is, the veterans of the Wehrmacht, would like to have as their archetype.

Audience Member: But you don't think it was realistic?

Dennis Showalter: It's realistic in spots. Certainly the depiction of a strong group identity was realistic. And, of course as you pointed out, primary groups form in war because they are necessary for survival—not because you like each other, not because you are members of some sworn brotherhood of arms, but because even if you've never seen your buddies until two days ago, you need to hang together to survive. In this context, note the portrayal of the Nazi as an outcast. We've seen this in many movies and TV shows, from *The Guns of Navarone* to *The Enemy Below* to a *Star Trek* remake of *The Enemy Below.* But as Omer Bartov has pointed out, the Wehrmacht was progressively Nazified, particularly in the latter part of the war and not least because Nazi propaganda fit the reality of the Russian front. I have said elsewhere that World War II was a war of flush toilets and toothbrushes as much as it was a war of ideologies, but these men had to know they were better men than the Russians or they might as well commit suicide or surrender immediately. Nazi ideology provided the sense of superiority they needed. So there's a certain element of what you might call wish fulfillment in this depiction of the Nazi as outcast. *Cross of Iron* is to a great degree *The Wild Bunch* in Wehrmacht drag, but it has certain points of validity and it's certainly the way the German veterans of World War II would like to see themselves.

Paul Fussell: On this matter, we're not holding the conclusion of a university course. But I can't resist adding a slight bibliographical note in relation to this last question. There's a superb memoir of a German soldier on the Eastern Front which I would recommend to everyone. It's called *The Forgotten Soldier* and it's by an Alsatian named Guy Sajer. It's utterly unpolitical, purely military, and delightful. I've read it several times and I recommend it to everyone. And I think you'd find it extremely useful in part because it knows that, for the common soldier, war has nothing to do with politics whatever. It has to do with survival. It has to do with doing well for the sake of your parents behind the line and your fellows next to you—politics is the last thing you're thinking about. And that's why the book is so refreshing.

The Fortress Peace: Germany in the Great War
Daniel Moran

My theme this afternoon is the so-called "Fortress Peace," an expression used to characterize political and social arrangements in Germany during the First World War. The phrase refers to a traditional practice dating from medieval times: when a city or a castle found itself besieged, the inhabitants were expected to set their private disputes and grievances aside in order to join forces against a common enemy. Some of Germany's opponents had similar slogans, with different psychological resonances: the French spoke of a "sacred union" against a presumably unholy foe, the British, more phlegmatically, of carrying on "business as usual" despite the war. All these catch-phrases were coined by politicians early in the war, and by the time the war ended all had become synonymous with naiveté and empty optimism, mocking the spirit of national determination they were supposed to capture.

Yet it almost goes without saying that the persistence of just such a spirit is what ultimately allowed the First World War to achieve its distinctive historical shape. None of the images that come to mind when we think of the war—the trenches, the gas, the endless bombardments, the waves of men moving forward toward industrialized destruction—none of them could have existed if the major belligerents had not maintained a degree of social cohesion in the face of what, before the war, would have been deemed unimaginable losses. The point may seem perverse, but let me make it anyway: it is only because the civil societies of Europe failed to collapse under the strain of prolonged war, as they were expected to do, that European soldiers eventually found themselves completely bereft of strategic expedients, stuck in a conflict of a kind that many of them had long dreaded, but which scarcely any of them knew how to fight effectively.

It is thus to the domestic histories of the major belligerents that we must turn if we seriously want to investigate two of the most fundamental questions about the Great War: why, given such unprecedented military futility, did it last so long; and why, having lasted so long, did it finally end? Such questions can never be fully addressed by studying only one side, or one aspect of the conflict. But even granting that, I still think that studying the internal history of Germany during the war is a good way into problems of this kind, for at least two reasons.

87

The first is that the immediate, personal suffering of civilians in Germany was worse than what generally occurred elsewhere—Russia being the major exception—which must have put a correspondingly greater strain on the bonds that held German society together. Immediately after the war, the German public health office calculated that Germany had suffered 763,000 "excess" civilian deaths during the war (see table), meaning that 763,000 people had died who, by pre-war actuarial standards, would have been expected to live. This calculation has been subjected to a good deal of analysis, but one straightforward way to interpret it is as a crude index of the effectiveness of the Fortress Peace. The domestic institutions and civil populations of Germany's Western opponents never underwent any comparable test.

"Excess" German civilian deaths in World War I

    1918–21 study 763,000
    1944 [Swiss] study 733,000
German military deaths in World War I 2,037,000

* * *

German civilian deaths in World War II

    From the strategic bombing
        campaign 300–600,000
    From all causes................................... 1,000,000
German military deaths in World War II 3,500,000

Those in Russia did, with catastrophic results. And although I will argue below that the Fortress Peace finally broke down in Germany, it is important to see the failure in context. 763,000 deaths is a high number, even when they aren't the result of violent contact with the enemy. Most people's impressions of the First World War don't include such massive civilian casualties. Yet, as you can see, German civilian losses from 1914 through 1918 exceed the high estimate of deaths attributable to the strategic bombing campaign of 1942–45. One German civilian died for every three German soldiers in the First World War, pretty much the same result that was obtained by more direct methods twenty years later.

One reason to investigate the Fortress Peace, then, is as a case study in the maintenance of morale and civil order in wartime, and also in the consequences of economic warfare vigorously pursued. I confess I am sometimes puzzled by the appeal that blockades and similar measures hold for public opinion in democratic countries, where "economic sanctions" are commonly viewed as nothing more than nonviolent extensions of diplomatic pressure. They can be that, of course; but, when seriously carried out, they can also be instruments of great and deadly coercive power, as the German experience shows.

Which brings us to the second reason why the Fortress Peace is worth studying: because in the end it does begin to fail, and in so doing contributes to Germany's decision to stop fighting in the fall of 1918. And here one must admittedly tread carefully, since the notion that Germany's armed forces did not really lose the war, but were rather "stabbed in the back" by feckless civilians, would become one of the most pernicious political myths of the postwar period. The myth is false, but like all myths it contains an element of truth, without which it would never have been believed by so many otherwise sensible people.

Germany suffered a classic military defeat in 1918, in precisely the terms described by Clausewitz a century earlier: the country had not been rendered literally defenseless—the least likely outcome of war, in Clausewitz's view—but it had been put in a position where its future defenselessness had become manifestly probable. The element of truth in the stab-in-the-back myth is simply that the best vantage point from which to view this looming probability was behind the lines, a fact that would subsequently be distorted into an image of an intact army betrayed by the people back home. The German war effort, from start to finish, involved the full range of Germany's social resources. The same can be said of Germany's defeat.

For purposes of analysis it makes sense to distinguish three essential components of the Fortress Peace, three areas of civil life where it was widely accepted that, if things went badly wrong, Germany could lose the war even if the army performed well. The first critical area was the management of party politics to secure parliamentary support for the war, and avoid dissension and criticism of the government, which would at a minimum give aid and comfort to the enemy, and might lead to serious unrest or even revolution if left unchecked. The second great problem was industrial production, which had to be expanded and reorganized in line with military priorities, and also adjusted to account for shortages of key raw materials. The third was how to maintain an adequate supply of food for the army and the civil population.

I don't want to make too much of these distinctions, which are obviously artificial. They certainly don't represent categories

into which specific policies fall, and the mutual dependencies linking political order, industrial production, and food supply are much
too intricate for anyone to disentangle them completely. Nevertheless, I think it is broadly true that, when judged in relation to the
overall goal of prosecuting the war, Germany does well enough to
get by in the first two of these areas, but much less well in the
third. This is not to suggest that much more should have been
done, simply that it was in the agricultural sector that Germany's
domestic arrangements would prove most inadequate.

Which, it's safe to say, is not where the smart money would
have been before the war began. In evaluating the Fortress Peace, it
is essential to keep in mind that, no less than the Schlieffen Plan, it
was predicated on the notion that the war would be short, meaning
that its length would be measured in months rather than years.
(The Russo-Japanese war, which lasted thirteen months on land,
was considered a "long" war by military planners in Germany and
elsewhere before 1914.) Given this assumption, the greatest domestic danger in the short run lay in the political arena, specifically in
the possibility that the Social Democratic Party (SPD) would refuse
to support the war, by voting against war credits and calling for a
general strike. If this had happened the army could not have been
mobilized, and Germany would have been left naked to its enemies.

The term "Fortress Peace" was initially coined with reference
to the political deal, struck on the day war was declared, by which
these grim possibilities were averted. At the time the agreement
was regarded as an unexpectedly easy victory for the German state,
which was able to dispense with a lot of potentially demoralizing
measures—the rounding up and imprisoning of trade unionists,
the suppression of opposition newspapers, and so forth. Instead,
the emperor could celebrate the triumph of community over class
and ideology. In retrospect, however, it is easy to see that the danger of revolutionary upheaval motivated by principled pacifism, or
even by crass political opportunism, was never very great at any
time during the war. Although the SPD had retained the rhetoric of
a revolutionary party, it and its membership had much too great a
stake in the existing system to seriously wish to take their chances
by turning it upside down (which is, after all, one of the meanings
of "revolution"). To which add that at least a third of the German
working class could expect to be immediately conscripted into the
army, thus becoming hostages for the patriotic behavior of their
comrades. This fact weighed heavily with trade union leaders contemplating the feasibility of a general strike.

Although political dissension inevitably mounted as the war
dragged on, groups like the Independent Socialists, who actively

sought to oppose the government on fundamental issues, were effectively driven to the sidelines. Mainstream debate focused on war aims, and also on political reforms like the introduction of a democratic franchise in Prussia; reforms that bore no relation to the conduct of the war itself, except in the sense that they were regarded as just recompense for the nation's military efforts. Which highlights an important feature of Germany's wartime politics: unlike the inhabitants of besieged medieval cities, who set their prewar quarrels aside only for the duration, most Germans, regardless of their politics, expected that life after the war would be markedly different from what it had been before, and sought as best they could to use wartime conditions to improve their chances. Wartime politics, in other words, was not just about how to prosecute the war. It was also, indeed primarily, about what the postwar world would be like. This general tendency, which is equally evident in the political histories of France and Great Britain, helped keep public controversy within acceptable—which is to say reformist rather than revolutionary—bounds, at least until Germany's military defeat had become plain.

The mobilization of German industry for war was intimately linked to the problem of maintaining political order, and can really be distinguished from it only in the sense that more was involved than simply keeping the working class in line—a necessary but by no means sufficient basis for military success. Germany also suffered from serious shortages of raw materials, and from the financial consequences of being cut off from world markets. All of which could have been, and was, foreseen before the war, only to be discounted on the grounds that the conflict would be over before these difficulties could make themselves felt.

That Germany should have begun the First World War with no more than a six months' supply of basic raw materials was at least consistent with Germany's overall strategy. The surprising thing is how quickly the nation's vulnerability in this area was recognized and addressed. Only five days after war was declared, long before the failure of the Schlieffen Plan could have been guessed, Walter Rathenau, head of Germany's General Electric Corporation, went to the Minister of War, Erich von Falkenhayn, with a proposal to create a Raw Materials Section within the ministry to organize the distribution of resources among German industries. It is no exaggeration to say that, but for Falkenhayn's acceptance of Rathenau's proposal, the war really would have been over by Christmas.

In the event, however, the Raw Materials Section was merely the first of a whole slew of agencies charged with managing the war economy. This proliferation of overlapping and conflicting authorities was lamented by pretty much everyone who had to work with them, and can be seen in retrospect as a consequence of poor prewar planning, and, more fundamentally, of the assumption, never seriously challenged, that the German economy, like all other aspects of the war effort, should be under the control of the German army. This was a task for which the army proved singularly ill-suited, both organizationally and psychologically.

Michael Howard once observed, apropos of the preeminence of "procurement" among the peacetime activities of soldiers today, that it is not easy to make swordsmen out of blacksmiths—meaning that people who spend all their time buying and selling things may lose the knack for fighting. The German experience in the First World War suggests that the opposite is also true: it's not easy to make blacksmiths out of swordsmen, either. The officers in charge of regulating the war economy regarded the rapidly changing needs of the army in the field as the sole determinant of industrial priorities, and never really grasped the degree to which industrial firms rely on predictable demand, long-term contracts, and economies of scale to organize their activities. German industrialists, for their part, never lost their knack for driving a hard bargain, and treated the government more or less as they would any customer caught in a tight spot. They always demanded high profits as recompense for their aggravation, and usually got them, with inflationary results that only became fully apparent after the war was over.

Apart from raw materials, the main resource that required careful allocation was human labor. And here the needs of the fighting front and the home front did not simply trip over each other, they conflicted directly since every man employed in war industry was by definition a man exempted from military service, and every casualty was a loss to both. Although the resulting shortfall of industrial labor could be partly filled by the mobilization of women, there was never a moment when the demand for skilled workers did not exceed the supply the army was willing to release from active duty. The result was a substantial rise in the real wages of skilled workers at the expense of unskilled laborers, agricultural workers, and lower-level white-collar types, whose real incomes declined during the war; and also a progressive subjugation of the civilian work force to quasi-military discipline, which limited the rights of workers to change jobs, to strike, and so on.

Labor unrest had been rising sharply in Germany before 1914, and putting an end to it was an indispensable element of the Fortress Peace. Until its logistical infrastructure was fully developed, the army was correctly seen as profoundly vulnerable to any sort of industrial disruption. The fact that there were virtually no organized work stoppages in Germany between the outbreak of the war and the spring of 1916 was crucial to Germany's ability to carry on the war. From April of 1916 onward, however, the prewar pattern of escalating work stoppages resumed, and by 1917 the German economy was losing more work days to strikes than in any period before the war.

These developments coincided with other signs of crisis in German society, including the so-called "Turnip Winter" and the passage of the Reichstag Peace Resolution, and are sometimes taken as an indication that, by the middle of the war, the Fortress Peace had ceased to exist. This is true enough if one takes as one's standard the emperor's original pronouncement that he no longer recognized parties or classes, only Germans. But if one judges the Fortress Peace in light of its strategic purpose, which was not to promote social harmony or political reform, but to prosecute the war, it is fairly clear that by the time industrial unrest becomes truly widespread the war economy is sufficiently resilient to stand the strain.

Like the British, the Germans suffer their worst logistical problems early in the war, when the deficiencies of prewar planning had not yet been overcome. Labor problems later on remain a serious matter, but they are viewed differently. One can only be struck by the extent to which Germany's military and political leadership, including some Socialists, viewed the strikes of 1916–17 not as a warning that the war needed to be wrapped up on whatever terms might be available, but as evidence that anything less than a clear victory would have disastrous consequences, since the people would feel that they had been asked to make great sacrifices in vain. A colossal misjudgment, perhaps; but the fact remains that, when Germany finally did stop fighting, it was not because the army was running out of ammunition.

Whether it was because Germany itself was running out of food is more difficult to say. Food was not a critical problem at the outset of the war, in the sense that immediate supplies were adequate and invulnerable to political disruption. As in the industrial sector, however, it could be foreseen that, if the war dragged on into the following year, serious shortages would arise. Again, the speed of the German response is impressive when viewed in light of prewar complacency: like industrial raw materials, bread and other basic foodstuffs were already being rationed in Germany at the start of 1915.

In the long run, however, the food problem was not all that amenable to the kinds of managerial solutions that were applied to industry. Like some other advanced industrial countries, Germany had imported a large fraction of its food supply before the war; and

while these missing imports did not need to be made up completely—people, after all, could eat less—the German population
nevertheless presented its leaders with a basic, inelastic demand
for food that had to be met continuously. On the whole, Germany
does seem to have met this demand—barely—at most times during
the war, by using rationing to impose different dietary patterns, by
expanding land use, and so on. No society ever manages these
sorts of trade-offs perfectly. More might have been done, but only
at the expense of other aspects of the war effort. Nitrates necessary
for ammunition could not be used for fertilizer, for instance. Manpower policies, administered by boards dominated by industrial
and trade union interests, strongly tended to favor exemptions for
industrial labor, in part because it was easier to mobilize women to
do farm work—though the net result was still that the agricultural
work force shrank by 60 percent over the course of the war.

Most historians would agree that Germany was not starved
into defeat. Some Germans did starve, however. Others suffered
from the indirect consequences of malnutrition, which accounts
for the bulk of the 763,000 "excess deaths" mentioned earlier. A
majority, including nearly all the inhabitants of German cities, eventually experienced a kind of profound hunger unfamiliar to advanced societies. This sort of thing could be mastered for a while
by camaraderie and gallows humor. One woman living in Leipzig
noted in her diary that she had heard a rumor that there was rat
meat in the sausages; she then added that it was not the rat meat,
but the rat substitute that really concerned her. In the long run,
however, the corrosive effects of food shortages on civilian morale
made themselves felt at the highest levels of German strategic de-
cision-making. The U-boat campaign of 1917 was clearly conceived
in large part as an indirect response to hunger on the home front,
the idea being to inflict similar suffering on the enemy. Whether
the same can be said of the decision to give up the fight the following year is more controversial, but the case to be made is strong. In
October of 1918, when General Erich Ludendorff turned to the
leader of the SPD, Philip Scheidemann, and asked whether it might
still be possible to obtain additional reinforcements for the army,
whose resistance to the Allied advance was now stiffening,
Scheidemann could only reply, "That is a question of potatoes."

Even questions of potatoes, however, admit of different answers at different times, and must be viewed in light of the overall
strategic situation. Which is why it is ultimately impossible to
accept the legend of the stab in the back, which holds that the
army stopped fighting because the Fortress Peace collapsed into
revolution. That does not seem to be what happened. Rather, the

German home front suffered a kind of gradual attrition, which was continuing but not accelerating when the war ended. What did seem to be changing rapidly during the last months of the war is the political atmosphere, which constituted a kind of lens through which material sacrifices were inevitably viewed. This change is usually attributed to the failure of the Ludendorff Offensive, which became obvious to the German public by mid-August. As a kind of speculative conclusion, however—if such a thing is possible—I would argue that if we want to understand the final breakdown of civilian morale in Germany we need to start a little earlier, and to focus, more closely than is usually done, on the war with Russia, or rather on its absence.

It is scarcely possible to overestimate Russia's contribution to the Fortress Peace. Russia's preemptive mobilization in July of 1914 confirmed the average German's impression that his country's cause was just, and that the war to come was defensive in nature—that Germany really was a besieged fortress. That Russia appeared to be the aggressor was also essential to securing the support of the SPD and the working class, who were easily persuaded that, however dubious the present system might seem, no good would come from a victory by Europe's most reactionary regime. Germany's stunning victories at Tannenberg and the Masurian Lakes contrasted strongly with the emerging stalemate in the West, and created an enduring residue of public confidence that, whatever else might be going on, Germany was winning the war in the East.

This residue, based on a realistic prospect of victory (though perhaps compounded by cultural arrogance toward a Slavic opponent), was an important component of the psychological glue that held the Fortress Peace together. Which may be why, once the war in the East ended in a Germany victory, morale in Germany itself became more fragile and not more robust. By the spring of 1918 Germans were eating rat substitute not to win "the" war, but half a war, in an arena where they had long since learned to regard all claims of progress as illusory. Under these circumstances it is hard to imagine a worse strategic miscalculation than the launching of the Ludendorff Offensive. If one takes Germany's internal condition fully into account, it becomes obvious that, in the aftermath of Russia's defeat, the only strategic alternative still open to Germany was a determined defensive in the West, conducted on the shortest and most formidable lines possible, intended to bring about peace based on the status quo ante, modified as far as possible by the terms of Brest-Litovsk.

Whether such a strategy would have succeeded may, of course, be doubted. Once America entered the war the chances for any kind of compromise peace declined, not simply because the Allies became more confident of final victory, but because America's own objectives included a total recasting of the international system which would have been impossible in the context of any sort of agreement based on prewar conditions. Nevertheless, such a strategy would at least have had whatever advantages coherence can offer. As it was, it is obvious that by the end of the war German military strategy had departed absolutely from the social and political base on which it necessarily rested. It was the failure of Germany's military leadership to see this that finally broke the Fortress Peace, and Germany with it.

Q&A

Q. *What was Germany's tax policy during the war? Did taxes go up or remain stationary?*

A. Taxes in Germany did go up during the war, but not as much as they did in the countries of the Allied coalition. The reason for this is due in part to the fact that it is the German Lände and not the central government that control the collection of direct taxes such as income taxes. But also, in general, the Germans preferred to finance the war by borrowing money. Everybody borrows some money and everybody has big war debts, except for America, at the end. But in Germany the proportion of borrowed money-to-taxed revenue was higher, and this was one of the causes of the big inflationary bump that occurred in the postwar period.

If you want to compare Germany to a country that raises taxes much more in line with the war effort, you want to look at England, which was much more willing to tax well-off people directly to support the war.

Q. *Germany was a recently unified country in 1914. Were there not in fact sectional differences within the country during the war?*

A. Most decidedly. In fact, there were efforts by the Bavarian government to seek a separate peace with Germany's enemies. On the whole, however, that danger is more symbolic than real. It's certainly true that Germany was a recently unified country, but the basic dynamics of wartime psychology—the sense of having a common enemy, the shared violence, the shared peril, the shared suffering—tends to overwhelm separatist sentiments. But the Bavarians actually did seek to foment a movement for a separate peace or a compromise peace in the middle of the war.

Q. To what extent did knowledge of Wilson's Fourteen Points affect the desire of Germans and Austrians to seek a separate peace?

A. I don't believe that Austrian efforts to conclude a separate peace, which were ongoing from 1916, were influenced by the Fourteen Points. However, I couldn't tell you how much impact Wilson's proposals had on German public opinion. Needless to say, the Fourteen Points were very well known in Germany. And they were ideally suited, it seems to me, to the kind of atmosphere that I see in Germany in 1918. The Germans kind of think that the Treaty of Brest-Litovsk was based on semi-Wilsonian principles; and they could have been easily persuaded that a similar treaty could be concluded to preserve the status quo in the West, after which everyone could turn against the Communists. Such a treaty could have worked in terms of German public opinion. And, clearly, Wilson's Fourteen Points contribute to the softening up of civilian morale. They do so decisively at the end, when the political people in charge saw that the proposals provided justification for kicking the kaiser out and doing everything else that's necessary to really end the war.

Q. I was wondering if you have any figures showing how the acquisition of Ukrainian wheat in the final months of the war may have helped the Central Powers feed their people. Did the wheat have a noticeable impact on the German and Austrian home fronts? Did it alleviate the starvation that gripped the civilian populations?

A. It's hard to get such figures. Most of what we know about food and other problems in Germany is based on local evidence, which can be piled pretty high but doesn't provide a comprehensive picture of the whole country. In general, if the war had gone on longer, Germany might have been in a position to incorporate those resources into their food program—which is what they did in the next war, when they conquered significant agricultural resources quite early on.

I'd be surprised, however, if Ukrainian wheat would have made a difference in the short run. I say that because the blockade did not end with the Armistice. The effect this had on German public opinion—the disappointment it caused—cannot be underestimated. The shooting stopped on November 11, 1918, but the war continued if by "war" you mean the starving of the German population. It was the blockade that kept the Germans' feet to the fire until they signed the Treaty of Versailles, which was the real surrender.

The blockade of 1918–19 had severe consequences for Germany. The suffering leveled off because there was no army consuming extra food, which meant that civilian malnutrition was no longer accelerating. Conditions just kind of hit bottom and stayed there. But I would doubt that Germany could have put together the resource base needed to mount offensive operations, especially after the Ludendorff Offensive. And that's the problem with the Ludendorff Offensive: even if it had succeeded, there could be no follow-up, not in 1919, not ever.

Q. *How successful were the efforts to circumvent the embargo by going through neutral countries such as Holland and Switzerland?*

A. I think they were fairly successful with small-scale items, that is, rare resources and industrial commodities. It's very difficult to do that with food. Food is big and hard to hide. It rots when it gets wet. It's actually a difficult business to handle food—it's hard to stockpile, it doesn't last, and so forth. I don't think that smuggling was a significant source of relief for the food problem in Germany because of the nature of the stuff you had to smuggle.

Q. *Can you make a neat, balanced equation between German civilian deaths and the blockade?*

A. No. I think you make a sloppy equation. The figure of 763,000 civilian deaths was, as I said, calculated on a sort of actuarial basis. So the figure can be manipulated in various ways.

I've seen one study, for instance, which for reasons I don't fully understand eliminated Alsace-Lorraine as part of the picture. It didn't count the deaths of civilians in Alsace-Lorraine. I suppose the reason for that is obvious—this is a study done at the end of the 1920s. But the study also decided not to include children who died in Germany. And I don't understand why the deaths of children would be regarded as less of a hardship than the deaths of, say, old people. But the figure itself must be regarded as a measure of the biological consequences, if you will, of Germany's ultimate economic inferiority in the war. And that economic inferiority was intensified by the blockade. That, I think, is as far as one can go. Very few German civilian deaths were caused by contact with enemy soldiers, and so you're left with a general picture.

These deaths are more evenly distributed through the population than you might imagine. It is not just the young and the very old who die, or just the sick and the poor. It really is more general than that. The death rates for young adults, for instance, which are normally very low, went up markedly during the war, so that the same people who were dying at the front, young men, if they didn't go to the front, they might still end up dying at home. If they were too sickly to fight in the war, the blockade might get them anyway.

I should say that the figure of 763,000 does not include deaths attributable to the influenza epidemic of 1918–1919. Approximately 209,000 Germans died of the flu in those two years. How much of that number you could read back into the blockade is anybody's guess.

Comment

Robert Cowley: The statistic of 763,000 civilian deaths in Germany during the war really gives new meaning to the phrase "home front." And a real mark, I think, of how badly beaten Germany was in the end is the apparent lack, in the autumn of 1918, of any war plan for 1919. There was nothing. They were beaten.

Paul Fussell: I was equally fascinated with the food-distribution substructure of the German war . . . with the economics and politics which are always there and which the melodrama and the romance—if one has to use that word—of military operations tends to obscure.

Edward Coffman: Dan Moran underscores the concept of the thirty years' war by making a connection between the civilian deaths from naval blockade in World War I and civilian deaths from strategic bombardment in World War II. He also points to the fact that in this century you're really getting into total war, war on civilians. He also alludes to the questions and problems that ensue when you impose economic sanctions on a country. Who are you really punishing with such sanctions? What are you really trying to achieve?

Paul Fussell: May I comment about the sources for assessing civilian morale? I would say that public sources are of no use at all unless they're interpreted in an absolutely reverse way than they're meant to be interpreted. The way to assess civilian morale is by private, internal, that is domestic, correspondences which have never been censored and which are written sincerely from one person to another with a sort of private implicit trust between them. That's the only way I think to get at the truth of the matter.

PART 4

KNIGHT AND KNAVE

Who Killed Manfred von Richthofen?
An Inquiry into the Events of 21 April 1918
Philip Markham

(Note: Philip Markham was unable to attend the conference. His paper was presented by Frederick Gaffin, the 1992 historian of the Canadian War Museum and author of several books on military history. Gaffin also fielded questions afterwards. The text of Philip Markham's paper first appeared in the summer 1993 issue of Over the Front, *the journal of the League of World War I Aviation Historians. It is reprinted with the permission of that organization. Ed.)*

Introduction

This research, or rather this reexamination and analysis of available documentation, was initiated by a request from Wing Commander Ralph Manning D.F.C., RCAF, who was at that time intending to write a book on Arthur Roy Brown. For the action on 21 April 1918, in which Manfred von Richthofen lost his life, Manning required an assessment of the time between Brown's attack and the time at which von Richthofen pulled up sharply into the turn from which he crashed. Manning was considering the possibility that von Richthofen could have been mortally wounded by Brown and not killed outright by some other marksmen. This thesis was also proposed by Dr. Bruce M. Cameron in his article in the *Houston Chronicle,* 30 April 1978. I was quite skeptical about this theory, but the task was straightforward, requiring only a review of the statements made by the witnesses, a topographical map, the appropriate meteorological report, and some performance figures for the Fokker Dr.I.

Having established the final flight path of von Richthofen's Dr.I and finding that its furthest point of advance was over or only just beyond the Bray-Corbie road, and having, incidentally, read the medical evidence, it appeared highly improbable that the presently accepted claimant, Gunner Robert Buie, of the 53rd Battery, Australian Field Artillery, had ever been in a position to fire the fatal shot.

At this point curiosity took over, and it was decided to take a closer look at the matter. As a result, several aspects of the incident were examined in depth. Comprehensive notes were prepared on each of these, and the narrative which follows is essentially a summary of these individual studies, with much of the detail eliminated.

103

Research

Initially I was quite ignorant about the matter. It seemed to me to be an incident which had been investigated to death, and had never had any particular interest for me; so I had no preconceived ideas, and was intrigued by the way in which each new fact enlarged, and often changed, the picture as it developed.

The initial literature search produced a number of references, which I began to acquire and read. This was an interesting exercise, because the more I read, the clearer it became that the primary issue was "who killed von Richthofen," and that emotion rather than reason was governing the writing. It certainly seemed that no one had carried out a thoughtful analysis of the available information, or even questioned its validity.

From the air aspect, the combat reports of the pilots of No. 209 Squadron RAF and No. 3 Squadron AFC, together with the Squadron Order Books, are readily available. German records are less easy to find, but letters and documents were obtained, and correspondence and telephone calls helped to fill the gaps and sort the wheat from the chaff. Gradually a much clearer picture of the aerial activity was pieced together, which was more complete and differed in a number of respects from the way it has been described previously.

On the ground, by 16 April 1918 it had become clear that the lull following the German attack and advance on Amiens in March and early April would be short-lived, and that another attack would soon be launched with the object of taking the city. It was expected that it would start early on 24 April, which, in fact, it did. This attack, which was centered on Villers-Bretonneux, was repulsed; the limit of the German attack in the Amiens area had been reached.

However, on Sunday, 21 April 1918, this attack was still a few days ahead and the Australian Corps was resting and regrouping. The troops were enjoying good weather and were living well in what had so recently been rear areas. The air fight which developed over their positions during the morning was obviously not a threat and was probably regarded with little interest by the troops. It seems that very few of them had even a fleeting glimpse of May, von Richthofen, and Brown during the two minutes or less of their fast-moving, low-level combat. Certainly no one seems to have noticed the similar pursuit of Mellersh by Wolff and Karjus across Corbie and Brown's firing at this German pair. The fact that von Richthofen was involved undoubtedly influenced both recollections and research.

In order to make a credible assessment of the action it was essential to establish the locations of the witnesses, and relate their statements to the terrain. Only in this way could the validity of their observations be checked and the flight paths of the aircraft determined. Not surprisingly, very few of these statements, painstakingly collected by Bean, Carisella, and Titler, for example, were in any way relevant. However, it must be kept in mind that most of them were made many years after the event and with the benefit of hindsight. It should also be appreciated that the witnesses were watching two aircraft flying at about one hundred miles per hour, fifty to one hundred feet above the ground, from positions where their views were restricted, so that in most cases only a fleeting impression of the chase could have been obtained. Most of the later statements include a reference to the fact that no aircraft other than May's Camel and von Richthofen's triplane were to be seen in the vicinity when von Richthofen crashed, as if a question on this matter had been asked specifically, as no doubt it was.

However, in spite of the fact that four grid references were found for the location of Sergeant C. B. Popkin, that three are given for the crash site, and that the grid on a 1916 map sheet was found to be displaced by about one hundred yards from that on a 1918 edition, it was possible to determine the flight paths of the aircraft and the locations of the key witnesses on the ground with a fair degree of accuracy. This exercise was greatly aided by the fact that the British used the same map series, with the same grid, from 1916 to the end of the war, and that all reconnaissance photographs taken by the RFC/RAF were annotated with a grid reference. Thus it was possible to obtain from the Imperial War Museum photographs of the appropriate area showing the locations of key items, such as the 53rd Battery AFA and the Ste.-Collette brickworks; and, as a matter of interest, it was possible to locate the aerodrome at Cappy and establish the location of *Jagdgeschwader* 1.

In addition to documentary analysis, the general area of the combat was driven and walked over, particular attention being paid to the view from the locations reported occupied by Gunners Buie and Evans, Sergeant Popkin, and Lieutenant Travers. Also, thanks to the generosity of my friend *Dr.-Ing.* Niedermeyer, it was possible to fly over the area in his Piper Comanche and follow the track flown by May and von Richthofen up the side of the Morlancourt Ridge to the west of Vaux-sur-Somme. It was clear that the final turn of Dr.I 425/17 was unlikely to have taken it beyond the Bray-Corbie road if it was to end up in front of the Ste.-Collette brickworks.

By this time sufficient material had been accumulated to make some sketches and do a few sums to establish the time from Brown's attack to von Richthofen pulling up from his pursuit of May, Brown's subsequent flight path, and what Buie and Popkin could have seen from where they were.

In addition, a Fokker Dr.I cockpit model was made in order to demonstrate the range of angles relative to von Richthofen's aircraft from which the fatal bullet must have arrived. This was based on an artist's mannequin, which, after estimating the height of Manfred von Richthofen, resulted in a very odd scale! The mannequin was seated in two different positions: looking straight forward, and turned to the right to look over its right shoulder. It was determined that the bullet entered above the ninth rib, which it broke, implying that it might have come from a slightly higher angle and been deflected.

Now a description of the action can be given, and some conclusions can be drawn from the facts which have been established.

Air Activity from 0900 to 1105 hours, 21 April 1918

At 0900 hours on 21 April 1918 a flight of Albatros D.Va aircraft of *Jagdstaffel* 6, probably led by *Obltn.* Richard Flascher, were airborne from Cappy. They headed west for the front in the vicinity of the Morlancourt Ridge, which was held by the Australian Corps.

The weather was misty initially, but cleared into a bright sunny day with scattered clouds; the wind was from the east—which was unusual—at about twenty miles per hour.

At Bertangles, thirty-six kilometers west of Cappy, about half an hour later, fifteen Sopwith Camels of No. 209 Squadron, RAF, took off, A Flight (Captain A. R. Brown) at 0935, C Flight (Captain O. W. Redgate) at 0940, and B Flight (Captain O. C. LeBoutillier) at 0945 hours. They too headed for the lines on a high offensive patrol.

A second flight of *Jasta* 5, possibly led by *Ltn.* Wilhelm Lehman, and including *Offz. Stu.* Josef Mai, left Cappy at 1009 to join the others, and, at about the same time, two R.E.8 aircraft of No. 3 Squadron Australian Flying Corps (Lieutenants S. G. Garrett and A. V. Barrow, and Lieutenants T. L. Simpson and E. C. Banks) left Poulainville, immediately adjacent to Bertangles, for photographic reconnaissance in the vicinity of Hamel.

At 1025, LeBoutillier, Foster, and Taylor of B Flight attacked two two-seaters (reportedly Albatros, but more probably L.V.G. C.V.—POW report) over Le Quesnel, and downed one in flames which crashed at Ignaueourt. This aircraft was from *Fliegerabteilung (A)* 203 at Hangest, commanded by Hauptmann Victor Carganico, who was von Richthofen's CO in *Jasta* 8 at Verdun. *Ltn.d.R.* Kurt Fischer, pilot, and *Ltn.d.R.* Rudolf Rubinius, observer, were both killed.

At 1030, while this action was taking place, *Jasta* 11, one flight led by *Rittm.* Manfred von Richthofen, commander of *Jagdgeschwader* 1 (six aircraft) and the other (four aircraft) by *Ltn.* Hans Weiss, the

Staffelführer, took off from Cappy, with Weiss's flight in the lead. They too headed for the Morlancourt area.

At 1040 Weiss's flight attacked the two No. 3 Squadron R.E.8 aircraft, which were now taking photographs from about seven thousand feet in the vicinity of Hamel. This combat was indecisive, but the rudder controls of Weiss's aircraft were damaged by gunfire, apparently from Barrow in R.E.8, B6576, and he had to return to Cappy. The others joined von Richthofen, who was now involved with No. 209 Squadron, and the R.E.8s continued their photography.

The dogfight in the vicinity of Cerisy started at about 1045, when Brown led No. 209 Squadron, now at twelve thousand feet, in a dive onto *Jastas* 5 and 11, which were some five thousand feet lower. This combat lasted about fifteen minutes, but although Lieutenant W. J. Mackenzie was wounded, the only aircraft lost was Fokker Dr.I 425/17, and the only fatal casualty was Manfred von Richthofen.

Lieutenant W. R. May, a newcomer to Brown's flight, had been instructed to stay out of any fight during the patrol, but went in, fired head-on at one triplane and then at another, missing both, and finally dived out over the lines. In doing so he was seen and followed by von Richthofen himself, who chased after him over the Australian positions.

Brown, after evading two triplanes which had got on his tail, saw May in trouble and dived to attack von Richthofen, overtaking him, firing one long burst and breaking off. This attack took place at low level just to the east of Vaux-sur-Somme. May, still pursued by Richthofen, who continued to fire short bursts, flew on over the village and up the slope of the ridge, passing Sergeant C. B. Popkin of the 24th Machine Gun Company on his right, and heading directly towards the 53rd Battery, Australian Field Artillery, which was located on the reverse slope. As they passed, Popkin fired a burst at the triplane, but did not think that it was hit. However, before reaching the crest, von Richthofen pulled up into a steep turn to his right, then dived back towards the east, turning to his left just before his aircraft struck the ground beside the Bray-Corbie road and opposite the Ste.-Collette brickworks. The time was 1050.

May continued on over the 53rd Battery and, turning to his right, saw von Richthofen crash. He then joined up with Brown and Lieutenant F. J. W. Mellersh, who had just evaded two *Jasta* 11 triplanes flown by Wolff and Karjus. Mellersh had also seen von Richthofen crash. They flew directly back to Bertangles, picking up the wounded Mackenzie on the way, and landed at 1105 hours.

1048 to 1050 hours

When May dived out of the fight, he crossed the lines just north of Hamel, roughly over Bouzencourt, and it seems to be at this point that von Richthofen caught up with him. The two aircraft then flew on towards Vaux-sur-Somme.

May's Bentley-engined Camel should have been able to out-run von Richthofen's Dr.I, but his evasive action would certainly have slowed him down. Nevertheless, von Richthofen must have flown a much straighter course, cutting corners, in order to keep up. This would require concentration on his quarry and may well explain why he failed to see Brown's approach.

Brown, noticing May in trouble, had dived steeply out of the fight, closed rapidly with von Richthofen from the northeast, and thus attacked him from his starboard quarter. This attack took place immediately to the east of Vaux-sur-Somme. It was witnessed by Lieutenant J. J. R. Punch and Gunner F. Rhodes of the 53rd Battery from their observation point near the stone windmill just east of Vaux, by Lieutenant R. A. Wood of the 51st Battalion in Vaux, and by Captain O. C. LeBoutillier of No. 209 Squadron, who was overhead. Rounds from Brown's guns are alleged to have hit a field cooker in Vaux!

Brown, who was flying much faster than von Richthofen, broke to his left and continued towards the bend in the Somme, where he climbed and fired at two triplanes (Wolff and Karjus) which were chasing Mellersh. He did not hit them but, according to Wolff, they broke off the chase and headed back to Cappy from the vicinity of Bray-sur-Somme. Brown then set course for Bertangles, picking up Mellersh, May, and the wounded Mackenzie on the way.

Following Brown's attack, May, still pursued by von Richthofen, passed over Vaux and headed up the side of the Morlancourt Ridge in the general direction of Bonnay. Sergeant Popkin, with his Vickers gun, fired a burst at von Richthofen as the aircraft approached the wood in and close to which Lieutenants D. L. Fraser and G. M. Travers were located. May crossed the crest of the ridge and continued on over the 53rd Battery, which was sited on the reverse slope; but beside the wood von Richthofen pulled up suddenly to his right, apparently breaking off the chase and heading back for the lines. His farthest point of advance was just about over the Bray-Corbie road, some three hundred yards in front of the 53rd Battery. As the triplane pulled up, it was fired at frontally and then from its port side by Gunners Buie and Evans of the 53rd Battery, who were manning Lewis guns at the battery site. Partway through the turn the nose of the Dr.I dropped, and, although the aircraft appeared to be pulling out of its dive, it crashed into the ground south of the Bray-Corbie road, opposite the Ste.-Collette brickworks.

Who Killed Manfred von Richthofen?
I. Captain A. R. Brown D.S.C., No. 209 Squadron, RAF

The cockpit model clearly demonstrates that von Richthofen was killed by a bullet which came from the starboard side at a horizontal angle between eleven degrees forward and fifty-eight degrees aft and a vertical angle between horizontal—possibly higher—and twelve degrees down. However, it is highly unlikely that the bullet was deflected off the spine as Colonels Sinclair and Nixon surmised, because the exit wound was small, indicating that the bullet was not tumbling and because of the high kinetic energy of the bullet. Doctors whom I have consulted agree with the assumption of Captains Graham and Downs that the bullet passed straight through the chest. In consequence, the range of angles from which the bullet came changes to a horizontal angle between thirty-seven and fifty-eight degrees aft and a vertical angle essentially flat. This is entirely consistent with Brown's attack from von Richthofen's starboard quarter.

From the point at which Brown attacked him to the point over the wood at which von Richthofen pulled up is approximately fifteen hundred yards and uphill. Assuming that his speed was falling between these points and averaged, say, one hundred miles per hour (the French meteorological reports for 21 April 1918 indicate that the wind was from the southeast at fifteen to twenty miles per hour), then the time taken would have been about thirty seconds.

Dr. Denton A. Cooley, the noted heart surgeon, attests to the fact that von Richthofen could have lived for at least sixty seconds after suffering a wound such as that described by the doctors who examined his body, and his opinion is shared by other members of the medical profession in the United States and Canada. The bullet passed through the pericardium and the heart, leaving small holes through which blood was pumped out of the heart into the pericardium and the thoracic cavity. Pressure would have built up in the pericardium and embarrassed the operation of the heart, causing blood pressure to fall. The rate at which it fell would determine how long von Richthofen could continue to function before he became unconscious. Consequently, it is reasonable to conclude that he could have continued to pursue and fire at May after he had been fatally wounded by Brown, and until it became physically impossible to carry on.

It should be noted that the flight of the triplane as it approached the wood was described as unsteady or wobbly, which may well indicate that von Richthofen was losing his faculties but still determined to carry on the fight. This was before he was fired at by either Popkin or Buie.

At this point it may be of interest to look at a graph which illustrates the deflection required at various ranges to hit an aircraft flying at right angles to the gun. The improbability of the aiming points is evident, and makes it very clear that the airman, firing from the rear with virtually no deflection and a low closing speed, had a very much better chance to hit his target than any ground gunner, although he seldom did!

It is also interesting to note that bullets from a fixed machine gun with a rate of fire of, say, six hundred rounds per minute and fired at right angles to an aircraft flying at ninety miles per hour, would be spaced at intervals of 13.2 feet. Close groups can only be obtained if the target is tracked, holding the correct deflection. This is extremely difficult for a ground gunner because the deflection is changing rapidly as the aircraft flies by; and so is the range, which must be estimated accurately in the first place.

II. Sergeant C. B. Popkin, 24th Machine Gun Company, AEF

As has been stated, four different locations can be found for Sergeant Popkin, but the one which seems most logical is that which he gave himself. This places him in the open area between the brickworks and the wood over which von Richthofen pulled up. Thus he would have been on the starboard side of the Dr.I as it passed his position. However, he did not think that he had hit it at this time.

Popkin thought that he had hit von Richthofen after he had turned back and appeared to be about to attack the machine gun site. But this was clearly not the case since the fatal bullet came from the rear.

III. Gunner R. Buie, 53rd Battery, AEF

It is abundantly clear from the flight path of von Richthofen's aircraft and from the medical evidence that neither Buie nor Evans had the opportunity to fire a bullet which would hit the starboard side of Dr.I 425/17. Furthermore, although strikes on the front of the aircraft were claimed, the engine, for example, which is in the Imperial War Museum, shows no sign of any bullet damage.

Conclusions

It will be seen from my interpretation of the facts that the contention of the Australians that there was no third aircraft within two thousand yards of von Richthofen when he crashed is not contradicted and, as it turns out, is irrelevant.

On the basis of this analysis it is evident that Manfred von Richthofen was not killed by Lieutenant Barrow, the observer in R.E.8 AS661, or by Gunner Buie at the 53rd Battery; nor, on his own evidence, does it seem that he could have been hit by Sergeant Popkin from the field south of the brickworks.

Also, paying due regard to the circumstances, it has to be extremely unlikely that he was hit by some unknown soldier who took a quick shot at the passing aircraft.

On the other hand, it has been clearly demonstrated that the thesis of Wing Commander Manning and Dr. Cameron that von Richthofen was hit by Brown but did not die immediately is not only possible, but very probable.

Consequently, although I make no claim to have proved the case, my own conclusion is that *the fatal bullet was fired by Captain Arthur Roy Brown of No. 209 Squadron, Royal Air Force.*

Postscript

The extensive bibliography for this work proved to be largely irrelevant, and for the primary documents I refer the reader to Frank McGuire's excellent compilation of the "Documents Relating to Richthofen's Last Battle" in *Over the Front,* Vol. 2, No. 2, and Vol. 7, No. 4, although I do not agree with all his interpretations. Little reference has been made to sources in the narrative, which I feel to be self-explanatory, and consequently I have not included a long list of references or annotated the text. However, if anyone wishes to question any statement, I would be delighted to correspond on the matter, either directly or through *Over the Front.*

It should be noted that Allied time has been used throughout, German time, which was one hour ahead, being corrected to correspond.

Acknowledgments

As a very inexperienced air historian I was surprised and delighted by the readiness of almost all my correspondents to answer my questions, no matter how elementary, to share their own knowledge, documents, and photographs with me, and to offer constructive comments. Without this generous assistance I could not possibly have assembled the relevant facts necessary to produce an acceptable account of this incident. My grateful thanks to them all, but especially to Bill Bailey, Neal W. O'Connor, the late Dr. Gustav Bock, *Dr.-Ing.* Niedermeyer, and my good friend and mentor, Ed Ferko.

One of Those Distractions

The following note is not directly related to my analysis but, knowing about the effect of rotary engines on handling characteristics, I was curious to know what might have happened if Richthofen had died at the start of the final turn; in fact, whether the turn might not have been a deliberate breaking off of the chase, but the result of a physical spasm preceding death. Just a provoking thought!

FOKKER DR.I 425/17: The Final Flight Path

The engine and propeller of Fokker Dr.I aircraft were right-handed, that is, they turned counter-clockwise, viewed from the front. This means that the reaction of the propeller torque on the airframe would bank the aircraft to the left.

On the other hand, if the nose of the aircraft was pulled up, the gyroscopic effect produced by the angular acceleration would turn the aircraft to the right.

This gives a possible explanation for the final flight path of 425/17, in which the aircraft pulled up and turned to the right through about 140 degrees, and then started to turn to the left shortly before striking the ground.

If the control column were pulled straight back, the aircraft would commence a climbing turn to the right, even if no rudder or aileron was applied. However, when the pressure relaxed, the gyroscopic effect would diminish, or even reverse if the nose fell, and the torque would become effective, turning the aircraft to the left. If no correction was applied to maintain a climbing turn, the nose would drop, and a flight path similar to that described above would result.

The trim characteristics of the Dr.I are not available, but either nose-up trim or increasing speed would cause the aircraft to recover from its dive, given sufficient height. The radius of turn must have been quite large—about six hundred feet—and it is unlikely that the angle of bank ever exceeded forty-five degrees. The speed evidently stayed high enough to avoid a spin.

This could have happened without any further action from Richthofen after the nose had been pulled up. He could have been unconscious or dead.

Q&A

Q. Why has it taken so long to get to the truth about von Richthofen's death?

A. The Canadians, of course, thought Brown was responsible. The Australians wanted to claim responsibility for their gunners. And there was an autopsy by the Australians and another autopsy by the British, and the doctors had contradicting opinions of what happened. A lot of the evidence was lost or mixed up. I think they're still trying to find some of the reports, which are buried away in the Australian War Memorial Museum. The various witnesses and the different reports . . . it's like watching an accident happen. You have people who saw the incident who later reinterpreted it to what they thought they saw or thought happened. It's a whodunit, and the possibilities of error are great.

Research is still going on. There have been a lot of books on the subject, and there are more in the works and more articles coming out. I don't think the subject is ever going to go away.

Comment

Paul Fussell: The talk about Richthofen brought up the problem of obtaining the details about an incident in a wartime situation, and problems associated with testimony and memory years after the fact. It seemed to assume that eyewitness testimony can be trusted. It's too often trusted by historians, but when questions of moment are at issue it is not trusted by juries, and that is a useful thing to remember.

Tim Travers: I spent a couple of months this summer in the Australian archives going through C. E. W. Bean's papers. Bean was the official Australian historian, and he was very much taken with the Richthofen business. Of course, he wanted to claim Richthofen's death for the Australian Lewis gunners and infantry on the ground.

In 1932, his papers say that Richthofen was shot down by the Australians because he had eyewitnesses who told him there were only two planes in the sky, and that was Richthofen pursuing May. So

Bean figured that Richthofen had to have been shot down from the ground—it couldn't have happened any other way. Then he was disconcerted to learn that there was another plane involved, Captain Bryant, and that Bryant was following Richthofen who was following May.

But he still believed that the Australians had shot him down from the ground. And for good reason. After all, why did Richthofen continue to fly on presumably after he had been shot and Bryant had stopped firing? Well, we heard the lecture which said you can fly pretty well for sixty seconds after you've been shot through the heart. I sort of doubt that because Richthofen also did a maneuver after he was supposedly shot—he turned. That's something to consider. Also, because his plane was very low to the ground, the Australian gunners may have been firing almost level at the plane. So the business of the angles may not be quite correct. But I think it's a controversy that's not likely to end too soon.

Audience Member: I'd like to comment about Richthofen's death from the viewpoint of a forensic pathologist who has examined several hundred fatal gunshot wounds. If what was said about his wound is correct, it's certainly possible that he could have lived for a minute or so and have been conscious and in control of his plane—particularly if the bullet went through the atrial or filling chambers of the heart instead of the ventricles or pumping chambers. His heart could continue to beat automatically and supply the brain with enough blood to enable him to stay conscious and maneuver his plane. It would be a matter of time as to how long it would take before blood leaked out of the hole in his heart, filled up the pericardial sac, and stripped the heart to the point it could no longer fill with blood and stop pumping. But there have been many cases recorded in both military combat and civilian life of people who have sustained horrific wounds to the heart and terrible head wounds that destroyed a good part of the brain—wounds you'd think would render the person immediately unconscious. And yet it's been documented that they were able to move or walk or talk, and to accomplish various acts before finally succumbing to their wounds.

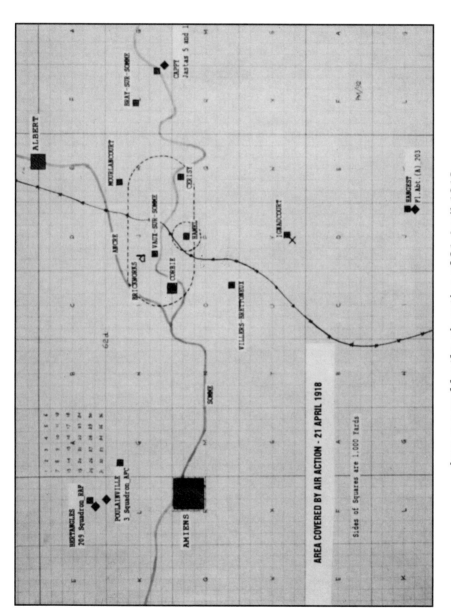

Area covered by the air action of 21 April 1918.

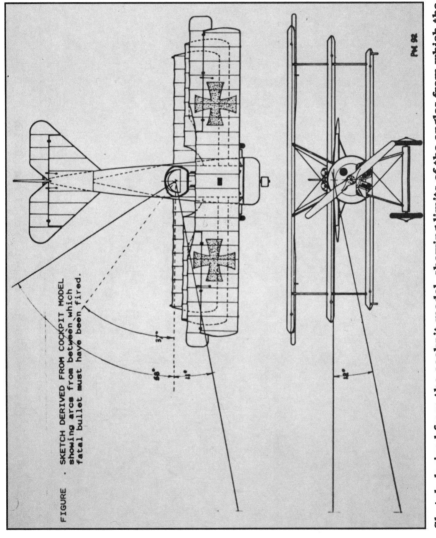

FIGURE . SKETCH DERIVED FROM COCKPIT MODEL showing arcs from between which fatal bullet must have been fired.

Sketch derived from the cockpit model, showing limits of the angles from which the fatal bullet was fired.

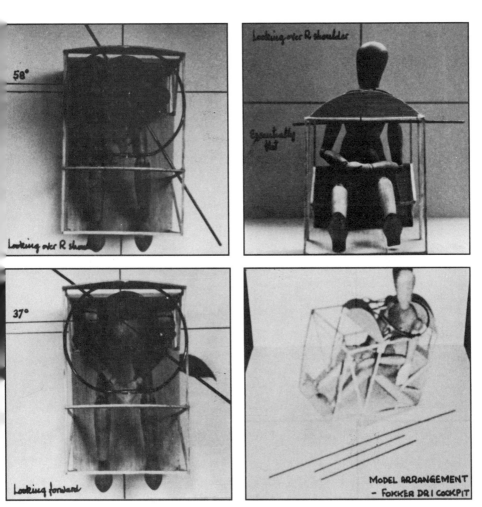

Model of Dr.I cockpit section used to estimate the angles relative to the aircraft from which the fatal bullet was fired.

118

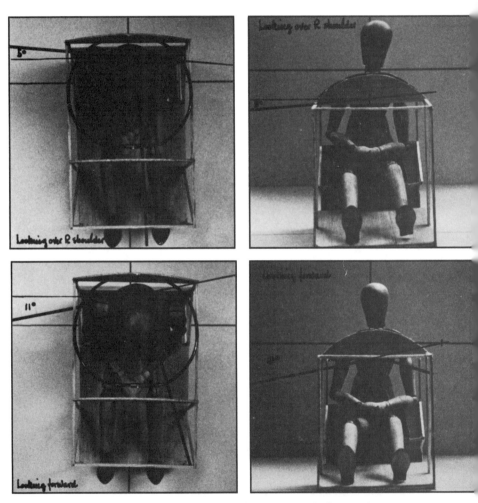

Another view of the model Dr.I cockpit section.

Gunner Robert Buie of the 53rd Battery, Australian Field Artillery, fired his Lewis gun at von Richthofen's Dr.I as the aircraft pulled up over the wood near the battery site.

Flanked by his crew, Sergeant C. B. Popkin of the 24th Machine Gun Company poses at the controls of his Vickers machine gun.

Captain Arthur Roy Brown of No. 209 Squadron tangled with the Red Baron in what proved to be the German ace's last dogfight. He is shown here with the Sopwith Camel he flew in that encounter.

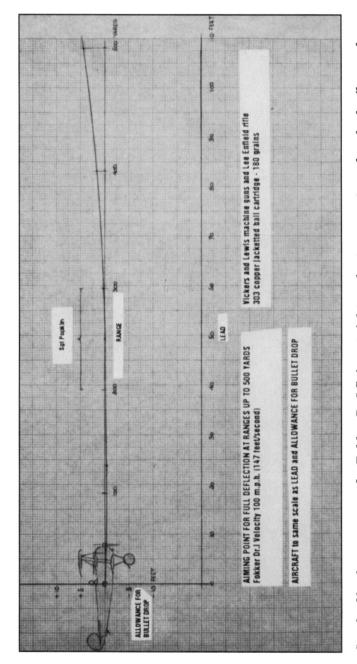

Graph of lead versus range for Fokker Dr.I flying at right angles to a gun at one hundred miles per hour. Aircraft is drawn to scale.

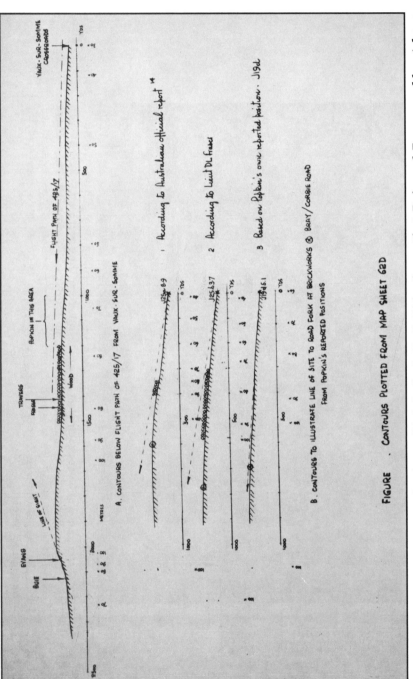

FIGURE . CONTOURS PLOTTED FROM MAP SHEET 62D

Contours below the flight path of von Richthofen's Dr.I. This shows that Buie and Evans could not have seen the aircraft until it had pulled into its final turn, and then only for a few seconds.

124

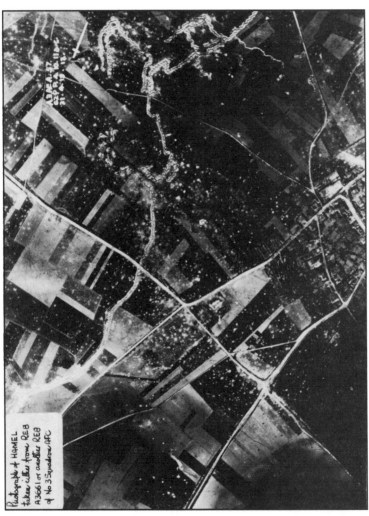

Photograph of Hamel and vicinity taken on 21 April by one of the two No. 3 Squadron reconnaissance aircraft, moments before they were attacked by von Richthofen's *Jasta* 11. A few minutes later, von Richthofen was dead. The camera caught this sector of the Western Front in a characteristically ravaged state, with shell holes and trenchworks (which show up here as crenellated lines) scarring the ground below.

Manfred von Richthofen with nurse Katie Otersdorf. The photograph, which was taken in the summer of 1917 while he was recovering from a head wound, permits comparison of his measured height—five-feet, five inches—with the known height of the pilot's badge. This was done to scale the mannikin used in determining the angle of the bullet that struck and killed him on 21 April.

Sidney Reilly, Master Spy:
A Reappraisal of His Role in the Lockhart Plot
Richard B. Spence

Anyone acquainted with the history of modern espionage has doubtless encountered the name of Sidney Reilly. His exploits as a secret agent have been the subject of several books, a television mini-series, and are the basis, in part, for the fictional James Bond.[1] Despite such attention or, indeed, because of it, Reilly remains as mysterious today as he was in 1925, the year he vanished into Soviet Russia. His career, replete with rumor and outright disinformation, is difficult to summarize. For the uninitiated, it must suffice to say that Sidney George Reilly was the chief *nomme de guerre* of Sigmund Grigor'evich Rosenblum, the scion of a prosperous Polish-Jewish family born in 1874. Leaving the Russian Empire in the early 1890s, young Rosenblum emigrated to Britain where, through uncertain agencies, he quickly rose in social and economic circles. In 1899 he obtained a passport under the name Sidney Reilly, and thus a legend was born.

From the turn of the century through the early 1920s, Reilly was involved in a bewildering array of clandestine affairs in Europe, America, and the Far East. He most often acted as an agent for British intelligence and of certain branches thereof, but he also functioned, sometimes simultaneously, as an agent for Germany, Russia, and Japan.[2] As a spy, Reilly was the consummate double—and sometimes triple or quadruple—agent. He was a mercenary at heart, and his primary motivations were the pursuit of wealth, power, and revenge. In these pursuits he was utterly ruthless and amoral, and was perfectly willing to employ murder to achieve his ends. By and large, however, he manipulated friend and foe by exploiting their own ambitions and avarice, and he frequently employed blackmail. His 1918 activities in Russia conform to this *modus operandi*.

While almost every aspect of Reilly's career is worthy of fresh analysis, this paper will limit itself to a reconsideration of his role in the so-called "Lockhart Plot" of 1918. Again, for those unfamiliar with that episode, a brief introduction must suffice. The Lockhart Plot *(Zagovor Lokarta)*, also known as the "Ambassadors' Plot" *(Zagovor poslov)*, centered on the alleged efforts of Allied agents, including Reilly, to overthrow the Soviet government in the summer of 1918. Soviet history has tended to link their efforts to an array of anti-Bolshevik actions that occurred in the same period, often at the same time.[3]

126

Western authors, while acknowledging the involvement of certain Allied officials in the anti-Bolshevik plots, have generally discounted the notion that these were the result of any coherent Allied plan. Beyond the reasonable suspicion that Reilly was somehow linked to some of the many subplots, his exact role—or roles—has remained obscure. Some writers, most notably Richard K. Debo, have argued that, at bottom, the conspiracy was an elaborate provocation by Soviet secret police (Cheka) chief Feliks Dzerzhinskii to discredit the Allies and the opposition in one fell swoop, Reilly being a rather minor player.[4] In contrast, Edward Van der Rhoer has argued that Reilly was a Soviet "mole" inside the Allied array, a conclusion also reached by the Soviet dissident writer Revolt Pimenov.[5] A more recent reassessment of the plot by Allen and Rachel Douglas comes to the conclusion that the above events were the work of an unholy collusion between British agents, especially Reilly, and the Soviet Cheka.[6] I will argue that, to one extent or another, they are all correct, but that they are all incorrect in their actual assessment of Reilly's role.

The following scenario is based on both new information, some of it from the long-shrouded archives of the Cheka/KGB, as well as a critical reassessment of the old. Given that many of my interpretations rest on circumstantial evidence, I do not claim that it is the absolute truth, but that it is closer to the truth than any previous account.

Following the Bolshevik seizure of power in late 1917, opinion in Allied governments was split over what attitude to take towards the new regime. Given Lenin's determination to make peace with the Central Powers, many argued that the Bolsheviks were traitors to the Allied cause and should be removed from power. Conversely, others advocated a conciliatory approach in the hope that the Soviet leaders could be persuaded to return to the Allied fold. In pursuit of the latter course, on January 1, 1918, His Majesty's Government (HMG) sent a young man named Robert Bruce Lockhart to Russia. Lockhart, a former commercial attaché, was to contact Soviet leaders and persuade them to renew war with Germany or, at least, not to make peace. Although familiar with Russia, Lockhart was inexperienced at this sort of diplomacy and, in the view of some, too inclined to sympathize with the Bolsheviks.[7] As acting consul, his presence was resented by the British intelligence agents in Russia, men such as Lieutenant Ernest Boyce and Captain George A. Hill, who regarded him, at best, as a misguided political interloper.[8]

At first Lockhart seemed to enjoy some success; he established contact with Leon Trotskii, Soviet commissar for foreign affairs and head of the peace delegation at Brest-Litovsk. Trotskii rejected the demands of the Germans and, as the Brest-Litovsk negotiations stalled, he appeared to become receptive to Lockhart's opinion. But in late February the frustrated Germans resumed military action and swept virtually unopposed across the Ukraine to within less than a hundred miles of Petrograd. This provided Lenin with the leverage he needed to force Trotskii and other reluctant Bolsheviks to swallow their pride and bow to German terms. Even so, the Central Committee approved Lenin's motion by the narrowest of margins—a single vote.[9] The harsh Treaty of Brest-Litovsk was signed on March 3, leaving the shrunken Soviet Republic at the virtual mercy of the Central Powers. Some three weeks later, the German army launched its long-expected offensive on the Western Front. As the British army reeled before the German onslaught, men in London decided that a new and drastic approach was needed in Russia and an experienced and ruthless hand to guide it. They turned to Sidney Reilly.

To appreciate why Reilly was the perfect man for the job, it is necessary to consider his prior associations with many of his coming partners in conspiracy. By 1914 Reilly had amassed a wide array of personal, commercial, and official contacts in Russia; indeed, his influence reached into the highest echelons of tsarist Russia's commercial and political establishments.[10] Such connections entailed a working relationship with the tsarist secret police, the Okhrana.[11] At the same time, and consistent with Reilly's tactic of always playing both sides against each other, he cultivated contacts in the revolutionary demimonde and, of course, with those spies and provocateurs who moved between these camps. From 1909 to early 1914, Reilly lived in Petersburg where he was a technical and commercial agent *and* an agent for both British and German intelligence. During this period, Reilly played a pivotal role in securing Russian naval contracts for the German firm of Blohm & Voss.[12] The kaiser's naval attaché in Petersburg, and a central figure in the Blohm & Voss deal, was Captain (later Admiral) Paul von Hintze. Hintze also happened to be the chief of German intelligence in Russia and, in both respects, he had every reason to be satisfied with Reilly's work.

Reilly's prewar Russian acquaintances included the political magistrate Vladimir Orlov, the Okhrana-linked lawyer Aleksandr Grammatikov, and an obscure statistician at the Putilov naval works, Henrikh Iagoda.[13] It is also likely that Reilly's Petersburg contacts included a young horse artillery officer, Aleksandr V. Fride,[14] but if they did not meet then, they certainly did a few years hence in New York where Reilly was an independent contractor and military purchasing agent for the Russian government.[15] Many of Reilly's American contracts concerned artillery ammunition, and this brought him into close contact with Russian officers assigned to this sphere, among them Fride. Reilly was also involved in procuring trucks and automobiles for the Russian army, Red Cross, and Zemstvo organizations. Assisting him in these ventures was the Russian-born American businessman Xenophon Kalamatiano. Also connected to Reilly's American automotive contracts, and thus to Kalamatiano and to Fride, was the Russian official M. V. Trestar. Similarly, Reilly was familiar with another of Kalamatiano's agents, the former military prosecutor and judge General A. A. Zagriazhskii who, in turn, knew Orlov.[16]

In addition to his commercial schemes, Reilly continued to work as a British and German clandestine agent in America. In the latter case, he was recruited by his old pal Hintze to head, along with the German-American agent Kurt Jahnke, a special sabotage group aimed against Allied war supplies produced in the U.S.[17] Of course, with Reilly nothing was that simple, for he and Jahnke also functioned as British double agents inside the German apparatus. When America joined the war in April 1917, the U.S. became too hot for Reilly, and the local chief of Britain's MI1c (later MI6), Sir William Wiseman, sent him on a secret mission to Russia where he worked with another British agent, George Hill. Reilly remained in Russia until the eve of the Bolshevik coup and then, with the help of Kalamatiano (who was now employed by the American State Department), he quietly returned to Britain.[18] In January 1918, again with Wiseman's help, Reilly slipped back to New York, where he exploited his contacts with Russian emigrants for information concerning the Soviet-German peace talks and opposition to them in revolutionary circles. Through his New York office manager, Aleksandr Weinstein (Vainshtein), Reilly had a direct pipeline to the Manhattan offices of *Novyi Mir*.[19] This radical publication had recently employed Trotskii, Nikolai Bukharin, and Aleksandra Kollontai as well as other persons now associated with the Soviet regime, and it was a ready source of current news and opinion about events in Russia. Also through Weinstein Reilly had a link to Maksim Litvinov, the Soviet's representative in Britain. By such means Reilly confirmed that there was much dissatisfaction with the course of the new regime, both inside and outside Russia. Back in London he offered to return to Russia and mobilize resistance to Lenin and his supporters.

Thanks to Wiseman, Reilly had received a temporary commission as a second lieutenant in the Royal Flying Corps in late 1917.[20] In March 1918 the War Office, under whose authority MI1c nominally functioned, sanctioned Reilly's employment for "special missions" in conjunction with the Foreign Office and, on April 1, reassigned him to the Technical Branch of the Royal Air Force.[21] All of this set the stage for Reilly's return to Russia as a "special military agent."

The latter title was necessary because Lockhart was still courting Trotskii, and there were those in London who believed that he might yet succeed. Thus, Reilly's mission could not appear to duplicate or overlap Lockhart's. Moreover, there seems to have been a general concern that whatever Reilly did, he should avoid direct association with HMG, which meant keeping his distance from Lockhart.

Reilly's mission did not necessarily entail the outright overthrow of the Bolshevik government and its replacement with a pro-Allied one. Such a move, men in Whitehall feared, might drive the Bolsheviks further into Berlin's arms or, even worse, provoke a German military riposte that would place an even more obedient regime in Moscow.[22] The wisest and most subtle course would be to effect a change in leadership within the Soviet government, transferring power to those more resistant to Germany and more amenable to the Allies. Given that the Soviets' present policies seemed to stem from the influence of one man, Lenin, his removal seemed to offer the quickest remedy.

Before leaving England, Reilly visited Litvinov to secure a proper visa for his trip. Being old acquaintances, they doubtless discussed other matters as well. How much Reilly said about his pending mission is impossible to say, but Litvinov, himself a veteran of underground intrigues, must have suspected something. A critic of the Brest peace, Litvinov would have been a good guide to other like-minded individuals. At the very least, he supplied Reilly with an introduction to Lev Karakhan, the Soviets' deputy commissar for foreign affairs.

Armed with Litvinov's papers and with some coded messages supplied by MI1c, Reilly departed for Murmansk in early April. Curiously, although a military officer on an official mission, he traveled in civilian dress aboard a British merchant vessel. Clearly he was trying to hide from someone, but who? Most likely Lockhart or, rather, any British officials who might report his mission or presence to Lockhart. Curiously, about the same time in Russia some of the resident British agents had introduced the amorous Lockhart to a willing Russian beauty, Countess Moura Budberg. If the suppositions of G. L. Owen are correct, Budberg's task was to distract and monitor Lockhart.[23]

Another explanation is that Reilly's disguise was meant to conceal his movements from the Germans. However, Reilly, being a good double agent, could hardly embark on such a mission without the knowledge and approval of his German superior. As it happened, Admiral von Hintze was at that very moment deeply concerned with Russian affairs. As in London, Berlin's policy makers were divided on their approach to the Soviet regime. One faction, centered around the powerful First Quartermaster General Erich Ludendorff, wanted to overthrow the troublesome revolutionary regime and replace it with a puppet government of pro-German monarchists. Indeed, German agents in Russia were already preparing such a move.[24] Hintze, however, led an opposing clique that advocated continued German support for the Soviets as the surest means of controlling Russia and limiting Allied influence.[25] Hintze was already involved in the drafting of supplemental Russo-German economic treaties which, he argued, would guarantee Germany's gains in the East regardless of the outcome in the West.[26]

Thus, Hintze wanted no precipitous action against the Soviets, and Reilly could help ensure this. As a British agent he could frustrate the more aggressive German efforts without implicating Hintze. At the same time, Reilly would prevent the Allies from gaining influence in Russia and thus leave the Bolsheviks with no alternative to accepting Germany's additional demands.

Reilly landed in Murmansk in late April. The White Sea port was already controlled by British naval authorities who, noting Reilly's strange appearance and dubious papers, promptly arrested him. As it so happened, Stephen Alley, the outgoing MI1c chief in Russia, was passing through Murmansk and was asked to examine the prisoner. Revealing his coded message, Reilly convinced Alley of his authenticity, and the latter recommended that the traveler be allowed to proceed to Moscow.[27] Whether this meeting was as accidental as Alley suggests is uncertain. It is also interesting that Alley did not leave Russia but remained in Murmansk as resident intelligence officer.

On or about the beginning of May, Reilly arrived in Petrograd and promptly reported to Boyce, his official superior. Reilly also touched bases with the resident British naval attaché, Captain Francis N. A. Cromie, a man he likely knew from 1917. Cromie's sudden and unexpected appointment as acting naval attaché occurred in December 1917, precisely the moment that Reilly was conferring with MI1c chief Mansfield Smith-Cumming and other officials in London.[28] Immediately after Reilly's arrival, Cromie began to recruit ex-Russian naval officers for a scheme to sabotage the Russian Baltic Fleet lest it fall into German hands.

On May 7, Reilly showed up in Moscow and rather ostentatiously sought audiences with several Soviet officials. His first visit was paid to V. D. Bonch-Bruevich, another acquaintance from pre-revolution days and currently a close advisor to Lenin.[29] Through him Reilly also had access to his brother, General M. D. Bonch-Bruevich, a former intelligence officer in the old army now working for the Soviets.[30] The most important figure to receive Reilly, however, was Lev Karakhan. Significantly, Karakhan was another strong opponent of the Brest treaty. His initial talk with Reilly must have made him very curious about his visitor's true status in Russia, so he immediately rang Lockhart. London, however, had not informed Lockhart of Reilly's mission and the stunned consul "blew up in a storm of indignation."[31] Reilly sought to allay Lockhart's concerns, but the consul remained resentful and suspicious. Lockhart's exclusion was no accident. He was, per Reilly's instructions, being kept out of the loop. The question was, would Reilly be able to keep him out?

Lockhart had good reason to be alarmed. His talks with Trotskii had taken a positive turn and the latter had expressed his willingness to resume war with Germany, dependent on Allied support.[32] However, so far as certain of Reilly's superiors in London and Berlin were concerned, this was an unwelcome development. Thus, soon after Reilly's arrival, a strange thing began to happen. Lockhart's telegraphic communications with London, heretofore quite reliable, broke down. Messages that previously reached Britain in forty-eight hours now suffered unexplained delays of a week or more, and an increasing number never arrived at all.[33] Incoming messages were delayed, garbled, or lost. By June Lockhart was out of effective contact with his government and consequently forced into ever greater reliance on Reilly and his intelligence comrades.

Reilly, however, suffered no such difficulties in his contacts with the outside world; he was able to send telegrams to his wife in New York which reached her in little more than two days.[34] Reilly's and Lockhart's messages traveled by the same route, via British stations in Petrograd and Murmansk, stations respectively monitored by Reilly's fellow MI1c agents Boyce and Alley.

Following his arrival in early May, Reilly largely disappears from sight for the next three months. He was certainly up to something—but what? And how did it relate to the "Lockhart Plot" that would emerge in August? His primary mission was to effect a change of leadership in the Soviet regime, and that, logically, was the end he pursued in the coming weeks.

The Soviet position was a very fragile one. Beset with bitter internal divisions and faced by real or potential enemies on all sides, the regime possessed only the most limited military resources. With the Red Army still a thing of the future, Lenin's government relied

on half-trained detachments of volunteer Red Guards and few remnants of the old Russian army. The most important of the latter
was the so-called Latvian Rifle Division (Latdiviziia), some of whose
regiments constituted the main garrison of Moscow and the Kremlin guard. The dependability of the Latvians, however, was open to
question. Although there were committed communists in their
ranks, many had no deep commitment to the Soviets, especially
officers who had served in the old army. Furthermore, the much-
debated Brest peace had handed Latvia to the Germans, a fact that
not only alienated many of the Latvian soldiers but also made them
prey to German overtures.

To reconstruct Reilly's clandestine efforts, we must return to...

Because of the unreliability of the military sector, the true
"inner line" of the Soviet regime was the Cheka, or "Extraordinary
Commission."[35] Under the guidance of the shrewd and ruthless
Dzerzhinskii it rapidly developed an effective network of agents.
Realizing the threat posed by foreign subversion, as early as March
Dzerzhinskii had planted agents among the Latvians to ferret out
any such activities.[36] Dzerzhinskii's closest deputy was another
Latvian, Iakov Peters, presumably a loyal member of the party.[37]

To reconstruct Reilly's clandestine efforts, we must return to
his initial meeting with Karakhan. If statements made by Peters
after his 1937 arrest have any credibility,[38] then Karakhan was
Reilly's first recruit in his anti-Lenin conspiracy and Peters, it would
seem, was his second. Why would Karakhan and Peters have agreed
to collaborate? Beyond any ideological objections to Soviet policy,
both men were realists. They knew the position of the Latvian regiments was precarious and any wise man ought to hedge his bets.
In addition, the changes Reilly suggested did not require their removal; indeed, they presented opportunities for rapid promotion.

In the case of Peters, Reilly may have had the advantage of
blackmail. A little-known accusation stemming from Peters's prewar activities in the Latvian revolutionary underground held that,
following his arrest by the Okhrana in 1905, he turned informer
and provocateur and infiltrated the Latvian radical community in
London.[39] There is some subsequent evidence to support this accusation.[40] Given his intimate connections to the old Okhrana and
British officialdom, Reilly could have had proof of this charge, or
could credibly claim that he did. If nothing else, the accusation
suggests that Peters had a history of opportunistic double dealing.

Peters probably aided Reilly by suppressing or deflecting Cheka
investigations of British subjects and assuring Dzerzhinskii that
no incriminating information had been uncovered. However, possibly unknown to Peters, Dzerzhinskii had assigned two special
agents to this very task. They were the Latvians Ian Buikis and Ian
Sprogis, who operated under the aliases Shmidkhen and Bredis.

In addition to Boyce and Cromie, Reilly also established contact with George Hill, whom he knew from their joint missions in 1917. In the interim Hill had not only ingratiated himself with Trotskii, but had helped organize a fledgling Soviet military intelligence service.[41] Hill had ready access to vital military information as well as a liaison with M. D. Bonch-Bruevich, who, in turn, had contact with his brother inside the Kremlin.

Reilly also renewed contact with the American, Kalamatiano. The latter had recently become the chief of the American Information Service in Russia, a thinly disguised intelligence bureau overseen by the anti-Bolshevik U.S. consul, Dewitt C. Poole. Kalamatiano's small group of agents, many of them known to Reilly, not only provided another channel of information, but also an American "cover" for some of Reilly's activities. Reilly's chief liaison with Kalamatiano was their mutual friend Colonel Fride who, as it so happened, was attached to the Latvian artillery units in Moscow.

Reilly also contacted the Russian anti-Bolshevik leader, Boris Savinkov, a former revolutionary terrorist and acting war minister in the defunct Provisional Government. Now a determined enemy of Lenin, Savinkov had organized a loose-knit insurrectionary movement mostly composed of ex-army officers.[42] The treasurer of Savinkov's group was A. Vilenkin who, again, had been attached to the Russian wartime mission in New York, where he undoubtedly encountered Reilly.[43] Savinkov had established links to the Czechs and the French, who had given him money, but he was anxious to gain the backing of the British and Americans, something he hoped Reilly could facilitate. Savinkov, apparently on his own initiative, approached Lockhart, a move that undoubtedly displeased Reilly.[44] Savinkov was impatient, and impetuous to a fault. An uprising by his followers would probably fail and provoke unpredictable reactions from the Germans, the French, and the Bolsheviks. Reilly, therefore, wanted to exploit Savinkov's organization, but also restrain it.

By the latter half of May, Reilly had become the common denominator, the ringmaster so to speak, of a diverse array of groups and individuals. As was his practice, Reilly had assumed the pivotal position where he could play these elements against his opponents or against each other.

On the evening of May 22, gunmen from Savinkov's organization positioned themselves to assassinate Lenin as he left a speaking engagement at Moscow's Dorofev Factory.[45] Because of simple confusion, Lenin missed the engagement and in doing so probably saved his life.

The circumstances of this abortive attempt bear such similarity to the subsequent August 30 attempt that it deserves some careful attention. The would-be killers were armed with detailed information about Lenin's route and means of travel: details, seemingly, that only someone close to the Kremlin would have had. Did Peters pass this information to Reilly, who handed it to Savinkov? Perhaps. It is also interesting that in Petrograd, Cromie was finalizing plans to destroy the Baltic Fleet and waiting for word to act. But in the immediate aftermath of the failure against Lenin, the plan was suspended.

At this juncture, a number of curious events occurred. On May 23, General F. C. Poole arrived in Murmansk and assumed direct command of all British military operations in Russia, including those of "military agent" Reilly. What is more, Poole knew Reilly and Hill very well, having commanded both in 1917. Two days later, on May 25, the Czech Army Corps in Russia refused to obey a Soviet order to disarm, provoking general alarm in the Bolshevik and Allied camps. For good measure, the Allied ambassadors, heretofore lingering about in Vologda, departed for Archangel—a sign, it seemed, that the Allies had given up on Red Russia. Under such circumstances, Poole ordered Reilly to suspend any provocative action until the situation had sorted itself out. Indeed, at almost the same time Boyce received orders for Reilly that called on him to desist from any "political" activity and, for good measure, to avoid any contact with Lockhart.[46] On May 29, yet another blow fell when Savinkov's organization was forced to quit Moscow in the face of surprise Cheka raids. This last development was not entirely disadvantageous to Reilly. The reckless Savinkov had been pushed out into the provinces where he could still be useful, but not underfoot. And just where, one must wonder, did Peters receive his timely information about Savinkov's safe houses?

The unexpected events of late May derailed Reilly's hopes for a speedy and simple resolution of the "Bolshevik problem" and forced him to adjust his tactics. However, his strategy remained the same. He continued his efforts to recruit or subvert key elements in the Soviet regime and to co-opt or exploit the efforts of anti-Bolshevik forces with the ultimate aim of carrying out a swift decapitation of the Soviet leadership.

In order to conceal his efforts from his enemies, and even from his friends, Reilly adopted at least two alternate identities and shifted the locus of his activity from Moscow to Petrograd. One alias was Konstantin Pavlovich Massino, businessman, the guise which he hereafter employed in his goings and comings to Moscow; and the second was Comrade Pavel Relinskii, an officer of the Petrograd Cheka.[47] According to Reilly's later account, it was his friend Orlov who helped him obtain papers for both identities and, presumably, the job inside the Cheka. Orlov was then employed as chief of the Sixth Criminal Commission in Petrograd, which was not part of the Cheka per se, but rather a subordinated branch of the Commissariat of Justice.[48] Thus it is hard to see how Orlov would have had the power or position to achieve such bureaucratic handiwork. Moreover, Orlov himself admits that Dzerzhinskii, whom he had once sentenced to prison, knew he was working for the Soviets, and doubtless kept an eye on him.[49] More probably, Peters arranged Reilly's admission to the local Cheka via, of course, the proper channels.[50] A necessary one would have been the chief of the Petrograd Cheka, Moisei Uritskii. As such, he could have connected Peters to "Relinskii's" appointment, something that might explain Uritskii's subsequent fate.

However, Orlov certainly had his value to Reilly, not least because he was a secret agent for the German commercial attaché in Petrograd, Walter Bartels.[51] Bartels, in turn, passed his intelligence on to a special Russian section in the German Foreign Ministry, a section overseen by none other that Admiral von Hintze. Also, Orlov owed his job in the police to V. D. Bonch-Bruevich, which may suggest yet another tie to Reilly.[52]

A likely target of Reilly's attention in Petrograd was V. V. Volodarskii, People's Commissar for Propaganda and Agitation. A former Menshevik and an opponent of the Brest treaty, Volodarskii had lived in New York before the revolution and was another veteran of *Novyi Mir*. Here again, there is a very good chance that he knew Reilly, at least by reputation. That, in fact, made Volodarskii a rather dangerous individual, particularly if he refused Reilly's overtures. However, any such threat was eliminated on June 20 when Volodarskii conveniently was assassinated by an SR (Socialist Revolutionary) gunman.[53]

Volodarskii's death also might have played a role in protecting or advancing the career of another Reilly recruit, Henrikh Iagoda. Reilly probably encountered Iagoda in 1913 when the former was managing director of a Putilov subcontractor and the latter worked in the firm's insurance office, where he would have processed payments and forms supplied by Reilly. It is a thin connection to be sure, but Reilly was always on the lookout for the ambitious and corruptible, and Iagoda was definitely both.[54] In early 1918 Iagoda commanded Red Guards in Petrograd, but sometime in June or July he was transferred to Moscow where he assumed general command of the Red Guard there.[55] Thus he was at just the right place and time to assist Reilly.

Some mention also must be made of Reilly's various female operatives. While often cited as examples of his sexual magnetism, they played important roles in his conspiratorial nexus. In Petrograd Elena M. Boiuzhavskaia, an amorous acquaintance from pre-revolution days, played the role of "Mrs. Massino" and was an intermediary to Orlov and others. In Moscow Reilly established a complicated ménage with another former mistress, Dagmara "K." (Kalamatiano?), the niece of Grammatikov and, possibly, a relative of Kalamatiano's. Beyond this, Dagmara introduced Reilly to two other women, the actress Elizaveta Otten and Ol'ga Starzhevskaia. The latter was a secretary in the Soviet Central Executive Committee and, according to later testimony, provided Reilly and his associates with official passes to various buildings and installations.[56] Finally, there was Marie Fride, Colonel Fride's sister, who was recruited as a courier.

This web of interconnections, personal and institutional, was the means by which Reilly managed his conspiratorial circus. The practice, however, had its risks; if one branch was penetrated by opposing agents, such connections permitted the gradual "infection" of the others. Unknown to Reilly, this is precisely what was happening.

At this juncture Reilly was no doubt looking forward to the meeting of the Soviet Congress, slated for early July, as an excellent opportunity to bag the Bolshevik hierarchy in one swoop. He was not the only one with that ambition. The Left SRs, heretofore the restive junior partners of the Bolsheviks, also were plotting an uprising to coincide with the Congress and, out in the provinces, the restless Savinkov was readying his officers for action. Both groups were being encouraged by the French, a circumstance that Reilly was aware of, but about which he could do little. But there is also evidence that the Left SRs were being deliberately provoked into rebellion by Lenin and Dzerzhinskii.[57]

As events actually transpired, on July 6 two Left SR gunman assassinated the German ambassador in Moscow, Count von Mirbach-Harff, a move presumably designed to provoke a German declaration of war on the Soviet Republic. The attack then triggered, perhaps prematurely, a general Left SR rising in Moscow. Again, there is vague evidence connecting Reilly to the Left SRs, specifically with D. I. Popov, the Left SR Chekist who initiated the Moscow revolt.[58] In any event Reilly was in Moscow on July 6 and had advance warning of the revolt.[59] At almost the same time, Savinkov's followers attempted to seize control of Iaroslavl', Rybinsk, and other towns.

The net result was that these disjointed efforts failed and the Germans did not declare war. The last was due to the personal influence of Hintze, now the kaiser's foreign minister, who desperately wanted the Bolshevik's signatures on the pending commercial treaties. Indeed, the death of Mirbach, who had been a strident voice for anti-Bolshevik intervention, probably worked to Hintze's advantage. For Reilly, the fact that the assassination tripped up the plots of Savinkov and the Left SRs was also advantageous. Interestingly, the lead assassin, Iakov Bliumkin, while possibly an agent of Dzerzhinskii, also had close contact with British agent George Hill.[60]

One result of the July fiasco was that French credibility with the anti-Bolsheviks was shattered, yet another advantage so far as Reilly was concerned as it would make them more likely to cooperate with him. Encouraging Mirbach's murder would have been a classic Reilly move; whatever the result, he could claim credit for the "success" and simultaneously disclaim any responsibility for "failure." Another welcome result was that Dzerzhinskii, who had been captured briefly by the Left SRs, temporarily stepped down from the head of the Cheka. For the next several weeks, he was replaced by Peters. This development may have tempted Reilly to a bit of overconfidence for, in fact, Dzerzhinskii remained very active behind the scenes.

If nothing else, the July events convinced most Allied representatives in Russia that if the Bolsheviks were to be removed it would require their collaboration. By mid-July, in contrast to his earlier stance, Reilly had drawn Lockhart into his scheme, albeit in a peripheral role. In order to provide funds for his operations, Reilly needed rubles, and to get them he persuaded a Moscow-based British banker, William Comber-Higgs, to "buy" rubles from willing Russians in exchange for promissory notes guaranteeing subsequent payment in pounds sterling. To add credibility, Reilly convinced Lockhart to countersign the notes as the representative of HMG.[61]

Reilly, however, was employing Kalamatiano for the same purpose. Among those who traded his rubles for dollars was Reilly's and Kalamatiano's old business associate, Trestar. In addition, Trestar happened to be the manager of the main military motor pool in Moscow, which made him another valuable asset inside the Soviet infrastructure.[62] So too was another Reilly recruit, I. I. Khrizhanovskii, an official of the Central Supply Administration.[63] The above ruble scheme was the means by which Reilly raised the money he later distributed to the Latvians, which suggests that Reilly initiated the plan soon after the events of July 5–6. One factor directing Reilly towards the Latvians may have been his awareness of German overtures in the same direction. On July 10 German agents offered to grant an amnesty and repatriation to all Latvian troops in Soviet service in exchange for the latter's nonresistance to a German occupation of Moscow. To prevent this and thereby satisfy the wishes of his superiors in London and Berlin (i.e., Foreign Minister von Hintze), Reilly had to offer the Latvians a better deal.

Basically, Reilly's plan was as follows. Abetted by his collaborators in the Cheka, the Foreign Affairs commissariat, Soviet military intelligence, the Red Guard, and other agencies, he aimed to launch a lightning coup timed to coincide with another convention of the Soviet leadership scheduled for the end of August. The key to the whole affair was the subversion of the Latvian units, particularly the Kremlin guard. Reilly already had at least one agent among the Latvians, Colonel Fride, who, as we have seen, linked Reilly to Kalamatiano. On August 15, Lockhart introduced Reilly to another Lett, Colonel Eduard P. Berzin, and it was arranged that Reilly would use Berzin to funnel money to the Latvian units.[64]

It is here that we must reintroduce the agents employed by Dzerzhinskii months earlier, Shmidkhen and Bredis (Buikis and Sprogis). Berzin later claimed to have known Bredis from before the revolution and to have encountered him and Shmidkhen sometime in late May or early June 1918. It was not until August 8 that Berzin again met Shmidkhen, this time alone. What had become of Bredis is unclear, but it is possible that he may have been the Latvian officer Bredis who joined Savinkov's organization.[65] Shmidkhen now presented himself as the agent of an Allied-backed plot to overthrow Bolshevik rule and solicited Berzin to join. As evidence of his connections Shmidkhen presented a letter of introduction from Captain Cromie and offered to introduce Berzin to Lockhart.[66]

Thus Shmidkhen, the Cheka provocateur, had found his way to Cromie and Lockhart, but without encountering Reilly. How was this possible? Cromie, it appears, had recruited Bredis and Shmidkhen for the abortive Petrograd operation in May and thereafter remained in regular contact. During July Reilly employed Cromie and the offices of the British consulate as a distribution point for some of his clandestine funds. Through Cromie, Shmidkhen made contact with Lockhart. However, then and later Shmidkhen studiously avoided contact with Reilly. Here again we must ask, why? Would Reilly have recognized him as the Chekist Buikis or otherwise have realized his true purpose? Reilly may have wondered the same thing.

Whatever the case, the one thing that no one anticipated in this situation was an honest man. Berzin, as a loyal servant of Soviet regime, promptly reported Shmidkhen's offer to the proper authority, in this case Iakov Peters. For Peters it was both an awkward and advantageous situation. He almost certainly knew that Shmidkhen was Dzerzhinskii's agent and, as such, could not interfere with his operations; nor could Peters reveal any knowledge that might connect him to the Latvian scheme and, thereby, Reilly. According to Berzin's statement to the Cheka in September 1918, Peters enlisted Berzin as *his* personal informant and urged him to join and follow the plot wherever it might lead. In this way the opportunistic Peters could not only monitor the activities of Dzerzhinskii's men, but also keep an eye on his secretive ally Reilly. Moreover, Berzin would later provide evidence that Peters had behaved as a proper and loyal Chekist in the affair.[67]

On August 14 Shmidkhen and Berzin met Lockhart in his flat, and the consul agreed to introduce Berzin to "Konstantin," who would supply him with the funds necessary to purchase the cooperation of other Latvian officers. The following day, Shmidkhen having dropped from sight, Berzin met Reilly. They met several more times in the following days, and Reilly gradually brought the Latvian into his confidence. Indeed, Reilly was uncharacteristically talkative, going into every detail of the conspiracy, including supposed plans to execute Lenin and the other Soviet leaders. On the other hand, Reilly was curiously reluctant to hand over large sums of money to Berzin, providing only a fraction of the amount initially promised. This suggests that Reilly did not quite trust Berzin. Significantly, on August 21 Reilly was especially provocative in his statements and pointedly asked Berzin if he knew Peters. When Berzin admitted a slight acquaintance, Reilly cryptically replied that "a bullet was the only cure for Bolshevism."[68] Reilly had guessed that Berzin was someone's spy and was deliberately feeding him inflammatory information to see what result it might produce, or whom it would provoke. The above statement by Reilly may suggest that he suspected Peters's duplicity or, perhaps, he emphasized hostility towards Peters in order to divert suspicion from him.

But did Reilly suspect Dzerzhinskii's hand? Certainly he sensed some sort of double cross. A critical realization seems to have come on or about August 25, when Reilly went to the American consulate to convene with Kalamatiano, Consul Poole, the French naval attaché, Capitaine Henri Vertemont, and the French consul, Ferdnand Grenard. This was the first and only general meeting of the Allied agents involved in the plot, and it doubtless gave them an opportunity to share information about their individual contacts. As Reilly later recalled the event, he suspected that a French journalist present at the meeting, Rene Marchand, was a Soviet informant.[69] The more likely case is that someone revealed something about Shmidkhen and/or Berzin that finally allowed the pieces to fall together for Reilly.

Soon thereafter, perhaps that night, Peters was roused by an urgent phone call from Karakhan.[70] Rushing to Karakhan's residence, Peters was confronted by an enraged Reilly who accused him of betrayal by permitting the infiltration of Cheka agents into the Latvian plot. This, Reilly raged, had compromised British officials—an obvious reference to Lockhart—something that Peters had promised to prevent. Peters protested that the agents in question, certainly Shmidkhen and Bredis, were Dzerzhinskii's men and there was nothing he could do to stop their activities without arousing his superior's suspicion. Not satisfied with this excuse, Reilly threatened to "expose" Peters unless he took immediate steps to correct the situation. With Karakhan's intervention, Reilly calmed down, and the three began to plot their next move.[71] Reilly insisted that the present plan, centering on the Latvian gambit, would have to be "liquidated" at once. In addition, British involvement was to be obscured by shifting the blame to the French and Americans.

On August 27 Reilly abruptly ordered Berzin to go to Petrograd to deliver the funds to the leader of the local organization. In fact, Reilly directed Berzin to his own (Boiuzhavskaia's) residence where Berzin was kept uselessly waiting around for the next three days. This move was obviously designed to get Berzin out of Moscow so that he would have no idea as to what Reilly and Peters were up to and, of course, so that he could not talk with anyone else.

Meanwhile, in Moscow, Reilly and Peters hurriedly derailed the "Lockhart Plot" and covered their tracks. Peters initiated the process on August 29 by ordering a raid on the French consulate. This put all the Allied plotters on alert, including Kalamatiano who, perhaps warned by Reilly, fled Moscow for Samara. Other loose ends required more desperate measures, and at the same time Reilly and Peters plotted one last, desperate throw at a target of opportunity.

On August 29 Reilly was on his way to Petrograd. The following evening Moisei Uritskii, who might have established a link between Reilly and Peters, was killed by a lone SR assassin, acting, apparently, on his own initiative.[72] At almost the same time, Lenin was shot and wounded by a young woman SR, Fania Kaplan, as he left a speaking engagement in Moscow. Kaplan's hasty interrogation and execution were handled personally by Peters.[73] As for Reilly, he later claimed that one of his female agents was a friend of Kaplan's.[74] In Petrograd, Reilly, having sent the confused Berzin back to Moscow, assumed his guise as the Chekist Relinskii and established contact with Captain Cromie. According to Reilly's later account, he arrived at the consulate just in time to witness its storming by fellow Chekists. In the process, Cromie was shot dead. Despite Reilly's subsequent condemnation of this murder, Cromie's death eliminated another source of incriminating information and, perhaps, the man whose carelessness had led to the present state of affairs.[75]

In the immediate aftermath of the above events, Reilly went into hiding and, according to his version, managed to slip out of Russia some weeks later. That his actual departure was much quicker and smoother than he later admitted is another chapter of his saga. As for Lockhart, he was arrested and held for most of September, but was never put on trial or, in fact, subjected to any serious interrogation. Throughout his captivity he was repeatedly visited by Karakhan and Peters, who seem to have done their best to keep him as isolated and comfortable as possible. Just before his release, Peters told Lockhart that they really had "nothing" on him and that the Americans were the "worst compromised" by the August plot.[76] Indeed, Reilly could take some satisfaction that Lockhart, while indicted as an "enemy of people," was safely back in England when Kalamatiano and Fride were sentenced to death.[77] Thus British honor, while not unsullied, fared far better than it might have. As for Orlov and Grammatikov, they not only avoided arrest, but also any mention in the later trial.

And what of Reilly's German connections? Although Germany's subsequent defeat would undo all his hard work, Hintze had no reason to be displeased with Reilly's efforts; the Soviet regime had remained in power and had signed the supplemental treaties while Allied efforts to gain influence in Russia had utterly failed. Thus, for Sidney Reilly, his Russian adventures of 1918 were a very qualified success and, suitably edited and reshaped, formed an important part of his reputation as a "Master Spy." They also established connections that would have a very important impact on his subsequent career, particularly his return to Russia in 1925.

Q&A

Q. *What was Reilly's linguistic aptitude? Did he speak English with an accent?*

A. Yes.

Q. *If so, how could he pass as Reilly?*

A. There are at least two references to the fact that he spoke English with a very strong accent. Now, what these references don't say is what sort of accent it was. I don't think he could have passed for Irish. Not many people took him seriously as an Irishman—I mean he doesn't look Irish, for one thing. His looks, in fact, are fairly Mediterranean—olive skin, very dark eyes, dark hair. Many people thought he looked far more Italian than Jewish. The odd thing is, his story about being born in

Ireland seems to have been accepted by many people, especially in Britain, although, if actually questioned about it, none of them really believed it. It's a bit like the business with the passport. Somehow he gets a passport without being a citizen and then, years later, when someone figures out what he's done, they go, "Well, it's kind of curious, but let's not look too closely." There's no attempt to investigate how this man obtained the passport. Now, why is it that throughout his entire career people are inclined not to look too closely at what he's doing? I don't know. Influence of some kind?

Q. *You mentioned how he operated—how he used his great charm, and his ability to blackmail and murder people. But you didn't mention bribery.*

A. Oh yes. It was mentioned in the fact that I said his influence could include charm, murder, and blackmail, and, yes, what should indeed be included in that is bribery. By the way, from early 1915 through early 1917, he earned at least $2.2 million in commissions while working in the United States on the Russian War Contract Commission. And that's the minimum amount—it may have been closer to $4 or $5 million. Most of that money remained in the U.S., and this is interesting because later on in the 1920s—in 1922 and '23—Reilly will be telling the story in Britain that he's flat broke. He'll bum £200 off a friend in order to get steamship passage. And he's got at least $2 million in American banks at that point in time.

Q. *What happened to him?*

A. Well, Sidney Reilly, who, remember, never existed, ceases to exist in November of 1925 when he returns to the Soviet Union and is ostensibly arrested. And for his involvement in the 1918 episode I've just described, he's placed under sentence of death and executed. Now, that's what happens to Sidney Reilly, but Sidney Reilly isn't there. What happens to the man who played Sidney Reilly? He lives on for a while . . . but that's far too complicated a story to go into now.

Q. *Did Reilly ever have contacts with Sir Basil Zaharoff, the munitions dealer?*

A. Yes, he did. They were partners in the early 1920s in a number of business deals involving French banks and oil companies. And they probably had some mutual involvement in the Chinese Eastern Railway and the Russo-Asiatic Bank.

Q. *Was he in the same hotel as Colonel House in 1916?*

A. I don't think Reilly ever met Colonel House. He knew Wiseman. He didn't associate with Wiseman, since that would be not a very wise thing to do. Wiseman communicated with Reilly through Colonel Thwates, who was his go-between, and that was the person with whom Reilly had most of the connections.

Now, later in the 1920s, there are American FBI agents who do a little thing one day. They know that Wiseman knew Reilly earlier on, and one of the agents gets a young woman to call up Wiseman, who is now an investment banker in New York. (Wiseman later goes on, by the way, to be a producer at Paramount. If you've ever seen the film *Gunga Din*, he's responsible for that.) And she goes, "Oh, my brother was looking for Mr. Reilly and he knew him during the war. Do you know where he is?" And Wiseman goes, "Oh, yes, I know Sidney very well. We go way back." This is Wiseman's first confirmation that, yes, he indeed knows him, and this makes the Americans rather suspicious. But Wiseman kept his connection with Reilly and with many others quiet when he moved in certain circles, largely communicating through Thwates, who operated the New York office.

PART 5

VALOR AND SURVIVAL

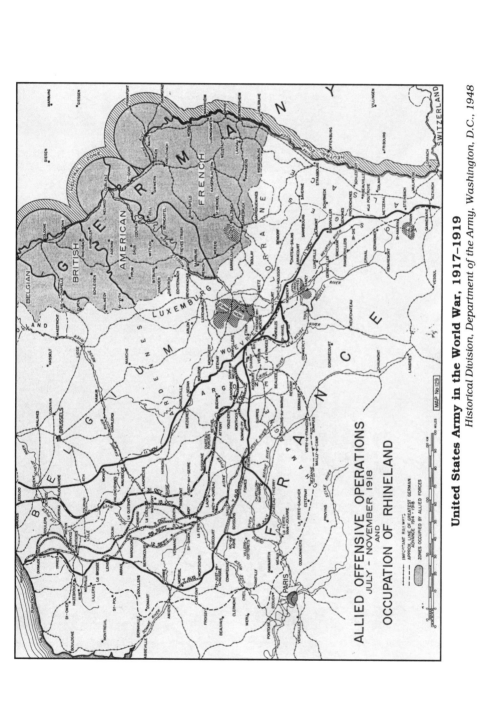

United States Army in the World War, 1917–1919

Historical Division, Department of the Army, Washington, D.C., 1948

The Medal of Honor and World War I
Edward F. Murphy

The Medal of Honor is America's highest award for combat valor. Awarded only 3,420 times in the 134 years of its existence, its prestige is such that President Harry S Truman once remarked, "I'd rather have this medal than be president." The criteria by which the medal is awarded are strict: recipients must be members of the armed forces who display the most conspicuous gallantry and intrepidity at the risk of their lives above and beyond the call of duty in armed conflict with an enemy.

The Medal of Honor came into being during the dark, early days of the Civil War. Navy Secretary Gideon Welles was looking for a way to recognize sailors and marines who performed bravely under fire and, at the same time, to inspire more reluctant members of the naval service to do their duty. At Welles's urging, Iowa Senator James W. Grimes introduced a bill into Congress in December 1861 providing for the creation of a "medal of honor." President Lincoln signed the bill into law on December 21, 1861. A few months later Massachusetts Senator Henry Wilson introduced a bill to create such a medal for the army, and that bill was signed into law on July 12, 1862.

The original Medal of Honor was designed by a Philadelphia silversmith firm, Wm. Wilson & Son. The medal was a bronze five-pointed star, hung with one point down. On the medal's face a figure representing the Spirit of Discord cowers before a larger female figure, the goddess Minerva, who represents the United States of America. Encircling them are thirty-four stars, the number of states in the Union. Both the army and navy medals were suspended from a ribbon with a blue horizontal top band above alternating vertical strips of red and white; however, the device from which the ribbon was suspended was different on each. The army's ribbon hung from an eagle with wings spread, perched on crossed cannon above stacked cannonballs; the navy's, from a rope-fouled anchor.

Prior to the First World War, Medals of Honor were given out with only minimal effort made to determine whether the recipients were worthy of the award. Most got it as a result of writing to the War Department to suggest they had performed a deed that had earned them a Medal of Honor. The War Department would typically ask the veteran for affidavits from witnesses to substantiate his claim. Upon receiving such documentation it would, more often than not, send him the medal.

149

Awarded almost indiscriminately, the medal consequently enjoyed little prestige outside the military. Few civilians had any idea what the medal was or how it was earned. The general public only became more aware of the medal around the turn of the century, when a Civil War veterans group, the Grand Army of the Republic, copied its design for a membership badge. To casual observers, the two were indistinguishable, prompting medal holders to request a redesign of the official military decoration. A Parisian jewelry firm, Mssrs. Arthur, Bertrand, and Berenger, prepared several designs. One was selected and, in 1904, the army adopted it. The navy did not change the design of its medal at this time.

The 1904 design retains the chief feature of its predecessor, the five-pointed star. But the two figures found on the old medal are gone, having been replaced by the helmeted head of Minerva surrounded by the legend, *The United States of America.* The star is encircled by an open laurel wreath, enameled in green, and green oak leaves fill the points of the star. Above the star is a bar bearing the word "VALOR." An eagle with wings spread is perched atop the bar. The ribbon is a blue watered-silk material spangled with thirteen white stars.

The onset of war in Europe led senior army officers to examine the army's lack of a decorations and award policy. Some officers felt that the Medal of Honor had been awarded too readily. As a result, a 1916 review board composed of general officers examined every one of the army's 2,364 awards given out since the medal's inception. The officers eventually recommended that 911 awards be revoked as unjustified. To prevent future abuses, they further recommended that the criteria for awarding the medal be spelled out in more detail and made more rigorous, and that lesser awards be created in order to recognize varying degrees of heroism. All the recommendations were acted upon. During World War I the army created the Distinguished Service Cross (DSC), ranking just below the Medal of Honor, and the Silver Star for heroic combat deeds not meriting a DSC.

Though the navy never reviewed its Medal of Honor awards *en masse,* it also created additional awards during World War I. Its equivalent to the DSC was the Navy Cross. The navy also awarded the Silver Star. Inasmuch as the navy allowed its Medal of Honor to be awarded for both non-combat and combat heroism, the navy brass decided to have two distinctive variants of its highest decoration. The award for non-combat heroism would be the original medal with the five-pointed-star; for heroism in combat, a new medal with a Maltese cross bearing an American eagle surrounded by four anchors. This medal, which was designed by Tiffany & Co., was suspended from a ribbon identical to that of the army's medal, but the inscription on the bar at the top—"VALOUR"—had the British spelling of the word. No explanation has ever been given for this discrepancy.

During World War I the U.S. Marine Corps Brigade served as a part of the army's 2nd Infantry Division. Five marines performed deeds sufficiently heroic to be awarded the Medal of Honor by the army. Several years later, the Navy Department decided to honor these marines with a navy Medal of Honor. Thus, these men became the only five in history to receive two Medals of Honor for the same deed.

The first Medal of Honor awarded for ground combat action in France was earned by a twenty-eight-year-old navy officer, Lieutenant Commander Alexander G. Lyle of Gloucester, Massachusetts. On April 23, 1918, while serving with a frontline marine unit about twenty miles southeast of Verdun, Lyle, ignoring an intense German artillery barrage, dashed into the open and rescued two wounded marines. With shells crashing around him, he carried the casualties back to the safety of his trench. There he provided lifesaving first aid to the stricken men. Commander Lyle went on to have a distinguished career in the navy, eventually heading the Navy Dental Corps and retiring as a vice admiral. He died in July 1955.

The first Marine Corps recipient of the Medal of Honor in World War I was Gunnery Sergeant Charles F. Hoffman, a forty-year-old career marine from New York City serving with the 5th Marines. On June 18, near Chateau-Thierry, Hoffman's company captured Hill 142. Before they could consolidate their positions, however, the Germans launched a counterattack. Hoffman spotted twelve Germans armed with five machine guns trying to outflank his position. Alone, he attacked the enemy and, using his bayonet, killed two of them. The rest fled. His actions prevented the Germans from recapturing the hill, a feat which earned him the Medal of Honor. The medal was awarded in 1921, at which time it was discovered that "Hoffman" was a pseudonym; his real name was Ernest Janson. It was, therefore, to Ernest Janson that the navy awarded its Medal of Honor. The army, however, awarded its Medal of Honor to Charles F. Hoffman. Hoffman/Janson remained in the Marine Corps after the war, rising to the rank of sergeant major. He died in New York City in 1940.

The first U.S. Army recipient of the Medal of Honor in World War I earned his decoration on July 4, 1918, during the Australian-American attack on the town of Hamel, in the Somme River valley north of Cantigny. Corporal Thomas Pope was a twenty-three-year-old Chicagoan serving with a company of the 33rd Infantry Division assigned to the Australian 4th Division. When a German machine-gun nest held up the advance of his company, Pope attacked it by himself, killing its occupants and capturing the gun. He then held the position against efforts to dislodge him until the rest of the company arrived, whereupon they drove the enemy from the battlefield. Pope returned to Chicago after the war and worked for the Veterans Administration. He died in 1989.

First Lieutenant George P. Hays was a forward observer for artillery with the 3rd Infantry Division when, on the night of July 14–15, a German artillery barrage cut the communication lines to his post near Graves Farm southeast of Chateau-Thierry. Disregarding the heavy German fire, the twenty-five-year-old Hays jumped on a horse and rode back and forth across the battlefield, carrying firing instructions to his battery and a nearby French battery. So effective was the fire of the two Allied batteries that a German infantry attack was halted. Hays had seven horses shot from under him that fearful night, and was himself badly wounded. Awarded the Medal of Honor for his actions, he had the distinction of being the last recipient recognized for a deed of valor involving a horse. Hays remained in the army after World War I, rising to the command of the famed 10th Mountain Division in World War II and retiring as a lieutenant general. He died in September 1978.

The most famous American aviators of the war, Eddie Rickenbacker and Frank Luke, were also Medal of Honor winners, but the first pilot to be so honored was an obscure naval ensign named Charles Hammann. A twenty-six-year-old from Baltimore, Maryland, Hammann was assigned to a naval squadron based in eastern Italy and equipped with Italian-built Macchi single-seat flying boats. On August 21, 1918, he participated in a bombing raid on Pola, Yugoslavia. During the return trip, a plane in Hammann's flight lost power and settled onto the turbulent waters of the Adriatic Sea less than two miles from enemy territory. Fearful that the downed plane's pilot, Ensign George Ludlow, might be captured, Hammann turned and flew back to the crash site, landing his plane in the rough water to rescue the man. With Hammann's help, Ludlow climbed aboard the seaplane and seated himself astride the fuselage between the engine and the cockpit. Despite Ludlow's added weight and the choppy water, Hammann managed to get the plane into the air with his passenger clinging to the inboard struts of the upper wing. Flying just a few feet above the water, Hammann made it back to base with both plane and passenger intact. Hammann's rescue of Ensign Ludlow earned him the Medal of Honor, though he never knew it: the medal was awarded posthumously, after he was killed in a plane crash on the Potomac River near Langley, Virginia in June 1919.

Private John Kelly was the youngest marine to perform a Medal of Honor-winning deed in World War I. He had just turned twenty when, in October 1918, his company of the 6th Marines went into combat in the Champagne sector, twenty miles east of Rheims. Near the town of Blanc Mont, Kelly's unit was pinned down by deadly accurate German machine-gun fire. Ignoring warnings from his buddies, Kelly leaped up and charged across one hundred yards of open ground. Armed only with his rifle, he attacked the first machine-gun position he came to, killing the gunners and capturing eight others. He then wheeled and captured two more Germans who had crept up to retake the position. Kelly was one of the five marines to receive both an army and a navy Medal of Honor for the same deed. Returning to civilian life, he found it difficult to forget the horrors of war; success eluded him, and he died in poverty in 1957.

Heroism is frequently a group act, and the history of the Medal of Honor is replete with examples of two or more individuals receiving the award for deeds done in concert. Such was the case for a pair of 30th (Tennessee) Division National Guardsmen, twenty-nine-year-old Sergeant James Karnes from Knoxville and twenty-year-old Private John C. Ward from Morristown. On October 8, 1918, while the division was operating north of Paris in the vicinity of St.-Quentin, the two men attacked a machine-gun nest that was holding up their company's advance, killing three Germans and capturing seven. Barnes returned to Tennessee and the quiet life of a farmer. He died in 1966. Ward, like John Kelly, had problems returning to the calm of civilian life. He committed suicide in December 1967.

Two marine aviators also earned the Medal of Honor in World War I for joint action against the enemy. Twenty-one-year-old Second Lieutenant Ralph Talbot from Massachusetts and twenty-two-year-old Gunnery Sergeant Robert G. Robinson from New York City were pilot and gunner, respectively, on a DeHaviland DH-4 that was attacked by nine German aircraft on October 8. In the ensuing dogfight, the intrepid pair each managed to shoot down one of their foe. Six days later, over Pitham, Belgium, their plane was attacked by twelve enemy fighters. Robinson was hit thirteen times in the dogfight but remained at his gun, blazing away at the attackers. At one point he even used his pistol, punching a hole in the fabric fuselage by his feet to fire the weapon at an enemy plane flying below them. A superb marksman, he brought down at least two German planes before action was broken off. Talbot not only exhibited exceptional flying skills in the encounter but excellent gunnery skills as well, and was also credited with downing two enemy planes. Robinson survived his wounds to wear his Medal of Honor, but Talbot was killed in action on October 25, 1918.

The backbone of the military is its career soldiers. One such soldier was a thirty-six-year-old army officer named Patrick Regan. A veteran of the Spanish-American War, the 1900 China campaign to suppress the Boxer Rebellion, and the Philippine Insurrection, Regan was commissioned a second lieutenant when the United States entered World War I. On October 8, 1918, near the Bois de Consenvoye, he commanded a company of the 29th Infantry Division in an attack on a machine-gun nest. After dispatching one of his platoons to flank the deadly weapon, he charged straight ahead. Although badly wounded when a burst of machine-gun fire tore into him, Regan continued on. He plunged headlong into the emplacement, killing several of the enemy and capturing thirty of their number along with four machine guns.

Last to receive the Medal of Honor in World War I was a twenty-one-year-old African-American corporal named Freddie Stowers, from Anderson, South Carolina. Stowers's company was attached to a French Division when it was ordered to assault Hill 188 near Sechault in the Champagne-Marne sector on September 28. Shortly after the attack began, the German defenders of the hill raised their hands in surrender. Stowers and his buddies rose from the ground and moved forward to take the Germans prisoner. Suddenly, several Germans who had remained concealed opened fire on the Americans. The surrender had been a ploy, and half of Stowers's company was killed in the ambush. Stowers was badly wounded but crawled forward, eliminating one position with rifle fire. He was advancing on a second position when he was cut down and killed by a hail of bullets.

Initially put forward for the Distinguished Service Cross, Stowers was later recommended for the Medal of Honor. The recommendation was never acted on, however, and Freddie Stowers was lost to history. But not forever. In 1988 the army, acting in response to accusations that its award policy for African-American members of the AEF was discriminatory, launched an investigation of the affair. A search of its records soon revealed that Stowers's paperwork was never processed. Further research indicated that Stowers fully deserved the highest award. Accordingly, on April 24, 1991, President George Bush presented the Medal of Honor to Stowers's surviving sisters—seventy-three years after he died earning it. He thus became the only African-American veteran of the First World War to be awarded the Medal of Honor.

As a group, the First World War recipients of America's most exalted military decoration were a virtual cross-section of the nation's diverse population, comprising doctors, lawyers, farmers, factory workers, college students and professors, and immigrants.

Before the war they were, for the most part, ordinary men living ordinary lives. During the war, however, each man, when thrust into the crucible of combat, drew upon previously untapped—and perhaps even unknown—reservoirs of courage to perform extraordinary deeds. As a result, they became members of that exclusive fraternity, those bravest of the brave who wear the Medal of Honor.

Q&A

Q. Are there any personality traits common to Medal of Honor recipients?

A. That's a good question. I usually answer it by saying the only common denominator among Medal of Honor recipients is the lack of a common denominator. There really is nothing you can point to that says this guy will do something that another wouldn't.

Q. Would you say that cultural definitions of bravery and gallantry have changed over the years?

A. Yes, I think there have been very definite changes as warfare has, if you will, progressed. And I think the nature of warfare has dictated that there will be different levels of heroism. And if you were to look at the citations from the Civil War through the Vietnam War or the most recent action in Somalia—where two army rangers got the Medal of Honor—you'll definitely see evidence of that. If there is one common thread, it's the willingness to sacrifice your own life in order to save the lives of others. One thing I can say about the Vietnam War is that many of the Medals of Honor awarded for service in that conflict went for saving lives rather than taking lives. That's certainly a change.

Q. Did political considerations play a role in the distribution of the awards?

A. To the best of my knowledge, no. The Medal of Honor is such a revered award that when an individual is recommended for one, political prejudices or concerns are generally set aside and the prospective recipient is judged from an objective standpoint.

Q. Can you discuss the different criteria for awarding the Medal of Honor, the Victoria Cross, and the Iron Cross?

A. The Victoria Cross is probably the closest foreign award to the Medal of Honor. We've awarded approximately 3,400 Medals of Honor to about 3,420 recipients. The Victoria Cross, I think,

has been awarded less than sixteen hundred times. So, if anything, the criteria for the Victoria Cross is much higher than it
is for the Medal of Honor. But I think you'd find a similarity in
the type of deeds that resulted in the award. I'm not real familiar with the Iron Cross, although I understand that its prestige
was somewhat diminished as time went by in both the First
and Second World Wars.

Q. *Which state has contributed the largest number of Medal of Honor
recipients?*

A. Generally I would say it was New York; although in recent years,
from World War II through Vietnam, it's probably California and
Texas. But overall, because of the large number of Civil War
awards and the large number of people from New York state
that served in the Civil War, it would be New York.

Comment

Edward M. Coffman: It is interesting to see what happens to Medal
of Honor winners later in life. The question is, to what extent was
the Medal of Honor a burden for these people? What did it mean to
them? You do a medal-winning deed in a moment or a few minutes, and then for the rest of your life you are a Medal of Honor
man. What does that really mean?

Tim Travers: Murphy's presentation reminded me of the awards
policy in the British Expeditionary Force. You all know very well
that medals are deserved by the great majority of men who receive
them, but I do recall coming across documents—letters from GHQ
to various divisions—saying, "We need the following number of recommendations for medals." So there was a kind of quota that had
to be filled, and it was. And it's no accident that senior generals
wound up with most of the medals. They recommended each other.

Paul Fussell: Something that fascinates me, as some of you know,
is the literary status of conventional writings of various kinds. Edward Murphy's talk made me curious about the literary status of
Medal of Honor citations. Now and then we come across reasons
why most historians seem so contemptuous of military history as a
branch. The reason they feel contemptuous is beautifully illustrated by a volume of the history of the United States Army in Europe in the Second World War, the one titled *Riviera to the Rhine.*
Here, citations for the Medal of Honor, the Silver Star, and so on
are actually used as historical evidence instead of evidence of

people's desires to be well thought of. I think the whole matter of what documents are useful in military history is one which doesn't get talked about enough.

Jeffrey Clarke*: Medal of Honor citations were *not* used as source material in *Riviera to the Rhine.* The one exception to this, I believe, is the citation for Audie Murphy. There are all kinds of reasons why I wouldn't use Medal of Honor citations for source material. It probably boils down to my personal experience. As a young infantry lieutenant in the 1st Infantry Division in Vietnam, somebody handed me the job to write Silver Star citations for a pile of officers. I wrote and I wrote and I wrote and, to make a long story short, I was never assigned to write a Medal of Honor citation.

One of my jobs was to review awards for valor. I got a stack of valor awards once a month. It took about six hours to review. For enlisted men, if a guy didn't run away in combat, he got approved for an Army Commendation Medal or a Bronze Star. For anything more than that, he got approved for Silver Star. As for officers—I looked at those awards very closely. In six months on the job, I didn't approve any valor awards for officers. But I felt bad about that because this was in 1968 and '69, and I knew that many of these officers were serving their second or third tours in Vietnam, and in some cases they should have received medals for what they did in 1965 and '66 . . . but because of the press of events and lack of paper, lack of time, they never got put in for anything. So, sometimes it was just chance whether you got written up or not.

*Jeffrey J. Clarke is Chief Historian, Center of Military History of the U.S. Army, and coauthor (with Robert Ross Smith) of *Riviera to the Rhine.* Ed.

Ensign Charles Hammann was the first American pilot from any service to win the Medal of Honor.

Edward Murphy

Alexander G. Lyle, seen here later in life, was a navy lieutenant commander when he became the first Medal of Honor winner for ground combat action in France during the Great War.

Edward Murphy

One man, two medals: Ernest Janson, known to the Marine Corps as Sergeant "Charles F. Hoffman," was awarded Medals of Honor from both the army and the navy for heroic actions at the Battle of Chateau-Thierry.

Edward Murphy

Patton, Eisenhower, and American Armor in the First World War
Dale E. Wilson

The Second World War saw Dwight D. Eisenhower and George S. Patton, Jr. accomplish their greatest deeds as soldiers and achieve lasting fame for the role they played in bringing about the defeat of Nazi Germany. Less well known is their service in the First World War, when both men were involved in the birth of a new form of warfare destined to revolutionize the battlefield and change the way wars were fought. As officers in the United States Army's fledgling Tank Corps, they helped develop the technology of tracked armored fighting vehicles as well as the doctrine that would later govern their use; and, in so doing, they also helped lay the groundwork for future victories in a conflict where the tank would come into its own as a weapon of decision. What follows is an overview of their involvement in the Tank Corps, both during the war and in its immediate aftermath.

* * *

Just four months prior to the Armistice, in July 1918, Patton was in France as the commander of the Tank Corps' 1st Tank Brigade. It was an assignment he had gotten in a roundabout manner. In October 1917, with service as General John B. Pershing's aide-de-camp during the 1916 Punitive Expedition in Mexico working in his favor, he wangled an appointment to AEF headquarters in Chaumont, France, as post adjutant and commander of the headquarters company. He wasn't there for long, however. He wanted to see action and, after some wavering while he contemplated seeking command of an infantry battalion, Patton became convinced that the army's nascent Tank Corps offered him the best way of achieving this goal. His subsequent application to Pershing for a transfer to tanks was granted on November 10, when he was ordered to report to the commandant of the army schools at Langres to establish a light tank school for the U.S. First Army. Patton, then a captain, thus became the first soldier in the U.S. Army assigned to work with tanks.

Soon thereafter, Patton acquired a mentor in the person of Samuel D. Rockenbach, a cavalry colonel who had previously served as quartermaster in charge of port operations at St.-Nazaire. There he had caught the eye of Pershing, who needed someone with experience in supply operations logistics to get the AEF Tank Corps up and running. Rockenbach fit the bill, and was accordingly appointed to command the corps on December 22, 1917. But it was Patton and other younger officers under Rockenbach's command who proved to be the real brains of the Tank Corps, creating the training programs and formulating the doctrine for using the tanks in battle in cooperation with their French and British allies.

In February 1918, Patton established the AEF's Light Tank School at Bourg, located five miles from Langres on the road to Dijon. Lacking tanks at the outset, Patton and his men were forced to make do with plywood mockups complete with a turret armed with a Hotchkiss 8mm machine gun. The entire contraption was mounted on a rocking device used to simulate movement over rough terrain while a trainee fired at a fixed target. It wasn't until March 23 that the unit received its first shipment of ten 7.4-ton Renault light tanks, with another fifteen following in May.

At Bourg, Patton demonstrated that he was a hands-on commander who liked to take part in all the training exercises with his men. He was quite strict when it came to saluting and drill, and he insisted that procedures which he formulated for maneuvering tanks in tactical formations be followed to the letter.

The 1st Light Tank Battalion was organized at Bourg on April 28, 1918, with Patton in command. By the first week of June, however, officers and men had been assigned to him in sufficient numbers to organize a second battalion. At about the same time, the two battalions were redesignated the 326th and 327th Tank Battalions, and command was given to Captains Joseph W. Viner and Sereno E. Brett, respectively. But at the end of August—just prior to the St.-Mihiel offensive, when the Tank Corps received its baptism of fire—Viner was made director of the tank center and school, a move which resulted in Brett assuming command of the 326th and Captain Ranulf Compton taking over the 327th.

Brett was a former infantry officer who was especially skilled in the use of the 37mm cannon which armed one variant of the Renault tank (a second variant was armed with an 8mm Hotchkiss machine gun), and had instructed Patton's men in the use of this weapon before assuming battalion command. Patton thought a great deal of him, but not so Compton, whom he regarded as an incompetent fool and disliked accordingly.

* * *

While Patton was setting up the armor training program at Langres and Bourg, Captain Dwight Eisenhower was similarly engaged in the United States. Eisenhower had gone to Camp Meade, Maryland, in February 1918 with the 65th Engineer Regiment, which had been activated to provide the organizational basis for the creation of the army's first heavy tank battalion. In mid-March the 1st Battalion, Heavy Tank Service (as it was then known) was ordered to prepare for movement overseas, and Eisenhower went to New York with the advance party to work out the details of embarkation and shipment with port authorities. The battalion shipped out on the night of March 26, but Eisenhower did not go with it. He had performed so well as an administrator that, upon his return to Camp Meade, he was told he would be staying in the United States, where his talent for logistics would be put to good use in establishing the army's primary tank training center at Camp Colt in Gettysburg, Pennsylvania.

Like Patton, Eisenhower also had a mentor—Lieutenant Colonel Ira C. Welborn, an infantry officer who had been awarded the Medal of Honor for service in Cuba during the Spanish-American War. On March 5, 1918, Secretary of War Newton D. Baker appointed Welborn to serve as director of the Tank Corps in the United States. Throughout the war, the army maintained a Tank Corps, AEF, which was distinct from the Tank Corps, United States, resulting in a divided command structure with two men—Rockenbach and Welborn— separately directing the development of the American armored arm.

Eisenhower went to Camp Colt as a captain in command of eighty men, but by September 1918 he was a lieutenant colonel commanding ten thousand men and eight hundred officers. Initially, the training program he established there was severely hampered by a lack of tanks—for a brief spell, he had but a single Renault which the AEF had sent from France so that his men could at least see what a tank looked like. Nevertheless, he accomplished a great deal with the meager resources at his disposal. For instance, he set up a telegraphy school, only to be told that the AEF didn't need telegraphers; whereupon he had the men trained as tank crewmen. Ironically, the first overseas draft from Camp Colt was made up of sixty-four men whose telegraphy skills were sorely needed in France. In addition, Eisenhower and his subordinates, again making the most of what little they had, developed a program for training tank crewmen in the use of machine guns. The weapons were mounted on flatbed trucks, which were driven around the camp grounds at speed while the trainees fired at Little Round Top to get a feel for shooting on the fly. A three-inch naval gun was used to familiarize crewmen with the larger caliber guns used in tanks.

* * *

The AEF Tank Corps was first committed to action in the offensive aimed at eliminating the Saint-Mihiel salient in September 1918. The operation was conducted by the U.S. First Army, organized into the I, IV, and V Corps; Patton, working with I Corps, attacked with two battalions of the 304th Tank Brigade, which was equipped with 144 Renaults obtained from the French. In support of the Americans were two *groupments* of Schneider and St. Chamond heavy tanks weighing 14.9 and 25.3 tons, respectively. These were manned by French crews. In all, First Army deployed 419 tanks, a figure that includes three French-crewed battalion-sized formations of Renaults and two additional company-sized elements of heavy tanks used in support of IV Corps.

Although the Americans accomplished their limited objective of eliminating the enemy salient, the offensive turned into a debacle for the Tank Corps, not so much because of anything the Germans did but rather because of mechanical failures and muddy conditions on the battlefield. By the time the fighting had run its course the battlefield was strewn with immobilized Renaults. Enemy action in the form of direct artillery hits claimed only three tanks; the rest, some forty in all, simply broke down or got stuck in the mud. The French quickly replaced the three knocked-out tanks and the others were quickly repaired, bringing the Tank Corps back up to full strength when the Meuse-Argonne campaign kicked off on September 26.

In the Saint-Mihiel offensive Patton learned that he couldn't count on army motorization to keep his armored units supplied with fuel. In the Meuse-Argonne campaign, therefore, he ordered his tank crews to strap two fifty-five-gallon fuel drums to the back of their machines. This entailed the obvious risk that a drum might be hit by shells or shrapnel, causing a fiery explosion which would incinerate the crewmen inside. Patton was well aware of the potential for disaster and, quite characteristically, ignored it. He felt that the loss of a few tanks and their crews to shellfire was preferable to the loss of many to a lack of fuel. Even so, he ordered that the drums be loosely tied to the tanks with ropes, the idea being that a fire would burn through the ropes and cause the drums to fall to the ground before exploding.

Given the propensity of the tanks for breaking down, maintenance was one of Patton's chief concerns. He was constantly after his men to keep their tanks in good running condition, a difficult task greatly hampered by a shortage of spare parts and the absence of repair facilities close to the battlefield. As it happened, it was neither Patton nor one of his officers, but rather a lowly private who came up with a solution to the problem. The private, whose name has long been forgotten, suggested that one tank in each company be converted into a sort of roving repair shop loaded with various spare parts (particularly fan belts) and equipped with towing apparatus to retrieve damaged, mired, or broken-down vehicles from the battlefield. Patton thought this an excellent idea and immediately saw to its implementation. This led to the creation of the first tank company maintenance team, which consisted of mechanics from battalion headquarters who were assigned to each tank company to operate the company's recovery vehicle. It was the beginning of a system that is still in use today in American armored units. And it is worth remembering that it was the brainchild of a private, which just goes to show how much Patton encouraged initiative in the ranks of the AEF Tank Corps.

Still, field maintenance was no easy proposition, in part because of the physical condition of the battlefield—muddy ground was a constant, hampering repair and combat operations alike— but also because the vehicles were breaking down in such large numbers. In the Meuse-Argonne campaign, which continued to the cessation of hostilities on November 11, the Tank Corps' vehicle attrition rate reached 123 percent, with only twenty-seven tanks lost to enemy action, chiefly artillery fire or mines—the rest were breakdowns. By the end of the Meuse-Argonne campaign the Tank Corps was down to less than fifty operating vehicles, a figure that can only begin to indicate the extent to which maintenance and logistics troops were kept busy trying to ensure that the AEF was able to field an armored force through to the end of the war.

Inter-tank communication also posed difficulties. As the tanks were not equipped with radios, unit commanders with orders to give and messages to deliver could do so only by leaving the safety of their own vehicles and making their way on foot to the other tanks. The Tank Corps tried to get around this problem by providing the crews with carrier pigeons, which were kept in bamboo cages on the floor of each tank behind the driver. The tank commander would stand on the cage, with predictable results: at some point during his machine's jolting passage over the broken ground of the typical First World War battlefield, he might inadvertently stomp down on the cage and crush its occupants. Finally, it was decided that junior officers would be delegated to walk alongside the tanks for the purpose of communicating orders and other information. Keeping up with the tanks was really no challenge, as the vehicles could manage a top speed of only four-and-a-half miles per hour under even the most optimal conditions. When the officers had instructions to impart they would simply rap on the hulls of the tanks until they got the attention of the men inside. The greatest problem leaders faced was, of course, exposure to enemy fire. Running messages back and forth between tanks, across open ground, in the thick of battle while the bullets were flying, required courage and devotion to duty—virtues which resulted in the awarding of Distinguished Service Crosses to several of those engaged in this hazardous enterprise.

The Tank Corps produced two Medal of Honor winners. In both instances the medal was awarded to men of Patton's brigade who performed lifesaving acts. One of them, Corporal Donald M. Call, was the driver of a tank that was hit by a 77mm artillery shell as it advanced along a road on the first day of the Meuse-Argonne offensive. Call escaped from the burning vehicle through the driver's hatch and scrambled to the roadside. However, the tank's commander, 2nd Lieutenant John Castles, got stuck as he tried to climb out of the turret. Call ran back to the tank and plunged into the flames to rescue the trapped man. While doing so he was hit and badly wounded by machine-gun fire, yet was still able to drag Castles to the side of the road before the tank exploded. He then carried Castles more than a mile to safety. In addition to the Medal of Honor, Call received a battlefield commission for his exploit. He eventually retired from the army as a full colonel.

The other Medal of Honor recipient was Corporal Harold W. Roberts, also a driver. On October 6, Roberts inadvertently drove his machine into a deep, water-filled ditch while trying to evade enemy fire. The tank overturned and began to sink. As it went down Roberts told his commander, "Well, only one of us can get out; out you go," and pushed the man through the turret hatch. The commander made it but Roberts did not; he drowned in his tank and was awarded the Medal of Honor posthumously for his self-sacrificing deed.

The ditch that claimed Roberts's life was known as a "water tank trap" and had been dug by the Germans for the purpose its name implied. The Germans were quick to develop other weapons and tactics for dealing with the Allied tanks. Antitank gunners armed with .75 caliber rifles firing armor-piercing rounds learned to aim for the engine compartments, which were only lightly armored and therefore vulnerable to penetration by large, high velocity rifle bullets. The Germans also employed 77mm field guns in the antitank role. Technique was less critical, as a shell of that size, no matter what part of a tank it hit, could usually stop the vehicle literally in its tracks if not destroy it outright.

Interestingly, the Germans found a rather devious way to exploit the preponderance in Allied armor to their own advantage. They did this by building wood-and-metal mockups of Allied tanks and placing them well behind the frontline trace. Allied pilots flying over the battlefield would see what appeared to be real tanks and, the Germans hoped, assume that they stood at the farthest point of the Allied advance. Pilots who fell for this ruse thus left the area and sought German positions elsewhere.

* * *

When the war ended on November 11, 1918, the AEF Tank Corps and Tank Corps units in the United States had a combined total of some twenty thousand officers and men. But these numbers were drastically reduced in the months that followed as the army demobilized. For a brief period, however, both Patton and Eisenhower remained involved in developing the armored arm, which found a temporary home at Camp Meade under Rockenbach's command. In particular, the two men formulated theory and doctrine for the use of tanks in mass formations to achieve breakthroughs and carry out exploitation. They met vigorous opposition to their ideas from senior army officers who favored the use of armor in support of infantry and not as a separate arm conducting independent operations. Congress took this view as well, enacting legislation in June 1920 that dissolved the Tank Corps as a separate entity. Not incidentally, funding for tank research and development was also cut to a bare minimum. Patton, convinced there was no future in tanks, applied for and received a transfer to the cavalry in September 1920. Eisenhower got out two years later, in January 1922, when he was assigned to the staff of an infantry brigade in Panama. Many other career-minded tank officers followed suit, and their defections dovetailed with further budgetary cuts and doctrinal conservatism which transformed the tank force to a shadow of the robust corps the AEF had deployed in the final weeks of the First World War. With few exceptions, the army's leadership virtually ignored the tank for the better part of the next two decades, until its ability to achieve decisive results on the battlefield was demonstrated by the Germans in their *blitz* campaigns of 1939–41.

Q&A

Q. Did the Americans use any British tanks such as the Mark IVs or Vs?

A. The 301st Heavy Tank Battalion commanded by Ralph Sasse was equipped with the British Mark V and Mark V Star.

Q. Did the Germans move artillery pieces forward for direct fire against tanks?

A. Yes, they did employ some direct-fire weapons at the front, firing over open sites at the tanks. They also had a seventy-five-caliber antitank rifle that fired an armor-piercing shell.

Q. *Were there any physical criteria for choosing Tank Corps men? Were only small men assigned to the corps?*

A. There's no indication of that in any of the records I came across. In fact, if you look at the way the army recruited for the Tank Corps—it's marvelous. The recruiters called the tanks "President Wilson's slaughterhouses," and they were looking for men who were willing to take the long chance. They were looking for guys who had a glint in their eye and made their womenfolk swoon, the big husky fellow, the big-game hunter type, and so on. The title of the book I wrote on the subject is *Treat 'Em Rough*—that's the slogan of the Tank Corps.

Q. *Was language a problem in coordinating Tank Corps actions with the French?*

A. Absolutely. Patton was one of the few Americans who spoke French.

Q. *How was the Renault's turret traversed?*

A. It used a hand-crank system. There were two cranks in the cupola, one for maneuvering the turret in azimuth and the other for handling the elevation of the machine gun.

Q. *What was the difference between Allied and German tactical doctrines concerning the use of tanks?*

A. Very briefly, the French saw the tank as mobile artillery. So they used their light tanks to accompany the infantry, moving forward with the infantry in the assault artillery role, while the heavier vehicles provided fire support instead of going forward to break the wire.

The British envisioned using the heavy tank alone, although later they employed the Medium A Whippet, and J. F. C. Fuller began to think more and more about using the Medium D for breakthrough and penetration. The British idea was to send the heavy tanks forward in advance of the infantry to destroy the wire. Then, with the infantry following through the gap they made, the tanks were to fan out behind enemy lines to exploit the breakthrough.

The Germans had similar ideas about the use of heavy tanks. They didn't think at all about light tanks. The Americans planned to send the heavy tanks forward to break the wire while the light tanks accompanied the infantry and provided suppressive fires for taking out machine guns and other strongpoints. And that was how we tried to use the tanks in the Saint Mihiel offensive and the Meuse-Argonne campaign.

Comment

Robert Cowley: One of the things that struck me about Dale Wilson's talk on Patton and Eisenhower is that one of the most important qualities of a good commander is a constant willingness, within limits, to improvise.

Paul Fussell: Dale Wilson told us about German antitank measures, but we didn't hear enough about mines. I'd like to know about early antitank mines. What were they made of? What set them off? And I'd like to hear a little more about tank armor. Was it that thick all around or was it thicker or thinner in certain places?

Dale Wilson:. The tanks had plate armor, and it varied in thickness from five-eighths of an inch to one and one-half inches, depending on the vehicle and the nation that manufactured it. The thickest armor was normally placed on the top and in front of the driver. The sides had three-quarter-inch or five-eighths-inch plate. The thinnest armor was always in the rear and on the bottom.

As far as I've been able to ascertain, the mines were metallic, filled with explosive pressure devices that were not sensitive to man but sensitive to large vehicles going over them.

Tim Travers: Tanks in World War I have gotten a pretty bad rap. But when they were used properly, when they had artillery and infantry support, they actually did pretty well, as was the case at Cambrai, Hamel, Amiens, and the opening of the Meuse-Argonne offensive. One thing that tended to really undermine them was the fact that there were very few reserve tanks available. Commanders didn't know about tanks, so they said, "We've got four hundred tanks, great. We'll put four hundred in the line." And after a couple of days there weren't four hundred tanks left, so what could you do? You really couldn't follow up their attacks with more tanks. Now, J. F. C. Fuller was the one who said you absolutely have to have reserves if you want to have successful tank battles.

In addition, although tanks did well, the war nevertheless ended in a traditional or at least semi-traditional way, which meant that armies in the interwar period by and large tended to go back to traditional or semi-traditional ways of thinking about the war.

Lieutenant Colonel George S. Patton, Jr. in front of a Renault light tank in France, July 1918.

Dale Wilson

Captain Dwight D. Eisenhower in front of a Renault light tank at Camp Meade, Maryland, summer 1920.

Dale Wilson

Wooden mockups of the turrets of Renault light tanks like these were used by AEF Tank Corps crews at the Light Tank School at Langres to simulate firing the Hotchkiss 8mm machine gun from a moving vehicle.

Dale Wilson

AEF Tank Corps trainees receive instruction on the mechanical operation of the Renault light tank at the 302d Tank Center at Bourg in the summer of 1918.

Dale Wilson

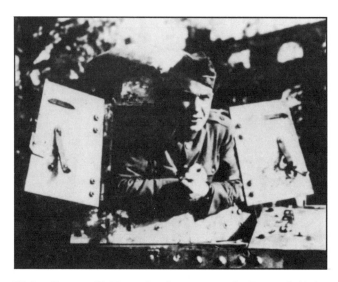

Major Sereno E. Brett in the turret of a Renault light tank in the summer of 1918. Brett commanded the 326th (later redesignated 344th) Light Tank Battalion in the St.-Mihiel and Meuse-Argonne offensives and took command of the 1st (later redesignated 304th) Tank Brigade after Colonel Patton was wounded on September 26, 1918.

Dale Wilson

Captain Ranulf Compton, commander of the 327th (later redesignated 345th) Light Tank Battalion in the St.-Mihiel and Meuse-Argonne offensives. A less aggressive leader than Brett, Compton was scorned by Patton, who criticized Compton's concern for creature comforts.

Dale Wilson

A 1st Tank Brigade Renault churns its way out of a muddy ditch near Seicheprey on the first day of the St.-Mihiel offensive, September 12, 1918.

Dale Wilson

Nineteenth- and twentieth-century warfare collide on the streets of Essey, France, as this 1st Tank Brigade Renault struggles against a tide of men, horses, and motorcars and trucks on its way to the front on the first day of the St.-Mihiel offensive.

Dale Wilson

Renault light tanks used by Patton's brigade at St.-Mihiel were transported by rail to the vicinity of the Argonne Forest in preparation for the climactic Meuse-Argonne campaign.

Dale Wilson

Renaults of the 344th Light Tank Battalion press forward in support of the 35th Infantry Division on September 26, 1918.

Dale Wilson

A combat artist's rendition of a 1st Tank Brigade Renault crew capturing a German machine-gun nest just east of the Argonne Forest in early October 1918.

Dale Wilson

These wood-and-metal mock-ups of Allied light and heavy tanks were used by the Germans in the Meuse-Argonne campaign in an effort to confuse Allied airmen as to the true location of the frontline trace.

Dale Wilson

The burned-out hulk of the Renault light tank that carried Corporal Donald M. Call and Second Lieutenant John Castles. Call returned to the blazing vehicle and dragged out Castles, who had gotten stuck in the turret while trying to escape after the tank was hit by a 77mm shell. Call, who was seriously wounded by machine gun fire during the rescue, was given a battlefield commission and awarded the Medal of Honor for his heroics.
Dale Wilson

This jumbled pile of metal is all that remains of a Renault light tank that hit a mine during the Meuse-Argonne campaign.
Dale Wilson

175

War-weary Renaults clutter a forward maintenance area during the waning days of the Meuse-Argonne campaign. The 1st Tank Brigade suffered a 123 percent vehicle attrition rate, testifying to the challenges faced by maintenance and supply personnel who struggled to keep a cohesive tank force operational throughout the hard-fought operation.

Dale Wilson

Canadian Fannigans in the Kaiser's Clutch: Canadian Prisoners of War, 1914–1919
Desmond Morton

In January 1919, Burlington House in London opened a splendid new exhibition of Canadian war art. Included were works by brilliant younger artists—C. Day Lewis, C. R. Nevinson, Augustus Johns—but pride of place went to a bronze frieze by sculptor Derwent Wood. It was, said the *Daily Express*, "the ghastliest thing in these rooms," a depiction of a Canadian sergeant, crucified on a huge door, as German soldiers drank and gambled at his feet.[1] *Canada's Golgotha* depicted the fate of a Canadian prisoner taken at Ypres in April 1915, reported in the *Times of London* by confirmed eyewitnesses, one of those special atrocities which explained not only why the war had to be fought but also why, at whatever terrible cost, it had to be won.

The truth of the story was, of course, unquestioned. Or was it? Already, since the Armistice, Germany's foreign affairs department had asked for the evidence. Canadian officials knew it would be found. But not easily. Unimpeachable firsthand sources turned out to have heard it from another unimpeachable source who, on inquiry, had heard it from someone else. Finally two actual witnesses were found. Corporal W. H. Metcalfe of the 16th Battalion, a Victoria Cross winner, had seen it with his own eyes as he came down the road from St. Julian. And Bandsman Leonard Vyvyan, a member of a distinguished British family, had seen it going up the Ste. Jeanne road. Marvelous—but the two, as any visitor to Ypres can testify—were in very different places![2] Sir Arthur Currie would not have been surprised. During the war, the Canadian Corps commander had tracked down every report of the crucified Canadian—the man would probably have been from his own brigade at Ypres—and found each story to be false. Canada's best-known prisoner of war had, almost certainly, never existed. Instead of its honored place in a New York exhibition, *Canada's Golgotha* was buried in the storage space at Canada's National Gallery, a symbol not of Hunnish horror but of lying Allied propaganda. There it remains, disturbed only when yet another claim arises that the government is "concealing an atrocity to curry favor or to deny some family compensation."

After 1918, the "Crucified Canadian" wasn't the only prisoner his fellow countrymen found embarrassing. In her wartime history of the Canadian Red Cross, Mary Macleod Moore assured her readers

176

that no Canadian had ever surrendered unless he was absolutely incapacitated.[3] That was not true. The two official histories had nothing to say about prisoners of war. The reminiscences of escapers were buried with other published wartime ephemera. The scars of beatings and salt sores, the suffering at Beienrode and K-47, the vestiges of starvation, and psychoneuroses of solitary confinement and "barbed wire disease" were left for oblivion.

There, perhaps, they should remain. Something—perhaps a reaction to current demands for compensation for former "enemy aliens" interned in Canada—led me to Canada's own *Kriegsgefangenen*, or the "fannigans" as they called themselves. How were they taken? How were they treated? Was there a basis to wartime claims of maltreatment? What, if any, were the aftereffects? All of this and more is the subject of a small book, and this talk may spare you the purchase price.[4]

Among the 3.67 million Allied prisoners in German hands, the vast majority of them Russians, 3,842 Canadian soldiers and a few civilians were a mere trace.[5] Civilian internees included students at German universities, tourists, sailors on Canadian merchant ships, and one luckless man who had lived all his life in Holland and Germany but whose parents were English and whose birthplace was the Magdalene Islands. The best known Canadian was Dr. Henri Béland, M.P. for Beauce and former Postmaster-General of Canada. The luckless politician, trapped in Belgium where he had just remarried, seemed to the Germans an ideal hostage and spent most of the war in a Berlin prison.[6]

How about soldiers? Some 377 Canadians in the British flying services survived crashes behind German lines, including Conn Smythe, a creator of the National Hockey League. Two survived Turkish prisons and another was a guest of the Bulgarians. In trench warfare, both sides tried to grab prisoners; others got lost on night patrols. At Vimy, Lens, and in the battles of the Last Hundred Days, intrepid attackers fell victim to German counterattacks. At least two Canadians deserted to the enemy.[7]

The largest loss was at Second Ypres on April 24, 1915, when the Germans assaulted the raw 1st Canadian Division with a yellowish cloud of chlorine gas and a far more devastating artillery barrage. Given their own inexperience, defective weapons, and baffled commanders, most Canadians fought with impressive courage, but performance was uneven. Deserted by its commanding officer, the 15th Battalion—Toronto's 48th Highlanders—dissolved. Half of British Columbia's 7th Battalion was overrun. By day's end the division had lost 6,036 men, half its infantry strength; 1,410 were German prisoners, 627 of them wounded, and 87 would die of their wounds.[8]

A year later, on June 2, the Germans unleashed a devastating assault on another new formation, the 3rd Division. Two battalions of Canadian Mounted Rifles virtually ceased to exist. Trapped in the forward trenches, the division commander was killed and Brigadier General Victor Williams was badly wounded. He and more than a hundred wounded were sheltered in a tunnel. "We were like rats in a trap," wrote the ranking officer, Lieutenant Colonel John Ussher.[9] He surrendered. So did 29 officers and 506 other ranks, among them the brigade chaplain and two medical officers.

At Vimy Ridge, Toronto's 75th Battalion suffered the only major setback at the otherwise successful battle of Vimy Ridge in April 1917; at Lens in August Manitoba's bad-luck battalion, the 44th, lost 258 men; 87 became prisoners. The Newfoundland Battalion, wiped out on the Somme in 1916, suffered a second disaster at Monchy-le-Preux on April 14, 1917. Among the few survivors were 150 prisoners.

* * *

Being captured is the most dangerous experience in a soldier's life. Blinded by blood lust or bent on avenging a comrade, soldiers may not accept surrender. Captors and captured alike are still under fire. Canadian prisoners recalled the cold-blooded killing of comrades. A wounded corporal at Mont Sorrel was shot in the shoulder by a German captain and left by the roadside; stretcher bearers found him later and he survived. Others insisted that frontline troops were kinder than German troops farther back, a common wartime observation. Jack Finnemore, wounded in the leg, was saved by a German who evacuated him under fire in a wheelbarrow.[10]

Germany was a signatory to the Hague Conventions of 1898 and 1907, a set of principles that promised, in the view of one jurist, to make prisoners "the spoilt children" of international law.[11] Wounded, exhausted Canadians who complained that they were forced-marched to the rear were benefitting from a requirement to remove prisoners from the battlefield as quickly as possible. German cavalry took over escort duties beyond rifle range using their lances to prod laggards and to menace sympathetic French or Belgian civilians. Despite the importance of prisoners as an information source, few Canadians claimed that threats or violence were used in interrogation. Most seem to have told all they knew willingly. Corporal Edwards of the Patricias recalled that the Germans knew more than he did of recent changes of command in his battalion. When General Williams recovered sufficiently to talk, his interrogation report revealed that he denounced British generalship and military competence, warned of the imminent offensive on the Somme, and insisted that Canadians had a friendly feeling for Germans.[12]

In 1915, at least, that feeling was not reciprocated. Canadians taken at Ypres recalled being beaten, harangued and threatened as *Geldsoldaten* or mercenaries who had no business fighting Germany. Lieutenant Edward Bellew was sentenced to death for firing after a white flag had gone up. He was later reprieved but news of his Victoria Cross was suppressed by the British until the end of the war.[13] Asked why he had come to kill Germans, a fellow officer of the 7th, Captain Tom Scudamore, summoned his half-forgotten German to explain "it was for fun."[14] He was promptly thrashed with the interrogator's riding whip. When train loads of Canadian captives passed through Germany, guards opened the doors to display their prisoners to angry German crowds. At Giessen, destination for most of the other ranks, a prisoner recalled how "one man was hit full in the face by all the spit a well-dressed woman could collect."[15] A year later, Mont Sorrel prisoners had no such experiences.

* * *

Although German war plans called for the envelopment of enemy armies and masses of prisoners, serious preparations had been neglected. Prisoners had spent the bitter winter of 1914–15 in tents and sheds, shivering in summer uniforms. A German policy of mixing prisoners of different nationalities meant that typhus among Russian prisoners spread to their reluctant French and British neighbors. At Wittenberg and Gardelagen, German guards simply fled the epidemic, leaving prisoners and a few Allied doctors to cope as well as they could. Reports of maltreatment and neglect added to Allied propaganda. Germans responded with their own stories. One beneficial result was that the American ambassador, James Gerard, inaugurated a system of neutral inspection of camps. Since inspectors had to give notice and see only what was permitted, prisoners were often critical of their neutral visitors; but inspection curbed the worst abuses and the wildest exaggerations.[16]

One feature of camp management was the extreme decentralization of German military administration among seven kingdoms and principalities and twenty-two army corps districts. Berlin issued guidelines but German military tradition was based on the doctrine *Alles hängt vom Kommandeur ab*, "all depends on the commander." Some districts left discipline to the prisoners' own NCOs; others left all authority to German guards, normally elderly reservists from the *Landwehr*. Most Canadians found themselves in the X Army Corps district, composed of Hannover and parts of Westphalia.[17]

By the time the Ypres prisoners reached Germany, the appalling conditions in the early months of the war had been corrected. Camps ranged in size from twenty to forty thousand men. Some were based on German barracks; most were barbed-wire enclosures, set in open field and scrub land. A board fence, ten to twelve feet high, set the prisoner's horizon. Camps were subdivided in "battalions" of two thousand Russian, French, Belgian, and British prisoners, housed in ten or a dozen low wooden barracks, with a few lean-tos housing latrines, wash stands, and a kitchen where the prison staples, soup and acorn coffee, were boiled. The huts were crowded with double-tiered bunks and prisoners' belongings. A first source of friction was ventilation: Russians insisted on a malodorous fug; the French hated the smells but feared a draft; while the tiny minority of British demanded fresh air. Latrine pails in the corner made that hopeless.[18]

Food was the other preoccupation. German rations called for 2,700 calories for light manual work and claimed that prisoners received plenty of soup, meat, fish, bread, and vegetables. Prisoners' recollections are quite consistent. Breakfast was acorn coffee. Dinner was soup, and supper at 5 p.m. was a thin gruel with occasionally a sausage or raw herring. The morning bread ration was issued at night and was eaten at once. Few Canadians ever acknowledged that the German army's rations were fit for human consumption.[19] They also accused French prisoners of monopolizing kitchen duties, serving their compatriots from the bottom of the pot while the British and Russians were given greasy liquid from the top.

So far as they possibly could, the Canadian and British prisoners subsisted on parcels from home and from the Red Cross. Thanks to neutrals, postal services worked between belligerents. Begun in 1914 with the first reports of suffering in the German camps, the flow of parcels began as a typically private response to need and developed, by 1916, into an official Red Cross function. By the end of 1916, in the name of censorship and preventing contraband, British authorities banned private parcels, at least to other-rank prisoners, and Canadians were eventually obliged by their own Red Cross to conform. Medical authorities helped design four standard, nutritionally balanced packages. The Red Cross undertook to deliver three ten-pound parcels to each prisoner every two weeks. Monthly, prisoners received a half-pound tin of tobacco and 250 cigarettes; every six months they got a supply of clothing and annually a new overcoat. Lady Evelyn Duff organized bakeries in Switzerland and later in Denmark that delivered loaves of white bread to British and Canadian camps. "Swiss dodgers" might be rock-hard or green with mold when they arrived, but hungry prisoners ate all they could. At the behest of

Sir Sam Hughes, Canadian prisoners were urged to make a monthly contribution. Few did, but almost every prisoner recognized that the parcels were life-savers. It was enough to see the starving Russian prisoners or to suffer periods when parcels were cut off to know what a difference the Red Cross made.[20]

Gratitude did not mean prisoners were well fed. The parcels delivered a diet of canned food. While it was amazing that starving Germans seldom if ever stole prisoners' food, the contents of the parcels could never be more than a supplement to an inadequate basic diet. As we shall see, many prisoners were cut off from parcels for long periods. Back in England, also suffering food shortages, reductions in the parcels and the bread supply were often considered but not implemented. Moldy or stale, Lady Duff's loaves nevertheless let Germany know that her enemies still enjoyed the peacetime luxury of white bread.

The Hague Convention was eloquent on the privileges of officer prisoners, and the Germans, on the whole, observed the terms. Officers were housed in schools, barracks, fortresses and lower-quality hotels, sleeping several to a room but always with orderlies from their own armies to attend to their needs. The German regulations promised them "a sufficient and nutritious fare." At Bischofswerda in 1915, Canadian officers reported a small white roll and dishwater coffee for breakfast; soup, meat, fish, potatoes, and bread for dinner; and a pickled herring for tea.[21] For fellow Canadians at Giessen, it might have seemed a treat.

Prison, of course, was prison. Canadian officers experienced two of the worst officers' camps, Clausthals and Holzminden, commanded by the brothers Carl and Heinrich Niemeyer, who had lived in the United States and tyrannized their captives with lengthy roll calls, surprise searches, and petty rules that kept solitary confinement cells filled. Whatever their rank, prisoners suffered from captivity. As the war dragged on, doctors began to talk of the neurotic symptoms they called "barbed wire disease." Walter Haight, one of the doctors captured at Mont Sorrel, emerged from Holzminden with acne, rotten teeth, and too mentally disoriented to continue a hitherto brilliant medical career.[22]

* * *

For other ranks at least, the Germans had a cure for barbed wire disease. The Hague Convention allowed them to put all but officers to work. The convention insisted that "the work shall not be excessive and shall have no connection with the operations of war," but that was a matter for Germans to judge.[23] In 1915, prison camps became depots supplying men for hundreds and soon thousands of

Arbeitkommandos. Employers in the X Army Corps ranged from Krupp and the huge Babcock and Wilcocks factory to farmers in need of a few hands. Contracts required prisoners to be paid—but almost all the money was promptly diverted to meet the cost of their food, shelter, and guards. By the end of 1916, Germany reported that 1.1 million prisoners were happily at work. Thanks to the food parcels, some of them were being subsisted at French and British expense.

Canadian prisoners chopped weeds, dug ditches and, at Bohmte, they dug a canal. At Vehnemoor they worked up to their knees in brown, fetid water, cutting peat. Others worked in steel mills and chemical factories. Still more labored in coal and salt mines, or swept streets and collected garbage in German cities. On the North Sea coast they built dikes. Wherever unskilled labor could be organized and guarded, prisoners could be employed.[24]

British prisoners—most of them regular soldiers taken between the battles of Mons and the Marne—resisted work, at least in support of Germany's war effort, and Canadians, taken at Ypres, identified with them and emulated their example. The patriotism that had induced the Canadians to enlist, the humiliation of capture, and the British roots of the great majority combined to make them want to defy their captors in solidarity with their fellow Britons. Such defiance accorded with their heroic view of war. The Germans were ready with a repertoire of punishment. When Charles Taylor, a thirty-one-year-old Torontonian, refused to work, "He was taken out of the line before the squad and beaten with rifle butts."[25] Fifteen years later, he could still feel the effects of the beating. Horace Pickering was beaten and sentenced to thirty days in punishment barracks, spending his nights in a tiny cell and his days sitting in silence on a low stool. The most common punishment was *Stillstanden,* two or more hours of standing rigidly at attention, preferably facing the sun. Spencer Symonds, a McGill student captured with the Patricias in 1916, endured eight hours in wet, cold weather. Exasperated guards threatened to shoot him. Instead, he died of bronchial pneumonia.[26]

At the Geisweid iron foundry, an obvious munitions industry, resisters there faced the steam room, a boxlike cell where exhaust from foundry boilers made life miserable and breathing almost impossible. Colin Earle, a nineteen-year-old who had endured savage beatings, gave up after a few hours. One tough prisoner lasted five days. Another punishment was *Stillstanden* close to the molten ore, with guards keeping their bayonets on prisoners' backs. Some Canadians at Giessen formed the Iron Twenty and challenged each other to take whatever punishment the Germans could hand out without buckling.[27]

The Hague Convention placed prisoners under their captors' military law and Germans considered resistance as mutiny. Giessen resisters were court-martialed and sentenced to long terms in military prisons at Butzbach and Cologne. Resisters under punishment were, of course, denied Red Cross parcels. Noncommissioned officers who insisted that they could not be obliged to work joined the so-called *nix arbeiters* (a corruption of *Nicht Arbeiters,* loosely translated as "work-refusers"). Their punishment was to be drilled, endlessly, in the awkward wooden clogs the Germans provided in lieu of boots. Other *nix arbeiters* were sent to hard-labor camps like Vehnemoor or Mettingen, where prisoners lived in dugouts and drained swampland. Prisoners learned the German word *langsam,* or "slow," and practiced it. Guards and overseers had the power to beat shirkers with rifle butts, bayonet scabbards, and rubber hoses.

At Bokelah in 1916, Canadians were charged as ringleaders in a strike that seems to have come as a climax of a campaign of sabotage and "go-slows." The culprits were court-martialed and given ten-year sentences. When General von Hanisch insisted on a death sentence, Fred "Tiny" Armstrong was the obvious choice. A McGill student from the West Indies, he had played the dangerous role of spokesman. A German court reduced the death sentence to thirteen years' solitary confinement, and American embassy officials advised Ottawa that there was no point in protesting. The German authorities were within their rights.[28] Armstrong died soon after his release in 1919. Another striker, Billy Brooke, died of pneumonia after nine days in punishment cells. His added offense was a letter home describing prison conditions and adding: "Mother, you know I am not George Washington." The censor, a German-American, got the double meaning.[29]

Some Canadians had relatively congenial experiences, living with farm families or working in factories where the pace was slow and supervisors were tolerant. Allan Beddoes perfected his sketching technique by drawing his German guards; Alex Yetman played in a camp orchestra. A few remembered that decent treatment from guards and overseers made them work harder and more cheerfully. More common was a brutally punitive atmosphere in which prisoners were expendable. At Wietze, Andrew Fernie worked with civilian convicts, shoveling oil sands through a grate into a hot furnace. The fumes were overpowering, he fainted often, and at the end of the war he was evacuated on a stretcher. In a foundry at Osnabrueck, fellow workers had goggles and masks. Frank Tilley, twenty years old, was given a piece of iron mesh to use as a mask. It didn't protect him. At the end of the war, his body was a mass of small burns and his eyesight was damaged.[30]

Canadians sent to the mines had the worst experiences. John O'Brien, captured with the 28th Battalion, spent a year at the Augusta-Victoria mine. After the working day, prisoners ran a gauntlet of German miners with knotted ropes if they had not met the day's quota. Elsewhere, they stayed below until they had met their target. At Beienrode, men of the 48th Highlanders worked eight-hour shifts in a salt mine, seven days a week, loading the sharp crystals into ore cars with their bare hands. A ten-man shift had to fill fifteen cars and, after September 1917, thirty cars. Salt-sores— boil-like eruptions—were the curse of salt mining. The camp doctor enjoyed lancing them, leaving them to bleed and absorb fresh salt. Another guard used a club to break boils.[31]

Brutality fed on itself. Guards and civilian miners casually beat prisoners. Lance Corporal Haley Jones described a fellow victim as "one mass of weals and blood was coming through the skin." Perhaps the saddest victim was Bill Lickers, a full-blooded Mohawk. From the moment of his capture in 1915, he seems to have been picked out for beatings as Germans, raised on Karl May, decided to find out for themselves whether an Indian felt pain. At the Celle camp he was beaten by a German officer for refusing to give his allegiance to the kaiser. At Beienrode he was routinely locked in a cell and visited by guards bent on administering discipline. A blow with a heavy lump of salt left Lickers partially paralyzed.[32]

In direct defiance of the Hague Convention, both sides held prisoners for work behind their lines. Canadian prisoners taken at the Somme until the end of the war labored on the trenches and dugouts of the Hindenburg Line, repaired roads and railways under shellfire, loaded supplies and ammunition, and camped in dugouts and open fields during the coldest winter in European memory. They went to Germany only when their health and strength had broken down; until then, their existence was either not admitted or their location was given as Limburg, one of the larger camps in Germany. Names of Canadian cavalrymen captured at Cambrai in November were not released until April. In Germany Canadians reported the arrival of behind-the-lines prisoners. On a bitter February day in 1917, Chaplain Wilken met the survivors of several hundred Somme prisoners: "living skeletons, frozen, hollow-cheeked human wrecks."[33] On October 8, 1918, Allan Beesley reported that 346 emaciated prisoners arrived. Within two months, 127 of them had died.[34]

* * *

Prisoners live for the end of their captivity. Some Canadians escaped—ninety-nine enlisted men and only a single officer, Major

Peter Anderson, a Danish-Canadian from Edmonton. Many more tried, one as many as eight times. The punishment on capture was routinely a beating followed by two weeks to a month of solitary confinement on bread and water—a psychological ordeal which affected some prisoners for the rest of their lives. Captain John Streight made three attempts, including jumping from a moving train at night. Recaptured, German police beat him so badly he was left with permanent head injuries and never resumed his pre-war business as a Toronto lumber merchant.[35] Mervyn Simmons, alone and hungry in a freezing steel-walled cell, felt close to death until, somehow, he regained control of his emotions.[36] Lieutenant John Thorn, an officer, decided after his third attempt that he would henceforth wait for internment in Switzerland.[37]

Internment was a more probable option for officers than for privates. As a humanitarian contribution to the European tragedy, the Swiss had begun by organizing a clearing house for prisoners' names and locations. Then it helped organize an exchange of the most seriously wounded prisoners. Finally, with a prudent eye to filling some of its own empty hotels, Switzerland agreed to hold less seriously sick and wounded prisoners on its own territory and in better conditions. In 1917, when the Netherlands replaced the United States as protecting power for British interests, it also offered to house prisoners from both sides. Since officers and NCOs could not work and merely absorbed scarce food and guards, Germany was willing to oblige, releasing those who had spent two years in captivity if they were ineligible or unfit for labor. Canadians shared in the British quotas. By the end of the war, officers and most of the NCOs captured at Ypres and Mont Sorrel had been released.[38]

Very belatedly, Canada extended its administrative concerns to include its prisoners. Until 1917, Ottawa had been content to leave such matters to the British. The furor over private parcels and the British failure to get Béland out of his prison cell raised Canadian concerns. The creation of the Overseas Ministry in 1916 gave Ottawa a means to act, though not before more urgent problems were tackled. By the end of 1917, Canadian missions had visited prisoners in Switzerland, and a year later Canada began to exert itself on behalf of its bored, resentful, and somewhat underfed internees in Holland. The news led, of course, to a flood of letters from worried parents and their political representatives, demanding prompt intervention to release a son or nephew. Canadians, even in captivity, had begun to feel special, reported the YMCA representative: "Life in the colonies has developed our men along sufficiently different lines from life in the Old Country that they call for special treatment. . . ."[39] Whether that included a special

$3,000 YMCA hut was another matter. The Armistice of November 11 interfered with more active intervention.

* * *

At the end of October 1918 there were 78 officers and 2,248 Canadian other ranks in Germany, 106 internees in Switzerland, and 42 officers and 286 other ranks in the Netherlands. In all, 28 officers and 255 other ranks had died in German hands and 100 had escaped. The Armistice required "immediate repatriation without reciprocity" of all Allied prisoners. In the chaos of postwar Germany, with the red flags of workers and soldiers committees popping up, that was easier promised than delivered. In a few camps prisoners complained that they were beaten when they refused to continue working after the Armistice, and one undersized prisoner was locked in a cupboard by a farmer when he announced he was going home.[40] In practice, repatriation was virtually complete by January 1919.

Prisoners were processed through camps at Calais and at Ripon in Yorkshire. The promise of twenty-eight days' leave, large sums of back pay, and the prospect of postwar London made bureaucratic delay intolerable. If prisoners had looked into the future, fewer would have reported "treatment good" and fewer medical boards would have scribbled "all systems normal." In Canada, ex-prisoners had no special place among the hundreds of thousands of veterans. If they were able-bodied, the government had a simple recipe for their reestablishment: let them sink or swim.

Some swam more easily than others. General Williams became Commissioner of the Ontario Provincial Police. When the Liberals formed a government in 1921, the long-suffering but reselected Henri Béland seemed a good choice as Minister of Soldiers' Civil Reestablishment. Conn Smythe, future owner of the Toronto Maple Leafs, recalled endless hours of playing cards and used his acquired skill in the expanding business of sports.[41] Ernest Macmillan became the great conductor of the Toronto Symphony Orchestra. Others fared worse, abandoning old jobs and losing new ones and wondering whether the months and years of captivity were a factor. Men who had been prisoners in their forties seemed universally unable to work but so did others, far younger, who had survived beatings and starvation with the apparent resiliency of youth.

Under sections 21 and 232 of the Treaty of Versailles, Germany was committed to paying reparations, and one of the grounds for payment was "maltreatment of prisoners of war." In 1931, R. B. Bennett gave the unfinished task of assigning prisoners' reparations to Errol McDougall, a tough-minded Montreal lawyer. McDougall took a hard view of the Treaty and the law.

Given conditions in Germany, malnutrition was not maltreatment. Neither were punishments, however brutal, for escapers. Nor was punishment for disobedience: the Hague Convention established the jurisdiction of German military law. Prisoners' statements and medical records from Ripon and Calais contradicted their claims of brutality and injury. A Vancouver claimant, Harry Howland, a much-punished ringleader of the Bokelah mutiny, annoyed McDougall as much as his German guards: "Claimant's demeanor before this Commission was truculent and defiant and not such as to rouse sympathy but rather created the impression that he was not only capable of inciting hostility but did arouse the active enmity of his captors."[42] As hundreds of prisoners brought their cases, he congratulated those who admitted that they had avoided punishment by keeping their mouths shut and doing as they were told.

McDougall, in short, was a tough judge. His tests were severe and his awards were small. The highest went to Bill Lickers, the semi-paralyzed Mohawk: $3,500. Major Clyde Scott, the army's Director of Records, was rewarded for an ankylosed knee and a smoothly prepared case. Those who had suffered at Beienrode and behind the lines got smaller awards, and so did the few survivors of the Iron Twenty from Giessen. McDougall's final report in 1933 closed the government's books on Canadian prisoners of war in the First World War. McDougall was promptly appointed to the bench, the third in an ancestral succession of judges.

More cosmic questions arise. Was there a connection between Germany's prisoner-of-war camps and the treatment of Allied prisoners in the First World War and Dachau and Bergen-Belsen in the Second World War? Were Canadians the precursors of those *Moorsoldaten* whose song became the anthem of the anti-Hitler resistance? Did Germany essentially meet its obligations under the Hague Convention, as Richard Speed has recently argued? Were the Canadians who suffered at Giessen and Beienrode merely victims of an unfamiliar but successful military culture, whose armies twice came close to European conquest? Were the Iron Twenty merely truculent troublemakers, as McDougall implied?

These are questions of judgment that anyone can answer. My own mood was caught by Michael Moynihan in his account of British prisoners in the Great War:

> Far from the spotlight of the fighting front, the silent battle being waged in these drab backwaters of war were against degradation and despair, physical collapse and mental stagnation. They were battles in which the chief enemy could be oneself and with which we may more readily identify than with those much-documented battles long ago waged with bullet and bayonet.[43]

<u>**Q&A**</u>

Q. Was there a psychology of escape among the Canadian prisoners? What sort of men attempted escape?

A. It appears to have been a minority culture among the prisoners. Some were escapers and most were not. The arguments against escape were fairly obvious. It wasn't easy for prisoners to travel through Germany. The one officer who escaped, a Major Anderson, was in fact a Danish-Canadian who posed as a Danish-American carpenter who was visiting Germany to find his fiancée. He could manage some German, but like many Danes he hated the Germans for the seizure of Schleswig-Holstein and other acts of aggression. But when he got back, because he was the first and only officer to escape, he was suspected of being a German agent. The poor man not only lost his business—his partners in Edmonton, Alberta, were busy stealing it from him—he found that no one gave him any respect until he was allowed to join the Canadian expedition to Archangel. There he earned the Military Cross and the Distinguished Service Order. He was able to recover his reputation by fighting not the Germans, but the Bolsheviks.

Ninety-nine other men got away in various circumstances, such as by escaping from work parties. Officers didn't have work parties, which sometimes provided good opportunities for escape. Work parties also gave men incentive to escape. Most of the escapes occurred from the salt mines and the coal mines. You didn't want to live there, you knew you might well die if you stayed. But the escapers constituted a culture. They're a culture of men, it seems to me, who were a little different, a little tough, a little hard to get along with when they were real soldiers. Many of them had conduct sheets that clean, nice soldiers wouldn't have. Obedient soldiers were obedient prisoners.

Q. Surrender was a perfectly acceptable option in earlier wars, particularly the wars of the later nineteenth and early twentieth centuries. For example, it was perfectly acceptable to the British during the Boer War and the Russian navy in the Russo-Japanese war. And yet, you pointed out, in World War I surrender was seen as a much less acceptable option from both a military and a moral standpoint. I wonder if you'd care to comment on the changing culture of surrender?

A. I think it's an aspect of what Dr. Anastaplo was saying about the will, the absolute fervency of the battle effort. I think there were romantic assumptions that soldiers didn't surrender, and a lot of that romanticism was carried into the Great War. The British took the attitude that their soldiers didn't surrender. "Other people surrender, but not us British." And Canadians in 1915 still identified themselves as British soldiers. They soon discovered that British soldiers do indeed surrender. When they came home, there was an undercurrent of opinion that maybe there's something wrong with you if you surrender. Remember, officers in the British army who surrendered were supposed to be court-martialed, a court-martial being an inquiry of a fairly fearsome kind into why you had done so. After the First World War, these courts-martial were set aside, but there were still inquiries. It was found that two Canadian soldiers who had surrendered were almost certainly deserters, so there was still some suspicion that you had done wrong by surrendering. But such were the numbers of men who surrendered, and such were the circumstances in which they had surrendered, that you could hardly blame them for what they had done. For instance, airmen who were shot down—clearly, nobody could blame a pilot for surviving and surrendering after he was brought down.

But I think the point you raise is a general one about will, about the romanticism of this war effort, about illusions that "our men never surrender." And that's very powerful in Canada. I mean, the woman who writes the Canadian Red Cross history has to explain why the Red Cross would worry about these otherwise disgraced men.

Q. *Where did escapees go?*

A. Well, Anderson got to Denmark; probably he had some reason for going there. Because most of the Canadians were in the X Corps district, the easiest escape route took them into Holland. If they could get across the border—one man, he discovered that he had crossed the Dutch border at night and then crossed back into Germany. His friend got caught and he realized his mistake in time to get back across the Dutch border. It was rather easy to do so. There were German patrols and barbed wire, and there were canals in places, but it was possible to do it.

Switzerland was a much more infrequent option for Canadians because of where they're held. Once across the Swiss border, prisoners were not routinely interned. They were sent back to their respective countries.

Comment

Tim Travers: Desmond Morton's paper reminded me that World War I was on the cusp of change. I'm thinking of the shooting of prisoners of war, for example, which was a very common phenomenon on the Western Front. Indeed, at the Somme in July 1916, there was a British division that shot all of its prisoners. Then Haig announced that he was going to come and visit the division and talk to the prisoners. This caused a certain problem for the men of the division, but what they did was, they bought prisoners from a neighboring division for two francs each.

Paul Fussell: As an ex-ground soldier, I was fascinated by Desmond Morton's talk on the way Canadian prisoners were treated, his version of the "crucified Canadian"—a well-known hoax—and his acute understanding of the problems of surrendering safely without being shot either accidentally by your own side or in a fury by the enemy. What my people used to do, my infantrymen in the Second World War, some of them, when a German would fire a machine gun for five minutes and kill many of their friends and then throw up his hands, they would say "Too late, pal," and shoot him. "Too late, pal, you can't surrender after causing all the damage you've done."

Robert Cowley: I'd like to comment a little more on what has been called that "dangerous moment" when people are taken prisoner. I have the feeling that it was a lot more dangerous than people like to admit. Paul Fussell asked, "When did you kill a man who was surrendering?" About twenty years ago my London landlord, who had been at the Somme, told me that the rule of thumb was, if somebody had been shooting at you and causing casualties, there was no mercy. If someone just put up his hands and you knew he hadn't done anything, he was spared.

Audience Member: I have a two-part question for Dr. Fussell which links the issue of treatment of prisoners to his idea, which I believe is correct, that the war followed a plot of revenge and humiliation. First, in the Second World War a very unusual situation developed in which the Germans, who were so brutal toward almost everyone else, treated American prisoners well enough that 99 out of 100 returned from captivity relatively intact. The Japanese, on the other hand, killed 53 out of a 100, and the remaining 47 came home as virtual living skeletons. What was the reason for this disparity? My second question concerns the atomic bomb. Did America use the bomb specifically to punish and humiliate the Japanese—to show them that those who sow the whirlwind shall reap the storm?

Paul Fussell: Let me try to deal with the first question first. Clearly, the mores and ethics built into prewar Japanese culture made it possible for them to treat prisoners in a way very different from what was considered proper in the West. The Japanese regarded prisoners as trash, as riffraff. Because prisoners had surrendered, they had foregone their honor; so they were not soldiers anymore, they were junk. Therefore, what happened to them was of no consequence or interest to the Japanese.

One thing that fascinates me: the Germans, who were quietly executing Jews and Gypsies, women and children, played extremely fair in other instances. The war-to-the-death mandated by Hitler, a war in which he made himself the final victim, is conducted, curiously, by a set of rules emanating from Switzerland, of all places.

As to the matter of Hiroshima and the bomb . . . I think Truman was sincere when he said the bomb was "just another weapon." It was another weapon designed to win the war and to put the Japanese out of their misery, which it did; and to avert an invasion of Japan, which it also did. To the degree that the whole American moral spirit was very largely one of racist revenge against the Japanese, the Hiroshima bomb was a weapon in that enterprise. The Pacific war was very much a war fought to inflict humiliation on these terrible little people who wore glasses, and to avenge the destruction they had wrought on the great United States Navy. This was unforgivable, and the only way to deal with them was to wipe them out. This becomes the motif of the Allies' war against Japan. It is a motif that doesn't operate at all in the German war, although it probably ought to have.

I'm frequently asked why we didn't drop the bomb on the Germans. Of course, it wasn't ready. It was tested in July 1945 and the war against Germany ended in May. People express disbelief that we would have dropped it on the Germans because they were a white-skinned people. I deny that absolutely. We certainly would have dropped it on the Germans, whether it would have ended the war or not. We would have dropped it on them because it was a very powerful weapon and it would have ended the war in Europe just as fast as it ended the war in the Pacific.

Audience Member: I've been to Auschwitz and Bergen and I know what the Germans did there; and yet, when my wife and I went to the First World War cemetery near Belleau Wood, we found Stars of David standing intact over the graves of American-Jewish soldiers even though the area was overrun by the Germans in World War II. We asked the cemetery superintendent about that, and he said the German commanders told their troops that, since those men died in combat, their graves were not to be disturbed.

Paul Fussell: That's very interesting. And as far as I know, in World War II American Jews captured by the Germans were treated the same as everyone else.

Audience Member: But the Germans didn't extend the policy of honorable treatment to Russian prisoners.

Paul Fussell: That's certainly true. What to say about that I don't know, except that the Germans did terrible things in Russia, and even the lowest Russian soldier knew that and was anxious for revenge. One thing I'd like to emphasize in this context is the irrational element to war. The histories we write and the interpretations we provide, even on occasions like this, are much too rational, in my view. War is a monstrous madness, just barely ordered by a set of rules or a set of conventions of discipline, and most accounts of it don't recognize this mad element.

Donald Abenheim: The Western Allies took a large number of German prisoners of war and the Germans were concerned about their fate. There was a kind of deterrent effect that acted to make German treatment of Americans more or less fair. And, in the Wehrmacht, there were certainly islands of tradition and sensibility and a willingness to adhere to the rules of land warfare. But Hitler made an announcement before Operation Barbarossa that the war against Russia would break with tradition in that it was to be a war of annihilation and of extermination linked, of course, to the annihilation of the Jews. Soviet prisoners of war were victims of that approach. But certainly, as an act of policy, mad as it was, a distinction was made between Western and Russian prisoners. The policy for Westerners reflected in part the deterrent effect of German prisoners in Allied hands; the policy for Russians was in part a reflection of the most evil and annihilatory impulse of the twentieth century.

Paul Fussell: Absolutely. And on that matter I'd just like to mention one word that helps suggest what was going on, and the word is "eugenics." Most people imagine that German conquests in the East were merely a matter of territory. It was a matter of people as well. You had to get the territory to round up the subhumans so you could exterminate them for the sake of the eugenic improvement of Europeans. This eugenic element, because it's very embarrassing and very nasty, is not often proposed as a motive equal to that of simply taking land. Nevertheless, the Germans had a powerful eugenic task to perform.

PART 6

EASTERN EUROPEAN PERSPECTIVES

The Emergence of the Great Nation: The United States, Past, Present, and Future As Viewed by the Russian Liberal Press During the Great War
Sergey V. Listikov

Examining Russian perceptions of American society and foreign policy from the start of the Great War through the revolutions of 1917 is critical to understanding relations between Russia and the United States during that period. In Russia, intellectuals and entrepreneurs wanted their country to follow the democratic path of development and looked to America to show them the way. They were represented by various newspapers and magazines such as the Constitutional Democratic Party's (Cadets) *Rech* and the Progressivists' *Utro Rossii* and *Russkoye Slovo*, which were patriotic but also liberal, and were therefore in accord with the liberal vision that informed the policies of the Wilson administration; and by *Novoie Vremiia*, also patriotic, but which viewed America from a conservative perspective.

The propensity of Russian liberals and businessmen to analyze the American experience for use as a guide to solving the problems that plagued their own society was evident before the overthrow of the tsar. For example, Russian observers of the American scene had closely followed the issue of "German intrigue," which came to the fore while the United States was still neutral, and had noted how it accentuated the social divisions in that country. This led many Russians to conclude that the popular conception of America as a melting pot where immigrants were assimilated into society was somewhat misleading, and hence of dubious value to Russia as a model for change. And so, even as *Russkoye Slovo* was editorializing that America's participation in the war would unite its disparate ethnic groups in common cause (much as the Spanish-American War had united a country still divided by the Civil War[1]), both the conservative *Novoie Vremiia* and the liberal *Rech* were asserting that the lessons of the American experience were inapplicable to a multinational state of Russia's size and complexity.[2]

After the spontaneous March revolution, the restraint that had previously characterized relations between the two countries was replaced by a spirit of active and enthusiastic cooperation. This occurred first in the economic sphere, where Professor B. Bakhmeteff and other advocates of the cooperative approach struggled to dispel

195

the doubts of those who feared American domination of Russian markets and basic branches of industry.[3] *Utro Rossii*, for example, reported that Russian liberals and businessmen regarded America as a place that offered optimal conditions for doing business. The newspaper further stated that Russia's system of bureaucratic controls stifled entrepreneurial initiative, a circumstance that argued for the establishment of an American-style market economy.[4]

In Professor I. Ozerov's opinion, expressed in the pages of *Novoie Vremiia*, Russia's bureaucratic controls constituted an artificial restraint on the development of modern, mass-production enterprises of the type found in America.[5] He cited the success of American agriculture in advocating the conversion and consolidation of big land holdings into modern, efficiently run—and, he assumed, productive—farms. Resolving the land question in this fashion, he wrote, would prove more beneficial to the economy than the much-touted alternative of breaking up the big holdings into smaller tracts for distribution to the peasants. However, Ozerov thought that smaller-tract distribution was inevitable because it offered the government a way of satisfying the insistent demands for land by peasants and soldiers for land, thus alleviating the conditions of social unrest and political crisis that wracked the nation.[6]

The March revolution also stimulated interest in, and enhanced the appeal of, the American political experience for Russians seeking models of political organization. The liberal press, for example, asserted that the idea of establishing a republican order of the French or American type was popular in Russia, as evidenced by political developments in Petrograd.[7] At the same time, however, there were aspects of the American system that caused Russians to doubt its workability. In particular, the events of February 1917, when President Wilson's initiative to arm merchant ships was blocked by a dozen senators, raised the question of whether the United States government had the mechanisms for effective leadership during a national emergency.[8]

This episode prompted Professor G. Vysheslavtsev to warn in *Utro Rossii* against a parliament with broad authority, or what he called "parliamentary tyranny."[9] A different but not dissimilar view was expressed in *Russkoye Slovo* by one of the Cadets' leaders, F. Kokoshkin, who said that investing sweeping powers in the presidency was a sure way to "republican absolutism."[10] Another participant in the discussion, Professor N. Alexeev, opined that the American political system was perfect. He explained that his colleagues' reservations about the republican form of government were typical of men who had spent so much of their lives fighting the tsarist autocracy.[11]

Not that the Russian press idealized American society. Far from it. The press often drew unfavorable comparisons between the American obsession with making money and the noble patriotism of the Entente nations. Russian liberals saw in America's "gold obesity"—a term coined by M. Petrov in *Russkoye Slovo*[12]—both a cause and a catalyst for social and political instability in American society. But the advocates of democracy and republican government recognized that such instability could not be compared to the social and political gulfs in Russia, where radicals associated the property owners' strata with reaction. "Aren't there generals, admirals, financiers, landowners, factory owners in France or in the United States of America?" asked a despairing writer in *Novoie Vremiia* at the end of March 1917; "are they dreaming of establishing unlimited monarchy in their countries?"[13] In implying that they were dreaming no such thing, one can argue that the opposite was true for Russia, where men of power frequently yearned, if not for a return to monarchy, than at least for the re-institution of authoritarian government.

In the summer and autumn of 1917, as the situation in Russia deteriorated, the question of what was to be done was an oft-discussed topic in the press. *Novoie Vremiia* asked the members of Russia's entrepreneurial class point-blank whether they were capable of leading the nation out of crisis. *Novoie Vremiia* answered its own question when it went on to compare Russian businessmen with their Western counterparts. Upon listing the formers' faults—fear of taking risks, sluggishness, lack of production facilities, an inability to organize labor, political apathy—the newspaper concluded that taking responsibility for society's destiny was too heavy a burden for the Russian bourgeoisie to bear.[14]

Aware of the growing power of the socialists and the soviets after March 1917, the liberals had no doubt as to who would lead Russia in the future. They could only complain that the Russian labor movement did not have the conservative and patriotic center provided in the United States by the American Federation of Labor under the leadership of its president, Samuel Gompers. With Gompers directing its actions, the AFL had demonstrated its patriotism by supporting employer efficiency drives. Russian liberals such as P. P. Riabushinskiy urged their country's labor movement to do the same. But this was unlikely. As I. Kulisher noted in *Utro Rossii,* the Russian labor movement was just then passing through a destructive stage of development where its workers were imbued with radical ideas and prone to mass, violent actions—a stage from which the labor movements in the Anglo-Saxon countries had emerged some time ago.[15]

The tragedy of Russia, as the liberals saw it, was that even with the socialists' rise to power and radical changes in property ownership, the situation was beyond salvaging. The liberals predicted that the socialist experiment would inevitably meet with hostility from the capitalist countries and was therefore doomed to failure. In *Novoie Vremiia*, a writer who went by the pen name of "Financier" addressed this issue when he observed that Russians "are not living on an island isolated from the outside world . . . [but instead] are connected with other countries by thousands of business ties" which made it virtually impossible to "establish the economic system of our own [choosing]." And if Russia develops along socialist lines, "Financier" continued, it will soon ". . . find it impossible to compete with [wealthier and more enlightened] countries, and our young and weak industry, fully dependent on foreign capital and initiative, will inevitably perish."[16]

As a result of such deliberations, the Russian patriotic press concluded that the American experience was not applicable to their country because of the chaotic changes and consequent growth of radicalism occurring there. Intellectuals and businessmen sensed that Russian and American societies were headed in opposite directions. Russia, they felt, was entering a period of internal strife and disintegration, and was thus losing its status as a great power; while the United States was going down the path of consolidation, in the process becoming a first-rate, if not yet the leading, world power.

Because U.S. foreign policy tended to support movement in the direction of consolidation, it was subjected to intensive scrutiny and analysis by the Russian patriotic press from the end of 1916. Previously, the press had focused its attention on the U.S. response to German "submarine terrorism." With regard to the latter, the assessments made by the press were contradictory, depending upon the success (or lack thereof) of President Wilson's policies. Sometimes the president was praised for diplomatic skill and firmness; sometimes he was accused of meaningless diplomatic maneuvering and pictured as an extreme pacifist ready to sacrifice national interests to keep his country out of war.[17] By the same token, American attempts in 1915 and 1916 to mediate the conflict met with little or no approval in Russia, where they were regarded as the expression of an unrealistic policy of reconciling the irreconcilable differences that prevented the Allies and the German block from making peace. Many Russians also believed that Wilson's mediatory efforts were undertaken for political ends— that is, to build his moral capital by presenting himself as a referee in the European contest, and thus compensate for his loss in public standing due to his inability to protect American citizens traveling on the high seas from U-boat attacks.[18]

On December 18, 1916, President Wilson sent messages to the belligerents asking them to declare their war aims as a basis for peace negotiations. In Russia, this action was thought to be the first step of a carefully planned policy—a perception that would have unpredictable consequences for the European military coalitions.[19] Liberals and conservatives differed as to what Wilson's subsequent "peace without victory" speech of January 22, 1917, meant with regard to America's preferences and aims. But both agreed that it signaled that country's desire to play an active part in the framing of the postwar world order; to strengthen its position internationally by making common cause with other nations in North and South America; and to present Monroe Doctrine principles as the basis for relations between members of the world community. To achieve this supposed goal, Washington was seen to have bypassed the world's political elites to make a direct appeal to world public opinion. This maneuver was known as the "new diplomacy," and it did not go unmentioned in the Russian press.[20]

Russian liberals and patriots were convinced that the United States would soon take its place among an elite group of nations whose policies and actions would determine the world's destiny. Inasmuch as they considered Wilson's League of Nations idea to be in line with the aspirations of the peoples of the *entente cordiale* for a stable and peaceful world order, they tried to convince others that the United States, as a country where militarism had never taken root, was for that reason the best guarantor of stability and peace.[21]

The more cautious Russians reminded their countrymen that the United States had resorted many times to armed intervention in Latin America. In early 1917 a popular *Novoie Vremiia* correspondent, M. Men'shikov, went so far as to speculate that the growing military strength of the United States might eventually whet Americans' appetite for war and conquest, with dire consequences for the rest of the world.[22] But the March revolution put an end to such speculation, and Russian patriots and liberals were accordingly pleased when the United States entered the war in April. When discussing what America could contribute to the Allied effort, however, they did not speak in the terms of military aid. *Russkoye Slovo* expressed the majority liberal view when it observed that America's strategic assets were of far greater value. It was a calculation that reflected a new understanding of war, derived from the present conflict, which recognized the importance of things other than troop numbers and tactical expertise to achieving victory on the battlefield.[23] Moral authority and material resources were also needed, and the United States was richly endowed with both, more so than any country in the world. With America providing them, it was felt, the Allies would finally have the means to defeat Germany.

And so, for a short time, Russian patriots saw a bright future for their country. They believed in the inevitability of victory over Germany and were full of praise for the way the newborn Russian and experienced American democracies were cooperating with each other. Any problems in that relationship (and problems were mounting as Russia's governmental crisis deepened) were viewed in the general context of relations with the Allies. When in the spring of 1917 the Socialists offered a formula for ending the war that called for immediate and universal peace without annexations and indemnities, it was denounced by the liberal newspapers as being at best the irresponsible fantasies of naive pacifists and at worst a product of German intrigue.[24] The same publications hailed President Wilson's message to the Petrograd Soviet of May 22, 1917, wherein he proposed practical and reasonable solutions to the issues at hand.[25] Wilson also stressed the necessity of prosecuting the war to a victorious end, a stance which was also in accord with the views of patriots, who were convinced that the Socialists were determined to conclude a separate peace with Germany. They thought a separate peace would be a moral disaster for the nation, for it meant reneging on commitments to the Allies—who would certainly condemn and revile Russia for deserting them.[26] Most liberals, on the other hand, believed that the actual damage done to the Allied cause by Russia's withdrawal would not prove critical because it would be more than offset by the intervention of the United States with its enormous manpower and material resources.

Inevitably, it became obvious to all concerned that Russia was facing not a bright future, but a tragic one: a future where it would be isolated, with practically no voice at the peace conference, its great sacrifices made in vain. In April 1917, Professor N. Alekseev accurately predicted the possibility of Allied economic and military sanctions against Russia when he declared that, "We shall be left without money, arms, and friends. [The] East is open to Japan. The U.S. joining [the Allies] creates even greater danger for our East Asian possessions. Our North with Archangel and Murmansk is absolutely defenseless."[27]

Q&A

Q. *You mentioned the role of the liberal press, that it was trying very hard to lead the Provisional Government out of its predicament. But what role today is the liberal press playing, and can you relate that role to the role of 1917?*

A. One of the reasons I undertook to study this topic is that I see many parallels between 1917 and the present. One of the very interesting and curious parallels is that, in 1917, Russian intellectuals were alienated from the Russian people. The people were tired of war and chiefly concerned with their everyday needs. They thought only about carrying out the reforms that were really needed, such as land reform and organizing food deliveries. And so, when Russian liberals tried to find some kind of American experience that would be applicable to Russia, or when they pronounced in noble-sounding phrases on the benefits of democracy, the people didn't hear them.

Unfortunately, today's situation resembles in many respects the situation in 1917. Now as in the past, the liberals have little power and influence among the people. The people do not support their efforts. The situation is very difficult for the common man. I see the intellectual strata working to improve it, but they remain alienated from the general public. And only a perceptible improvement in the living conditions of ordinary people will unite them and liberals and in common cause to solve the problems confronting Russia.

Q. *It intrigues me that Russian liberals were confused by the conflict in our government between the executive and the legislative branch, which we obviously haven't resolved. I just wonder if you'd like to extend your parallel there also.*

A. In the wake of the spontaneous March revolution, Russians were looking to America for a model to organize their government. The liberals and bourgeois circles—they were dreaming of power, they were looking for power, they were thirsty for power. But when power fell into their hands after this spontaneous revolution nobody could do anything practical with it. There were two centers of power at that time: the Petrograd Soviet, which really didn't want to take power, and the moderate socialists who headed the Provisional Government. But the moderate socialists were not prepared to offer any alternatives to the situation. They were desperately looking to other countries for experiences they could use in Russia. As for today's experience, I think the executive branch will find a way to cooperate with the parliament of Russia. But the problem is, the people are so tired of politics. And events of October 1993, when Boris Yeltsin used force to crush an uprising by Parliament, showed that there was a serious split between the executive and legislative branches. And there still is the problem of the division of power in our society.

Q. As a former journalist, I would be interested to know to what
extent the liberal press in Russia during the Great War actually
influenced public opinion. Did it make converts of those to whom
it preached or was it preaching only to those who were already
convinced of the worth of its political agenda?

A. As I said, the people were tired of war, tired of the terrible devastation the war had caused. They listened to the slogans that
were understandable to them. That's why the Bolsheviks won
the support of the people. If anybody said, for example, "I do
not want to prolong the war; I want to give the land to the peasants and the factories to the workers"—this was understandable to anybody, and it reflected the people's wishes, what they
really wanted.

As for the liberals, it is my impression that they had a terrible
problem connecting with the people and influencing public opinion. They influenced a very narrow strata of people and, unfortunately, they could not broaden their support because nobody listened to them.

Comment

Tim Travers: Sergey Listikov's lecture reminds us that 1917 was a
very bad year for the Allies. There were the French mutinies, Russia left the war, Caporetto was a defeat in Italy, the U-boat campaign was quite successful, British morale was quite low after
Passchendaele, and soon after that, in March 1918, there was the
very successful German offensive. Although we tend to think of
the war as almost a sort of foregone conclusion as to how it ended,
in fact, in late 1917, people were thinking the other way. One
tends to overlook that when you talk about the last year of the war.

Paul Fussell: There was something that fascinated me in Dr.
Listikov's very interesting talk about the Russian liberals and their
interest in the United States as a model of a racial and ethnic melting pot. He kept talking about the intelligentsia and businessmen
as if they were the same thing. But nothing's more noticeable after
the Bolsheviks seized power and began to exert their influence
upon the West than the sharp distinction leftists made between
intellectuals on the one hand and businessmen on the other. Think
of Sinclair Lewis and that whole American and British tradition of
intellectuals excoriating big business and businessmen.

Robert Cowley: Something just kept occurring to me as I listened to Dr. Listikov, and that's the question of how you connect the everyday aims of the people—I mean food, for instance, and just getting shoes—with the kind of idealism that motivated those Russian liberals.

Donald Abenheim: Professor Listikov's paper was suggestive of George Kennan's argument that the origins of the Cold War are in the First World War. I found extraordinary the ambivalence in Russian liberalism towards the United States and how Russian liberals began to make statements about an "American danger." This is all very reminiscent of the way Germany turned against America between the 1880s and 1890s. It's very disturbing.

Paradigm Changes in the Russian Historiography of the Great War

Viktor L. Mal'kov

In 1918, the Russian philosopher Nikolai Berjeyev wrote that, with the Great War, the world had "entered into a new historical dimension." In fact, although the Great War was the major crisis of the century and remains a traumatic historical experience, other crises directly or indirectly triggered by that conflict appear to have superseded it in importance. But numerous events of the past few years are modifying our image of the Great War.

In Russia, there is an abiding sense that the simultaneous globalization and fragmentation of world politics since the end of the Cold War is promoting a drift toward universal chaos not dissimilar from the descent into war that occurred in the summer of 1914. The feeling that present circumstances are somewhat analogous to that in which Europe found itself eighty years ago, coupled with the opening of Soviet archives—and the attendant release of information, previously undisclosed, about that bygone era—has stirred widespread public interest in the history of the Great War.

It has also changed the profession of history. Previously, Russian historians tended to view the Great War as an event of secondary importance to the revolutionary crises of 1917. Many have since adopted a different approach, one that rejects the vulgar chauvinistic dogma that places Russia at the center of world events while identifying the Great War as the focal point not only of Russian history but of twentieth-century history as well. Accordingly, they are devoting an increasing amount of space to explaining the connection between the war and major trends in politics and socioeconomic development from 1918 to the present.

The new approach demands a comprehensive reexamination of some of the basic methodological issues relevant to the study of twentieth-century history. The following three principles are regarded as critical to the process of reexamination. First, priority must be given to studying both the conflict's origins and such direct and distant consequences of the war as the rise of fascism and communism, the division of Europe, and the formation of the so-called national states. Second, the origins and character of the Great War must be studied because they are key to understanding subsequent conflicts and political developments, in particular the Second World War and its aftermath. Third, it is equally vital to study the relationship between the war's proximate and remote causes as a means of formulating a more complete picture of the military crisis, one that encompasses the course of the war, casualties, damage to infrastructure, and the consequences for society as a whole.

Not that the question of the war's origins is the sole province of the new Russian historiography. In the past ten years or so, it has been the subject of dozens of books published in several countries. But it exercises a special hold on Russians, who have turned the attempt to answer it into a search for the root causes of the misfortunes that have plagued their country in this century.

In recent years, Russian historians have lost much of their former fascination with economic factors as the main cause of the Great War. The historians' lack of interest in economic-based explanations is reflected in the new Russian historiography. The new Russian historiography exemplifies this point. Contemporary scholars have discovered that it is difficult to ascertain how economic factors affected the foreign policy of the Great Powers in general, and on the formation of European military and political blocs in particular. In that context, the notion that Russia was induced to join the Triple Entente by infusions of capital from France and Britain—once a stalwart of Russian historiography—is now taken seriously by almost no one. Nor are historians persuaded that Russia's problematic trade relations with Germany, sometimes cited to support this theory, had much to do with her choice of allies.

Historians have determined that, in some instances, Russian politicians did indeed make diplomatic, military, and strategic concessions to France in exchange for loans. But it does not follow that Russia's overall foreign policy was shaped by a need for capital. And although economic interests were certainly a factor in the conclusion of an alliance between France and Russia, they were not solely responsible for the military collaboration between the two countries. (By the same token, it is known that German industrialists pressured their rulers to adopt policies favorable to big business, but it would be naive to think that the industrialists actually pushed Germany into war.) Moreover, economic interests played only a small role in the formulation of Russian policy toward the Balkans, and had no influence on the actions of the Great Powers during the crisis of July 1914.

The present generation of Russian historians believe that relating what happened in Europe and the rest of the world to the events that occurred in Russia from July 1914 through November 1918 constitutes a major historiographical and philosophical problem which may indeed be unsolvable. Consider, for instance, the issue of the October Revolution's inevitability. Numerous scholars have examined it, but their discussions about the causal relationship between the war and the revolution have yielded unsatisfactory results. What has emerged from such discussions are still evolving ideas and conjectures based on studies of newly released archival material. These ideas can be summarized quickly and without much difficulty.

To begin with, Russia in the summer of 1914 was not on the brink of revolution. However, it is true that the labor movement was relatively active, and that Russia entered the war with its acute social, national, and political tensions under control but capable of exploding any time in the right circumstances. For that reason, State Council member Peter Durnovo, in a memo to the czar written in June 1914, warned that the country was economically and politically unprepared to fight a total war of lengthy duration. Durnovo stated his case forcefully and with great conviction, basing it on personal observation and his deeply held belief that war could and must be avoided. Whether the war was indeed avoidable is *the* crucial question for historians of the October Revolution, many of whom are now inclined to think it was.

The outbreak of the war at the end of July 1914 aroused patriotic fervor in all strata of Russian society. Together with government-orchestrated displays of patriotism there were spontaneous outpourings by the people in which they expressed solidarity with the army and their Serb cousins. National unity was achieved virtually overnight. In this regard, the new historiography stresses two noticeable and important developments: the sharp decline in strikes by the labor movement in the last five months of 1914, and the populace's almost total rejection of defeatist revolutionary ideology. In light of these developments, it is reasonable to assume that a little more flexibility by the czarist regime in the early years of the war would have altered conditions in Russia to the extent that the events of October 1917 might never have occurred. But the czar and his ministers remained rigidly uncompromising, rejecting measures aimed at liberalizing the government because of the loss of authority that would have entailed. Thus, proponents of czarism missed an opportunity to institute reforms that would have probably ensured the monarchy's survival.

In 1915, the crisis in Russia intensified. Russia's war economy began to break down, causing the burdens of war to be distributed inequitably among the social strata. At the same time, state institutions were weakening and the Romanov dynasty's prestige was in precipitous decline. Even so, the czar would not agree to share power with the younger industrialists and members of the liberal intelligentsia, members of an increasingly restive class who wanted a bigger say in how the nation was governed. Instead, he let it be known that reforms were to be postponed until victory was achieved. The result, at all levels of Russian society, was apathy, fatigue, disillusionment, pacifism and, finally, revolutionary activity in its most radical and violent forms. The war, it would seem, had given birth to a new type of revolutionary, a cynical extremist who rejected traditional Russian values and was armed with a machine gun that he was quite willing and eager to use in the furtherance of his cause.

Following the crisis of 1914, Russia's revolutionary parties revived and reconsolidated themselves. In 1915 and 1916, the Bolsheviks, Left Social Revolutionaries, and Mensheviks restored their underground organizations. At the same time, there was an enormous growth in the economic and political strike movements. Not all the strikes were revolutionary in nature. But the impact of the war on Russian society, combined with misgovernment by the intractable and increasingly unpopular monarchy, ensured that even the purely economic strikes—and especially the mass ones— would take on political overtones. In 1916 and 1917 the strike movement became increasingly political in the industrial and cultural centers, particularly Petrograd.

In the past, historians disregarded the Russian people's desire for change as the driving force of the revolutionary movement, instead crediting the monarchy's fall to the efforts of a small group of revolutionary "supermen." But this is now held to be incorrect, and attention is shifting to the study of national cohesion in an effort to explain the sudden collapse of the monarchy. It is now evident that the social explosion that resulted in the overthrow of the czar was spontaneous and unorganized. The Bolsheviks were nowhere to be seen when it occurred; there were no revolutionary conspiracies directing the events in Petrograd in March 1917.

Between March and October of 1917, the Provisional Government (under the leadership of Aleksandr Kerenskii), and the Allies lost an opportunity to consolidate, through joint effort, the forces of stability in Russia. This failure is the subject of a great deal of speculation, much of it focused on Russia's military collapse in the abortive offensive of July 1917. For instance, what was the strategic objective of the offensive? Was it launched as the opening move in what was intended to be a summer-long campaign? Was its disastrous outcome an inevitable consequence of Kerenskii's miscalculations vis-à-vis the diminishing capabilities of the Russian army? Were payouts of gold by the Germans a real factor in Russia's defeat, or did the Allies use them to explain away their failure to direct the course of events? These are only some questions from a long list which demand comprehensive answers from historians.

After the March revolution the people's movement in Russia, spurred on by the continuation of the war and economic and political chaos, marched in quick step with the Bolsheviks and the Left Social Revolutionaries. The events of October 1917 determined that Russia would leave the war, but the Treaty of Brest-Litovsk was followed by civil war and intervention by Allied troops. So the Great War led to revolution, and revolution in turn provoked a new round of bloodshed.

The changes that have taken place in my country in the past several years have stimulated a great deal of interest in the military history of Russia during the Great War. Such history was, for various reasons, decidedly unpopular with Soviet historians, and even today some historians regard it as devoid of value. But new research, conducted under the auspices of the recently founded Association for the Research of the Great War, has provided a different interpretation. In the first year (1992) of the association's existence, members showed that many aspects of Russia's Great War historiography need to be reinterpreted because they were so often based on false or misleading stereotypes which were accepted as fact for the better part of seventy-five years. The chief focus of their studies is the use of Russian troops and resources to relieve German pressure on the Western Allies and to otherwise render assistance on the general behalf of the Entente.

Such use of Russian troops can best be summarized in a chronological survey of Russian operations on the Eastern Front, starting with the outbreak of the war. In August 1914, troops stationed in European Russia were readied for combat and deployed for action by mid-month. In accordance with Allied strategy, Russia then launched an offensive into East Prussia even though her forces had not reached full strength. The purpose in doing so was to help the Western Allies recover from the critical defeat of French forces in the Battle of the Frontiers. On the right wing of the German offensive, French armies along with the British Expeditionary Force were falling back on Paris with the Germans in pursuit. The encroachment of Russian armies into East Prussia was a development which German military leaders had neither expected nor adequately planned for. In effect, it saved the Allies from defeat on the Marne because the German High Command was forced to weaken its attacking formations by transferring six infantry divisions and one cavalry division to meet the Russian threat. As a result, the Germans were unable to deliver a decisive blow at the junction of French and English armies, which would surely have led to the capture of Paris and the encirclement and annihilation of the remaining French field armies.

Russia, however, paid dearly for going on the offensive in August 1914. In the north, General Pavel Rennenkampf's First Army was thrown back and General Aleksandr Samsonov's Second Army was totally routed. These defeats were somewhat offset by successes in Galicia, where Russian forces inflicted enormous losses on invading Austro-Hungarian armies. By mid-September, counterattacking Russian forces in the Galician theater had advanced beyond the Vistula to the Hungarian and German frontiers, investing the fortress city of Przemyśl in passing and making menacing gestures toward the economically important region of German Silesia and Hungary itself. But they could go no further, though a major victory was seemingly within their grasp. Their inability to do so was in part attributable to supply shortages arising from the effort to sustain the beaten armies in the north. The setbacks on the Russian right flank had the effect of draining scarce resources away from the Galician armies, thus depriving them of the means to deliver a knock-out blow against Austro-Hungarian forces and thereby removing Austria-Hungary from the war. And yet, German successes in East Prussia notwithstanding, the 1914 campaign ended on a generally positive note for Russia. This is an important point, one worth emphasizing because it has somehow escaped the notice of many authors of books on the Great War, Russian and non-Russian alike. Also worth mentioning is the fact that, simultaneous to the dramatic events in East Prussia and Galicia, the German High Command's plan for achieving a quick and decisive victory in the West came to ruin on the Marne. For Germany, the defeat in France not only meant failure in the 1914 campaign but to a large extent determined the outcome of the entire war.

As mentioned earlier, Russia's sacrifices in the fields of East Prussia were made in response to the Allies' pleas for help in halting the advancing German armies in France. But these sacrifices served Russia's interests as well. General Headquarters, in the person of the Grand Duke Nikolai Nikolaevich, was well aware of the risks involved in mounting offensive operations in 1914. But the grand duke had no real choice in the matter. A German victory on the Marne would in all likelihood have led to the destruction of Allied forces in the West and the conclusion of a separate peace between France and Germany. Left to fend for itself in its struggle with the Central Powers, the Russian army almost certainly would have been subjected to an attack by the combined might of Germany and Austria-Hungary, resulting in an ordeal far more terrible and of far greater dimensions than the one it underwent in East Prussia.

The situation in the East created by the Russian army in its 1914 campaign compelled the German High Command to alter its strategic plan for the war. The Germans shifted their main effort to the Eastern Front, increasing their forces in that theater by the addition of thirty-seven infantry and ten cavalry divisions. This forced them to abandon for quite some time the idea of conducting large-scale offensive operations on the Western Front, which in turn enabled the Allies, particularly Britain, to accumulate forces and supplies for the offensive strategy it subsequently implemented.

In early May 1915, a powerful Austro-German army group commanded by General August von Mackensen breached the Russian lines in Galicia. But though the Central Powers inflicted heavy losses on the Russian army and forced it to retreat, decisive victory eluded them. To keep the offensive going, Germany was compelled to transfer more troops to the East from France, where force reductions necessitated a defensive posture. Austria was similarly obliged to move troops to the East rather than to the new front with Italy, which declared war on its neighbor on May 23. (It declared war on Germany on August 27, 1917.)

By mid-October 1915, there were seventy Austrian and fifty-six German infantry divisions on the Russian front, 63 and 33 percent of their total number, respectively, together with eleven German and nine Austro-Hungarian cavalry divisions. The lengthy deployment of large German and Austrian formations on the Eastern Front permitted an increase of British forces in the West to near-parity with the French and their takeover of a large sector of the front around Arras. It also alleviated pressure on the Italian front, which was manned by just two Austrian and two German infantry divisions. (At the same time, four Austrian and ten German infantry divisions, plus one German cavalry division, were deployed in Serbia, which was vanquished in December by a combined Central Powers offensive that included a Bulgarian army among the attacking forces.)

By the end of 1915, Russia's chief importance to the Allied cause lay in the fact that, due to its energetic actions thus far, her forces had tied up the bulk of the Austro-Hungarian army on the Eastern Front. Not only that, it had also tied up most of the Turkish army on the Caucasian Front.

The spring of 1916 found the Russian army much depleted by heavy losses suffered the previous summer during the retreat from Galicia. Moreover, it was evident, after nearly two years of fighting, that the war effort was beyond the means of the country to sustain. Nevertheless, the army resumed offensive operations in June, attacking in great force along a three hundred-kilometer front between Lutsk and Czernowitz. In the opening phase of this so-called Brusilov

Offensive (named for its commander, General Alexei Brusilov) the Russians inflicted a major defeat on the opposing Austro-Hungarian forces, rupturing the front and penetrating almost one hundred kilometers within the month. The success of the offensive was such that, by the beginning of July, advancing Russian forces posed a real threat of invasion to Hungary and Silesia.

To counteract that threat, the Central Powers were again compelled to transfer large forces from the other fronts. By November some 130 infantry and 33 cavalry divisions—fully 43 percent of the total number of divisions available to the Central Powers—had moved east from the Western Front and Italy. In the meantime Rumania, encouraged by Brusilov's success, had entered the war on the side of the Entente. Rumania declared against the Central Powers on August 28; shortly thereafter, in September, it suffered a severe defeat at the hands of an invading Austro-German army. The Rumanians appealed to Russia for assistance and Russian military leaders, previously unsupportive of initiatives to bring Rumania into the war, succumbed to governmental pressure to help their ailing ally. A Rumanian front was opened and stocked by three Russian armies diverted from other fronts. As expected, joint operations by Russian and Rumanian forces in Moldavia and Walachia resulted in heavy losses and the curtailing of activity in more important sectors. But victory for the Central Powers required further transfers of German and Austro-Hungarian division from fronts where they were sorely needed. On those fronts the resultant change in force correlations favored the Allies, to the extent that they were able to hold Verdun during the critical summer battles and achieve some success on the Somme and Isonzo fronts in the autumn. What is more, Russia reinforced the Western Allies by sending two infantry brigades to France and Salonika, respectively.

In contrast, the Allies' spring 1917 offensives on the Somme and in Champagne did almost nothing to reduce the number of German divisions, some seventy-five in all, on the Russian Front. The Russian army's July 1917 offensive along the Dniester, which was mainly intended to suppress revolutionary activities, ended in defeat; it was followed by a German counteroffensive which saw the use of a further fifteen divisions transferred from France. Thus, even after the March Revolution, the Russian front continued to make substantive demands on Central Powers' order of battle, with 38 percent of all German and Austro-Hungarian infantry divisions and nearly all the Austro-German cavalry formations deployed there. Even after the October Revolution, when Russia's armed forces became completely demoralized and then disintegrated, the Germans deployed 74 divisions on the Eastern Front, or 31 percent of the 238 divisions then at their disposal.

In conclusion, in three years of war the Russian army's active and self-sacrificing efforts on behalf of the Allied cause compelled the Germans to divert significant forces to the Eastern Front, to the advantage of the Western Allies. But despite her contributions—and losses which numbered upwards of five million dead—Russia was not destined to be counted as one of the victorious nations when the fighting stopped on November 11, 1918. The fact that Russia was a loser in a war her Allies had won—and the corresponding realization that its sacrifices had all been in vain—had a profoundly negative impact on the collective mentality of the Russian people, fostering in the years to come persistent misperceptions about the West's policy toward the new Soviet state. Another lost chance?

Q&A

Q. *You outlined the help that Russia gave to the Allies in their various offensives. Russia, in my opinion, committed the supreme sacrifice in World War I in that it sacrificed itself. Could you give your opinion of the relationship between the Allies and the Provisional Government from February through March of 1917? Do you feel that the Allies were right in demanding that the Russians stay in the war; or would it have been more prudent of them to permit Russia to leave the war in the spring of 1917?*

A. This is a subject for further exploration. However, I do agree with some scholars, including some foreign scholars, and I do agree with some Americans who lived at the time in Petrograd, that the Allies missed many opportunities to positively affect the course of events. Perhaps the Allies should have dissuaded Kerenskii and the Provisional Government from launching the abortive July offensive that practically ruined the army and contributed to the revolutionary mood in the country. And when we speak of the origins of the October Revolution, we certainly must begin with the July offensive and the subsequent defeat of the Russian army. After that offensive the Russian army had not only collapsed—it was simply gone.

Still, it *was* possible to control the situation. If you read British ambassador George Buchanan's memoirs and the memoirs of the French Ambassador, Maurice Paléologue, you realize that they saw this possibility, even though it might mean developing contacts with representatives of the leftist revolutionary forces. You will remember that Professor Spence, in his lecture about Reilly, told us about contacts between Reilly and Lockhart, especially Lockhart, with Trotskii and other Bolsheviks, and that was the cause of divisiveness in the British War Cabinet. So I think that some way to save Russia and preserve stability could have been devised.

Q. Do you think the revolution would have happened anyway, without the Great War?

A. Even before the war Russia was ready for a radical change. Czarism was outdated and all strata of Russian society were against the old institutions. The real question is not whether revolution was inevitable but what form it would take.

Comment

Paul Fussell: In listening to Dr. Mal'kov, I was struck by the startling new freedom now available for independent scholarship in Russia. But I was also made aware of how many generations it will require to accomplish a shift of intellectual habits. Only ten years ago I gave a paper at a conference in Moscow, but at the end of my presentation the paper was not discussed. The chairman of the conference stood and said, "We will not discuss Professor Fussell's paper because he departs so far from Leninist norms." He said this quite seriously, and nobody laughed. So I think it will take generations to get over that "yes sir" habit of mind to arrive at that "I'm going to say what I like" business which Americans are simply born with and is almost instinctual in us.

With all respect to Dr. Mal'kov—with whom, by the way, I've become very friendly—there is still a little trace of the U.S.S.R. attaching to his modes of thought. I welcome this because at one point he called attention to an issue that hasn't come up yet: that there might be something wrong with making private money out of the manufacture of materials of war to kill other people. That was a genuine socialist moment, it sort of slipped out unawares, and I was happy to see that somebody still had enough of the U.S.S.R. consciousness for that.

Tim Travers: I, too, have read George Buchanan's diary and notes, and what struck me about them was that the Allies, in this case the British, were really rather selfish. They were only interested in keeping Russia in the war. And they didn't really care, or perhaps didn't anticipate, what was actually going to happen in Russia later on in 1917.

Robert Cowley: In general we are neglectful of the impact the Eastern Front had on the Western Front. Consider the year 1915, when the Russians saved the bacon of the British and the French. If there hadn't been a tremendous threat from the Russians which caused the Germans to pull away all those troops in the spring of 1915, there would have been a huge offensive in the West hitting between the French and the British armies. And the British army at that time was nothing. The new troops hadn't begun to come in and the old troops were wasted.

The question of whether the revolution would have happened without the war is one of the crucial questions of this century.

Dennis Showalter: Several papers at this conference have highlighted not merely Russia's role in the First World War but its role in the making of twentieth-century history. They give rise to the question of whether Russia, and subsequently the Soviet Union, is the most Eastern of Western powers, or the most Western of Eastern powers. Dr. Mal'kov's comes down very firmly on the side of Russia as the most Western of Eastern powers, and in this sense prefigures the policies of Boris Yeltsin. But the Soviet Union from 1917 to 1990 wavered between these positions.

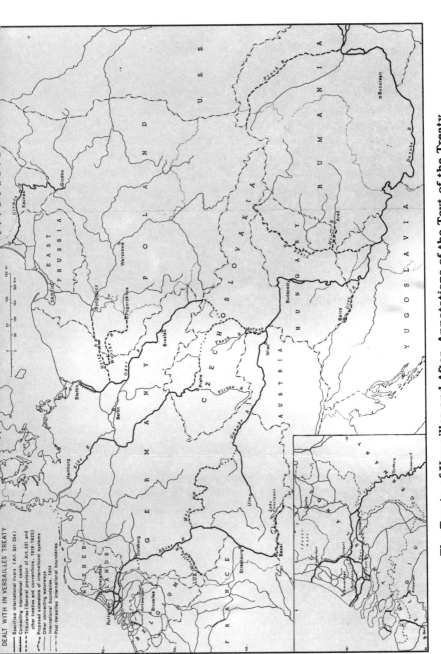

INTERNATIONAL WATERWAYS
DEALT WITH IN VERSAILLES TREATY

—▲—▲— Specified international rivers (Art. 331-354)
—▲▲▲— Connecting international canals
▲▲▲▲ Tributaries (General provision of Art. 331 and other treaties and conventions, 1919-1923)
——— Proposed extensions of international systems
——— Other connecting waterways
·········· International boundaries, 1914
- - - - Post-Versailles international boundaries

The Treaty of Versailles and After. Annotations of the Text of the Treaty
United States Government Printing Office, Washington, D.C.

A Wilsonian View of Self-Determination for Eastern Europe and Russia

Betty Miller Unterberger

Woodrow Wilson's vision of a world ruled by popular consent in which aggression would be prevented or punished by the collective action of the international community continues to ignite the hopes of humanity for a more peaceful world. Wilson's dream is a perennial one that George Bush rebaptized in the New World Order. Yet Wilson himself came to see the limitations in the principle of self-determination. And, in our own time, we have seen the disastrous effects resulting from the dissolution of the Soviet system after the Cold War and its release of national and ethnic aspirations and antagonisms deeply rooted in history. We have seen how those antagonisms have resulted in the disintegration of the Soviet Union and now of Yugoslavia while affecting separatist movements all across Europe, on both sides of the old Iron Curtain and indeed throughout the world. Certainly this was a state of affairs which Woodrow Wilson never intended.

The Wilsonian concept of self-determination cannot be understood apart from its historic evolution in the American experience. Self-determination refers to the right of a people to determine their own political destiny; but beyond this broad definition no legal criteria determine which group may legitimately claim this right in particular cases. No universally accepted standards mark the measure of freedom a group of people presumably must enjoy before they can exercise it. Nothing approaching a consensus exists regarding the feasibility of the principle itself. As a concept it cannot be stated in terms applicable to any given context. Consequently, it has been both a factor of cohesion and a source of disunity, depending on the circumstances in which the question has arisen. As one authority remarked, "Self-determination might mean incorporation into a state or some measure of autonomy within a state, or a somewhat larger degree of freedom in a federation or commonwealth or union, or it might mean complete independence."[1]

Both American historians and statesmen have frequently expressed America's historic attachment to the principle of self-determination. The revolt of the English colonies in North America has been defined as the first assertion of the right of national and democratic self-determination in the history of the world. The American colonists invoked natural law and the natural rights of man, drawing inspiration from the writings of John Locke to support their view.[2] In 1796, President Washington stated that his best wishes were "irresistibly excited" whenever, in any country, he saw an oppressed nation unfurl the banner of freedom.[3] Three years earlier Thomas Jefferson, then the American secretary of state, had said: "We surely cannot deny to any nation that right whereon our own government is founded, that everyone may govern itself according to whatever form it pleases and change those forms at its own will."[4]

Jefferson's view was widely accepted by the American public during the ensuing years although never actually followed as official policy. However, regardless of its original intent, the American Declaration of Independence provided a beacon of hope to European peoples struggling for independence against autocratic governments throughout both the nineteenth and the twentieth centuries. Innumerable peoples called upon that venerable document in support of their own struggles for independence from governments which denied them the right to life, liberty, and happiness.

But the attitude of the federal government changed at the outset of the Civil War, when the United States found itself in the embarrassing situation of using force to suppress the will of the minority of the nation seeking to establish its own independence. Southerners themselves contended that they were following the example of the American patriots of 1776 in fighting for their own self-determination as a nation.

The Polish insurrection of 1863 was the nineteenth century's last uprising in Eastern Europe which might have aroused the crusading zeal of the American people. But their attitude toward this insurrection was clearly affected by the Civil War in which they were currently engaged. In this case the United States had in effect denied the right of communities within a constituted federal union to determine their allegiance, and that denial had been enforced by military power.

By the turn of the century, the American conflict of principle in regard to self-determination might clearly be seen by comparing the two greatest heroes in American history. The popular reputation of George Washington rested less on his great work as the nation's first president than on the successful conduct of a struggle for self-determination, while Lincoln's rested on his success in suppressing such a struggle. Although pursuing diametrically opposite principles, both were judged right by posterity, even, in the main, by the descendants of the defeated side. Lincoln himself asserted that the Civil War was fought to maintain the Union—that is, to resist the claim of the Southern states to independence. Such a claim or right has its limits; and, to state the matter from the cold standpoint of political philosophy, the national government believed that in this case the claim was not within the limits where the principle properly applied.[5]

World War I and the leadership of President Wilson provided the nation an opportunity for a supreme effort to reconcile the principles of self-determination and national sovereignty in a way that might provide a lasting peace. The war brought the principle of self-determination to the forefront of international politics. Indeed, many referred to that conflict as the War of Self-determination. Small nationalities that were dominated by bigger ones had the opportunity for expressing their desire for freedom. The belligerents had within their own states peoples struggling for separate international personalities; both sides of the conflict appealed to the national sentiments of the minorities on the other side. Each tried to woo allies by promising them territories and populations that did not rightly belong to them.[6] Both were restrained at the initial stages of the war, for too much stress on self-determination might prove a boomerang.

Wilson's espousal of the principle of self-determination as a central element of the peace was not simply a reaction to Bolshevik initiatives and wartime exigencies, as some scholars have claimed.[7] He had early embraced this concept under his own favored expression of self-government and had referred to it in relation to the war as early as November 4, 1915.[8] Wilson defended the principle with missionary zeal and in the spirit of the American anti-colonial tradition which dated back to the War of Independence. His statements embodied the main tenets in Lincoln's "government of the people, by the people, and for the people," the Virginia Bill of Rights ("that all power is vested in and consequently derived from the people"), the Declaration of Independence, and the United States Constitution. His speeches clearly indicated that he had read and reread with a student's care and an evangelist's ardor the writings and speeches of the great men who formed the republic and built up the splendid fabric of her political philosophy.[9]

Wilson had an abiding faith in the capacities of all peoples for self-government because of their inherent character and capacity for growth. Thus, the Declaration of Independence, with its clarion call for national self-determination, was for him not merely a statement of political ideals but also a program for action. It was a vital piece of "practical business, not a piece of rhetoric." Now that the United States had become rich and powerful, it was important to use that influence, not for "aggrandizement and material benefit only," but to support, through moral influence, the legitimate aspirations of struggling peoples for self-government throughout the world.[10]

Although Wilson does not appear to have used the term "self-determination" publicly until February 11, 1918, his addresses of May 27, 1916, and January 22, 1917, as well as his early wartime addresses are permeated with the ideas later incorporated in the catch-all phrase "self-determination."[11] Wilson also recognized the importance of noninterference in the affairs of other nations. His difficult experiences in formulating policies during the Mexican Revolution had made him highly sensitive to the limitations of interference in the domestic affairs of other nations.[12] He came to recognize that the Mexican Revolution was not merely a personal struggle for power and profit but also a major social upheaval comparable to the French Revolution. After Huerta abdicated, Wilson saw the wisdom of permitting the Mexicans to settle their own internal affairs. There were in his judgment "no conceivable circumstances which would make it right for us to direct by force or threat of force the internal process of what is a profound revolution."[13]

In a draft of an address to Congress in 1916, Wilson wrote: "It does not lie with the American people to dictate to another people what their government shall be or what use shall be made of their resources, what laws or rules they shall have or what persons they shall encourage and favor."[14] From the moment on May 27, 1916, that Wilson announced as a fundamental principle "that every people has a right to choose the sovereignty under which they shall live," he was selected as leader by those who believed that the new frontiers drawn at the peace conference should be based on self-determination.[15]

However, as is shown by his repeated refusals to favor the petitions from subject nationalities which poured in on him later, as the war was ending, the president's words did not endorse the right of secession. His meaning appears, from the first, to have been that no change of sovereignty must be made by conquest and that such national groups as wished it should be autonomous within the state to which they belonged. Wilson did not contend that independent statehood was the only outcome consistent with an exercise of the right of self-determination. Neither did he believe that ethnic boundaries had to coincide with new political boundaries. Clearly, for him, the "self" in self-determination did not necessarily have to coincide with an ethnic group.[16]

During the following two years, Wilson continued to proclaim vigorously and with passionate conviction his version of the right of national self-determination: "No peace can last, or ought to last, which does not recognize and accept the principle that governments derive all their just powers from the consent of the governed," and "no right anywhere exists to hand peoples about from sovereignty to sovereignty as if they were property."[17] Although aspiring minorities within the Austro-Hungarian empire assumed that Wilson's program of national self-determination was based upon the dismemberment of empires, Wilson explained to Ambassador Jules Jusserand just a few weeks later that he had not intended to suggest the breakup of the Habsburg empire, but only broad autonomy for its subject nationalities.[18] On December 4, 1917, when Wilson requested a declaration of war on Austria from Congress, he reiterated this view: "We do not wish in any way to impair or rearrange the Austro-Hungarian Empire. It is no affair of ours what they do with their own life, either industrially or politically. We do not purpose or desire to dictate to them in any way. We only desire to see their affairs are left in their own hands, in all matters, great or small."[19]

On the very day that Wilson addressed Congress, the armistice between Russia and the Central Powers was signed. When the Bolshevik leaders, Lenin and Trotsky, had come to power in November 1917, they had demanded an immediate, general, and democratic peace with the Central Powers, based on no "annexations and contributions with the right of all nations to self-determination."[20] On December 3, the Russians suspended hostilities with Germany and its allies, a state that lasted until December 17. During this period, the Bolsheviks used the concept of self-determination heavily on behalf of peace. After a powerful propaganda campaign, they were finally able to convince their opponents to allow more time for the negotiations, so as to permit the Allies to define their war aims and to decide whether they wished to participate. During this period, the Bolsheviks published the six points for world peace they had laid down for the guidance of the peace conference. Five of the six points dealt with self-determination. Although the United States and the Allies failed to perceive it until Trotsky pointed it out to them, the points were directed at them as much as at the Central Powers. On December 29, with six days remaining during which the Entente Powers could exercise their option to participate in the negotiations, Trotsky sent them his longest and most impassioned appeal.[21] The address was clearly an ideological challenge. He pointed out that the Allies could no longer insist on fighting the war for the liberation of Belgium, the northern departments of France, Serbia, and other areas, since Germany and its allies had indicated a willingness to evacuate those areas at the conclusion of the universal peace.

Some response appeared to be necessary, for not only did Trotsky call for violent proletarian revolution against the Allied governments, but he had also shrewdly based his primary argument on

President Wilson's principle of self-determination. Indeed, his interpretation was a direct confrontation to the president's view of that principle. Yet, Trotsky's address was an even greater challenge to the Entente in terms of practice. Trotsky had charged that the Allies had not even "advanced that one step towards peace" made by the Central Powers.

Although the Allies could not publicly refute his statement, British Prime Minister Lloyd George had secured Allied support at the inter-Allied conference in December to investigate Austria-Hungary's latest peace offers. Those investigations seemed to indicate that Austria was "now in a mood to talk, apparently behind the back of her allies." Lloyd George now believed that a separate peace with Austria-Hungary was possible.[22] The timing of these events, then, became important. Lloyd George had learned of Austria-Hungary's apparent willingness to discuss a separate peace on the day after they had accepted the Soviet Peace Principles as a basis for peace discussions. Foreign Minister Ottokar Czernin's response to the Bolshevik overtures for peace on December 25 seemed to concede, at least as far as phraseology was concerned, all that the British were fighting for. It now became essential to ascertain what Czernin's utterances actually meant.[23] The War Cabinet recognized that if they were to pursue further fruitful discussions with Austria-Hungary for a separate peace, they must emphasize, as Wilson had advised, that Britain's objective "was not to destroy the enemy nations."[24] After considerable discussion within the War Cabinet, and the preparation of three drafts of a proposed statement, the cabinet members agreed on a final form which was approved by France.[25] That statement read: "Though we agree with President Wilson that the breakup of Austria-Hungary is no part of our war aims, we feel that unless genuine self-government on true democratic principles is granted to those Austro-Hungarian nationalities who have long desired it, it is impossible to hope for the removal of those causes of unrest in that part of Europe which have so long threatened its general peace." The final statement was as clear and precise an enunciation of Wilson's position on self-determination as had yet been made.[26]

Meanwhile, Wilson, too, had been pondering the entire issue of war aims. By this time, he had received two invitations from the Bolsheviks to join in general peace negotiations, or at least to state the Allies' reasons for continuing the war.[27] Wilson believed that "something would have to be done to counteract the Bolshevik propaganda and he might have to do it soon."[28] Moreover, Czernin's statement of possible peace terms in response to Bolshevik overtures was so similar in its essentials to the principles that Wilson had laid down that he felt he had to respond.[29] Wilson still cherished the hope that a carefully worded statement on self-determination might persuade Austria-Hungary to separate from its Allies.

While Wilson had been sympathetic to the principle of self-determination as enunciated by Lenin, he had no illusions concerning the German response to it. By the end of December 1917 it was evident that the German interpretation of self-determination justified the severance from Russia of the territories then occupied by the German army: Russian Poland, most of the Baltic provinces, and parts of Belorussia (White Russia). Indeed, by the middle of December, the State Department was aware that the Ukraine, Finland, and the Trans-Caucasus were in the process of declaring themselves independent. It seemed clear that if Petrograd were to have peace according to both the German interpretation of self-determination and the Russian implementation of Lenin's program, it was to be purchased at the price of the dismemberment of the empire.[30] Wilson was sternly opposed to such an interpretation. If Wilson's concept of self-determination did not anticipate the dismemberment of empires, what did it really mean? Trotsky had made it clear that to demand self-determination for the peoples of enemy states and to refuse it to the peoples within the Allied states or their own colonies would "mean the defense of the most naked, the most cynical imperialism."[31]

Trotsky's last invitation clearly presented an ideological challenge. Secretary of State Robert Lansing argued that the president should meet this challenge by refusing to make any response whatsoever to the Bolshevik appeals. On the other hand, he admitted that Trotsky's logic demanded some answer and that a restatement of American war aims in greater detail might well be expedient.[32] Lansing also sought to convince Wilson that self-determination was an undesirable means of settling territorial problems. He argued that the current concept of the sovereignty of states in international relations would be destroyed if the "mere expression of popular will" became the governing principle in territorial settlements. He reminded Wilson of the nation's decision in regard to popular sovereignty in its own civil war. "We, as a nation, are . . . committed to the principle that a national state may by force if necessary prevent a portion of its territory from seceding without its consent especially if it has long exercised sovereignty over it or if its national safety or vital interests would be endangered." The Bolshevik proposal, Lansing warned, would be "utterly destructive of the political fabric of society and would result in constant turmoil and change."[33]

One of the strongest points in Lansing's analysis was his dis-
covery that the whole discussion regarding self-determination up
to that point had a major ideological flaw. There was no definition
of the "distinguishing characteristic" of the unit to which the principle was to be applied. Trotsky had discussed the right of nationalities without defining what a nationality was. Was it based on
blood, habitation of a particular territory, language, or political af-
finity? Clearly, accurate definition of the word was necessary if the
terms proposed were to be properly interpreted; otherwise they
were far too vague to be considered intelligently. Lansing observed
that if the Bolsheviks intended to suggest that every community
could determine its own allegiance to a particular state, or to become independent, the political organization of the current world
would be shattered. The result, he said, would be international
anarchy. Lansing did not provide a definition of "nationalities." He
surely must have perceived that his criticism of the Bolsheviks
applied equally to Wilson's position.

Wilson now had before him two totally divergent views on self-
determination. Whereas Trotsky had pushed the political logic of
the principle to its limits, thereby advocating that all peoples, not
just a selected list, be liberated from foreign rule, Lansing had completely negated the usefulness of self-determination in settling world
issues. He insisted that if the present political and social order was
to be preserved, then the principle of the legal sovereignty of constituted states must take precedence over any consideration of the
popular will of minorities.

On January 2, 1918, the very day that Wilson received
Lansing's letter opposing the Bolsheviks and their concept of self-
determination, he also received a cabled report from Balfour about
the progress of British conversations with the Austrians on a separate peace. Balfour explained that the Austrians were very pleased
to know that the destruction of Austria "was no part of the British
war aims." They also seemed very sympathetic to the British desire
"to see the various nationalities of which the empire is composed
given an opportunity for autonomous development." To Balfour,
this sympathy reflected opinions in the "highest quarters."[34]

On January 3, Wilson revealed in a highly confidential conversation with Sir Cecil Spring Rice, the retiring British ambassador, his own concern over war aims. He had been pondering both
the impact of the Bolshevik peace appeal and Lansing's criticisms
of it.[35] He realized now that the problem was "in the main, a psychological one." He wanted to determine a course of action "which
commended itself to the great majority of the American people whose
interpreter he was."[36] Yet he could scarcely be unsympathetic to

the Bolshevik appeal to the peoples of the belligerent nations over the heads of their governments, since he had made a similar appeal to the German people "with the full consent of the American people." He recognized the tremendous power of the Bolshevik statement and its potentially devastating effect on the morale of the peoples of Italy, England, and France. He believed that if it was not counteracted, "the effect would be great and would increase." Wilson explained that while he sympathized with the Bolshevik desire to settle the war on the basis of self-determination, "In point of logic, of pure logic, this principle which was good in itself would lead to the complete independence of various small nationalities now forming part of various empires. Pushed to its extreme, the principle would mean the disruption of existing governments to an indefinable extent. . . ." This was already occurring in response to Lenin's decrees on self-determination. Moreover, if Petrograd accepted peace according to the German interpretation of self-determination, the price would be the dismemberment of Russia.[37]

Allied policy itself complicated Wilson's position. He believed that the Allies would find it extremely difficult to agree on any definite program that "did not look as if its main objective was aggression and conquest." Therefore, to evoke the enthusiastic approval of the American people, his own program had to represent the highest principles for which the United States was fighting. He had to oppose the aggressive war aims for which the Germans were fighting, distinguish between American and Allied war aims, make clear to the Russian people continued American sympathy, and support and pledge noninterference in their affairs.[38]

Lansing's advice and Balfour's report on peace discussions with Austria all tended to move him to clarify his concept of self-determination toward that empire, and to emphasize his opposition to the German dismemberment of Russia as a part of the peace settlement. He also wished to indicate his opposition to any Allied effort to intervene in Russia's affairs in a way that might deny to the Russian people the right of self-determination or result in the detachment of Russian territory. By this time, Wilson was deeply concerned over the Allied desire to sanction Japanese intervention in Siberia as their mandatory—a policy which he regarded as tantamount to giving Japan the right to do in the East what Germany was already doing in the West.[39]

As Wilson wrestled with the problem of responding to the Bolshevik peace appeals, additional peace feelers from Austria were being extended by Julius Meinl, an able, cultivated Vienna businessman and industrialist reputed to be a friend of Emperor Charles. Hugh R. Wilson, the American chargé in Switzerland, believed that

Meinl was acting on official instructions and had the complete confidence of the highest authorities. He enthusiastically endorsed Meinl's views, which, he said, advanced "a long stride in fact nearly all the way, towards our position."[40] Meinl's peace feelers seemed to confirm Balfour's report on the British conversations with Austria-Hungary concerning peace. Both offers reflected Wilson's desire to preserve the integrity of the empire, and also to provide for a government by the consent of the governed through a federation of autonomous states, a position that now appeared to have the sanction of Austria-Hungary as revealed in its agreement that the various nationalities of the Empire should be given *an opportunity for autonomous development.*"[41]

So it was that Point Ten of Wilson's Fourteen Points did not call for the dismemberment of Austria-Hungary, or for the independence of its people, but rather stated: "The peoples of Austria-Hungary, whose place among the nations of the world we wish to see safeguarded and assured, must be accorded the freest opportunity of autonomous development."[42] That Wilson clearly intended a federation of autonomous states within a strong and democratic Austria-Hungary is clearly indicated by his earlier discussion with Ambassador Jusserand and by his discussions with Lansing later on.[43]

Wilson's introduction to his Fourteen Points speech appeared to be a direct answer to the Brest-Litovsk summons. His deep concern with Russia's plight seems apparent from a reading of the passages concerning that nation. Recognizing Russia's prostration before the grim power of Germany, he sought to impress both the ruler and the ruled, and thus did not call for the overthrow of Bolshevik power as a condition for renewed cooperation; indeed he even seemed to hold out the faint hope of American assistance to Russia's present rulers. Wilson refused to abandon Russia's borderland to the tortured interpretation of self-determination put forth by the Central Powers. Thus the sixth of the Fourteen Points called for an evacuation of all Russian territory and the adoption of diplomacy by all other nations of the world, of actions that would permit an unhampered and unembarrassed opportunity for Russia's independent self-determination under institutions of its free choosing.[44] As Wilson was to reiterate at the Peace Conference, the sole criteria which he recognized for the principle of self-determination was "the consent of the governed."[45]

So it was that Point Six and Point Ten provided a reconciliation of the historic conflict of principle between national self-determination and sovereignty. Clearly Wilson envisioned both the Russian and Austro-Hungarian empires of the future to be great confederations of self-governing states.

Wilson was particularly anxious about the response of the Central Powers to his speech. The reaction in Vienna was generally favorable. There were, of course, many reasons for this. The most important were the bare realities of war, which by January 1918 had had a cataclysmic impact on Austro-Hungarian life. The nation had suffered nearly two million casualties on the Eastern Front. The army was exhausted, the internal situation confused, and Germany's firm grip over the monarchy's policy unshaken. Moreover, the people were starving and clamoring for peace. Given these considerations, Czernin had returned hurriedly from the peace negotiations at Brest-Litovsk on January 22 to answer Wilson's speech in the friendliest terms.[46] He declared that he would accept Wilson's proposals with "great pleasure."[47] As Czernin later wrote eloquently: "A new star had risen on the other side of the ocean, and all eyes were turned in that direction. A mighty man had come forward and with one powerful act had . . . reopened the gates for the peace of understanding."[48]

During the next five months, Wilson made heroic efforts through the good offices of George Herron in Europe and Professor Heinrich Lammasch of Austria-Hungary to persuade Emperor Charles to implement a program for the transformation of the Austro-Hungarian Empire into a Danubian Confederation of States. For a variety of reasons, that effort failed. Prominent among those reasons was the German domination of Austria-Hungary, the timidity of Emperor Charles, the strong national aspirations of the peoples of Austria-Hungary themselves, and the decision of Wilson's own Allies to agree in principle to the recognition of Czecho-Slovak independence.[49]

Perhaps the most decisive blow to the efforts at federation was the result of events in Russia. Once the Bolsheviks signed the Treaty of Brest-Litovsk, the Czecho-Slovak legion, organized in Russia to fight alongside the Russians against the Central Powers, found itself trapped in the interior of Russia. Placed under the command of the French, it was now forced to seek a passage across Siberia and indeed around the world in order to continue its struggle against the Central Powers in the hope of winning independence from the Austro-Hungarian Empire. Unbeknownst to President Wilson, both the French and British had made secret agreements with Edvard Benes, a leader of the Czecho-Slovak liberation movement, to permit the Czech forces to serve as the nucleus of a force to seek the reestablishment of an Eastern Front. Czech participation in this scheme was the quid pro quo for both British and French de facto recognition of an independent Czecho-Slovak state.[50]

In the meantime, the Allies, desperately seeking to find a way of alleviating their precarious military situation on the Western Front, had inaugurated a barrage of appeals to President Wilson seeking his agreement to send American forces to reestablish an Eastern Front or at least to approve of the Japanese acting as a mandatory of the Allies for this purpose. Wilson was adamantly against such a scheme, and for six months he opposed every Allied appeal. However, by May of 1918, the Allies had secured Japan's agreement to enter Siberia as their mandatory, and Japan itself had succeeded in signing a series of military agreements with the Chinese which in effect would permit them to enter Manchuria. Thus Japan was now in a position to invade not only eastern Siberia but Manchuria as well. Wilson had no illusions concerning the ultimate objectives of the Japanese in those areas. At the same time the Czechs, who were now en route on the Trans-Siberian railroad to reach Vladivostok where they hoped to be expedited to the Western Front, had come into collisions with Austro-Hungarian and German prisoners of war located in camps throughout Siberia. They were now pleading desperately for American aid through their leader, Thomas J. Masaryk, then in the United States. Masaryk had been seeking, without success, President Wilson's approval for the recognition of an independent state of Czecho-Slovakia. However, the situation was now in the process of change. Masaryk's desperate pleas for help to aid his Czechs, combined with his clear opposition to Japanese intervention or indeed to any Allied intervention in Russia, met with a sympathetic response from Wilson. He agreed to send American troops to "rescue" the Czechs and invited the Japanese to participate in a joint expedition for that purpose.[51]

Wilson justified those departures from his clearly enunciated principles on the ground that he was seeking to preserve the territorial integrity of both Russia and China and their ultimate right to self-determination "against suspected Japanese imperialism which would have resulted in the occupation and seizure of both these areas," while at the same time "rescuing the Czech legion allegedly trapped in Russia." But perhaps even more important, Wilson was seeking to retain the good will of the Allies, whose support was vital to the success of the League of Nations, the capstone of his Fourteen Points. Thus in order to block Japan and to further the League, Wilson followed a policy that appeared to be totally at variance not only with the principle of self-determination he had enunciated concerning Russia but also with the principles of his proposed League.[52] Wilson, above all the man of principle, had found himself caught, as had the nation itself many times since its inception, in a debatable situation where, despite deep convictions, none of his principles could be rigorously applied. So it was that Wilson's vision of the creation of two great self-governing confederations foundered on the rocks of coalition diplomacy.

As we review the tragic fate of those newly independent states created by the dissolution of the Austro-Hungarian empire and the dismemberment of the Russian empire at the close of World War I, and the extent to which the dissolution of the Soviet empire has released the same pent-up national and ethnic aspirations, it is clear that the time has come to reconsider the doctrine of self-determination and to incorporate the limitations that Wilson himself acknowledged and that the experience of the United States confirms. Clearly, the objective should not be to give every people the right to choose the sovereignty under which it should live. It should be, rather, wherever possible, to seek ways by which people of diverse ethnic, religious, and racial backgrounds can be brought to live together in harmony under the same sovereignty. This is all the more urgently the case in an era that will be marked more than ever before by the mixing of peoples. As the twentieth century draws to a close, a number of factors—the end of the Cold War, the development of swifter modes of communication and transport, the acceleration of population growth, the breakdown of traditional social structures, the flight from tyranny and from poverty, the dream of a better life somewhere else—converge to drive people as never before in mass migrations across national frontiers.

One answer to the question of how to provide a sovereignty which offers the promise of harmony for peoples of diverse ethnic, religious, and racial backgrounds has been, at least until recently, the United States. But today, even here, the outburst of multicultural zealotry threatens the spread of separate ethnic and racial communities, a new tribalism. Unless the United States can continue to provide the world an example of how to make a federal, multiethnic state work, then the future of the Wilsonian ideal will be dismal indeed.

Q&A

Q. How did Wilson's ideas on self-determination affect Masaryk's thinking about a sovereign Czech state?

A. Initially Masaryk did not intend to create an independent Czech state. His intention was to seek some kind of autonomy within the Austro-Hungarian Empire. In fact, when Masaryk went to England, he had never heard about ethnic aspirations as being a criteria for independent statehood. He was basing his claims primarily on what was then regarded as the single most important criteria for statehood, and that was the historical experience which bound a people of diverse backgrounds together and had done so over a very long period of time. But when he heard that ethnic considerations were for the first time in modern history actually being discussed, he decided that he ought to add that argument to his plea for autonomy for the Czechs. Ultimately, of course, he used it to seek independence as well.

Q. Did Wilson favor independence for Armenia?

A. Well, ultimately America refused to take Armenia as a mandate. Certainly Wilson was very sympathetic to Armenian aspirations and of course to the great misery that the Armenian people were going through. But he also saw a solution for the Russian empire in its becoming a great confederation of self-governing states.

Comment

Tim Travers: The talk about Wilson's ideas reminded me of what is being done about Ireland. I think it's not really necessary really to have either complete self-determination or integration within one empire or federation. With regard to Ireland, there are some thoughts about a condominium whereby the two parts can operate together without being either totally one country or independent from each other. There seem to be some possibilities in between.

Paul Fussell: Several of the papers today, including Betty Unterberger's, have forced us to confront again the whole theme of the United States versus Europe in style and in culture. We've heard about Wilson's highmindedness and his idealism and the way it was suborned and aborted, and so on. For the United States, things seemed very easy until they are tried. The Europeans have been trying them for two thousand years, and America for a little more than two hundred. Definitions, as Betty Unterberger reminded us, seem very easy until they face the test of actuality.

Edward M. Coffman: Woodrow Wilson has got to be one of the most interesting people to come down the pike. Here is a man who is very much the intellectual and yet he certainly gets hoist on his own petard when Trotsky starts really questioning the real meaning of self-determination. The question is, once he gets into this situation, has he become simply a propagandist?

PART 7

INTO MODERNITY

The Unreal City:
The Western Front Examined as the
World's Largest Metropolis
Robert Cowley

We live in an age defined by its fierce boundaries, military and political. Have any affected our lives more conclusively than the Western Front? The Great War trench line that stretched from the North Sea to the Swiss border gave us a modern metaphor for senseless slaughter, for stalemate without hope. It added indelible words and phrases to our language: the trenches, over the top, no-man's-land, three on a match. Here was the barrier on which were shattered traditions of humanism and refinement nurtured over centuries—not just a physical presence but one of the genuine dividing lines of history.

At a time when urbanization was becoming the dominant mode of civilization, was it an accident that the Western Front adhered to that mode and even turned into something of a paradigm for its rise and decline? "Unreal city under the brown fog," T. S. Eliot wrote in *The Waste Land.* He was describing London just after the war, but his words might have fit another recent unreal city just as well. Aviators flying along the Western Front were struck by the brown haze compounded of mist and dust, an inversion caused by a constant shellfire, that reached a height of several thousand feet above the trenches.

Alfred Hein, a German infantryman who survived to become a novelist, remembered Verdun. "A cold mathematical monstrosity had usurped the place of nature," he wrote. Writers have applied the same sort of imagery to the cityscapes of this century—though "mathematical" may be too grand a word for the grid plan of the Western Front, which seemed more like a demented spider's web. That, or the improvised urban nightmare we now know as Lagos, Calcutta, or Mexico City. You might call the Western Front, in the scientific jargon of doomsday, a premature ecological sink—and, indeed, I have seen photographs of places like the Passchendaele battlefield used to conjure the image of coming environmental disaster. The Western Front always seemed larger than the life it denied.

It is hardly as if the phenomenon that was the Western Front had emerged spontaneously, going in a single leap from mud-hut

233

cluster to metropolis without intermediate experiments in military urbanization. There was nothing new about trenches. They were as old as city sieges. Archaeologists recently found evidence of a trench outside the walls of ancient Troy; it dates back to the thirteenth century B.C.E., about when the Trojan War is supposed to have taken place. Its function may have been more to impede attackers and their siege engines than to protect defenders, but it was a trench nonetheless.

Even the familiar descriptive phrases of trench warfare are centuries old. When Swedish armies invaded Poland in the 1620s, Geoffrey Parker tells us in *The Military Revolution*, Polish propagandists scoffed at their siege techniques as "mole's work" and manifestations of a "grave-digger's courage"—while Polish military engineers hastened to copy the Swedes. There was nothing new about the lament of one Virginia officer at the siege of Petersburg in 1864: "This mole-like existence was killing the men." In the American Civil War, people liked to say that "spades were trumps."

On the Western Front, spades rapidly did become trumps. By the end of September 1914, the Front was already beginning to congeal into a more or less solid line. (For the record, the last gap in that line seems to have closed on October 15, 1914, when patrols of the Royal Scots Greys and the English 3rd Cavalry Division met at Kemmel, a few miles south of Ypres.) Soldiers on both sides began to connect rifle pits and scattered lengths of shallow freestanding trench. The digging not just of frontline trenches but of reserve trenches signaled that something different was happening. A *system* was taking shape, and one that soon had marks of permanence. What was different about this new world-class city was its length, depth, and variety, as well as its complexity of military and social organization.

*   *   *

Here, I want to digress for a moment to take up the relevant matter of dimensions. To begin with, the length of the Western Front from Nieuport-Bains on the North Sea to the Bec de Canard on the Swiss border was about 470 miles (the most trustworthy estimates of the line that was established by mid-autumn of 1914 range from 466 to 475 miles). The front would contract by about twenty-five miles in March 1917, when the Germans made their premeditated withdrawal to the Hindenburg Line—and would expand considerably when they made their gamble for victory in the spring and early summer of 1918. During those months the Western Front would briefly reach a maximum length of some six hundred miles, as mobility (though not true maneuver) returned to war.

By the end of the first year of trench warfare, the average combined width of the frontline systems, including no-man's-land, was between one and two miles. Gradually the front grew broader, and its distinctive coloration—brown, or the dead white of upturned chalk—spread across the landscape. The excavating intensified. Side trenches accommodated kitchens, latrines, trench mortars, and stacks of duckboards. Wired-in defensive strongpoints, connected to the main system by diagonal switch lines, were constructed to the rear, as well as added trench lines in case of future emergencies. You have the feeling that sometimes all this compounded effort was just digging for digging's sake, to keep thousands of men occupied. (British military engineers estimated that 450 men needed six hours to dig 250 yards of frontline trench; the factories of the empire rose to the challenge by providing the army with 10,683,000 spades and shovels during the fifty-one months of the war.) Both the French and the British experimented with gasoline-powered trench-digging machines. But these noisy and conspicuous devices were apparently used only in back areas, out of sight of enemy artillery. Manpower was still more reliable.

The German trench system tended to be far more intricate than the Allied one, and it was known to reach a depth of ten lines. It was not just that the Germans were better prepped in siege-warfare techniques. Forced to fight a two-front war that put them at a numerical disadvantage on either front, the Germans were by nature and necessity more defense-minded than their Western adversaries. In contrast, Allied military leaders insisted that trenches that looked too permanent undermined the spirit of attack. But the habits of the mole were hard to shake. When the Germans made their retreat to the Hindenburg line in 1917, the Allied pursuers who emerged from the relative safety of their underground city were so bewildered by their first taste of open warfare, and so overcautious, that they let the enemy slip clean away.

As much as anything, continuous fighting, concentrated in a single sector, accounted for the growing width of the Western Front. The French might take two lines; the Germans would dig three more—and then the process would start afresh. No one remembered who, or which side, had dug some of the oldest trenches: they seemed as ageless as the war itself. In July 1917, a British artillery officer named P. H. Pilditch took in the view from the summit of the Flanders hill called, somewhat grandiloquently, Mont Kemmel (it was barely five hundred feet high). Below, a "hideous six-mile-broad scar" stretched "brown and loathsome" as far as his eye could see. (That was before the Passchendaele offensive, which widened the scar in the crescent around Ypres by another five miles.)

The sector that could probably boast the greatest width of trenchworks was in Champagne, roughly between two geographic nonentities, the village of Tahure and the Ferme de Navarin fields. There, the combined width of the opposing systems reached twelve miles. On the Somme at the beginning of 1917, the trench lines approached a similar width—and if you add to that desert the intentional devastation bequeathed by the Germans retreating to the Hindenburg Line, you have a band of wasteland more than thirty miles across.

Henri Barbusse's novel *Le Feu* takes these figures a step farther. (The title means "the front" or "up front," a bit of soldier slang that the translator of the English version, *Under Fire*, was either ignorant of or chose to ignore.) Set during the Artois offensives of 1915, the novel has among its characters a *poilu* named Cocon, who at one point makes some calculations that provide a memorable picture of the trench system. Barbusse's "Man of Figures" begins:

> In the sector occupied by our regiment, there are fifteen lines of French trenches. Some are abandoned, invaded by grass, and half leveled; the others solidly unkept and bristling with men. These parallels are joined up by innumerable galleries which hook and crook themselves like ancient streets. The system is much more dense than we believe who live inside it. On the twenty-five kilometers' width that forms the army front, one must count on a thousand kilometers of hollowed line—trenches and saps of all sorts.

He goes on to estimate that on the French front alone there are about ten thousand kilometers—6,250 miles—of trenches, "and as much again on the German side": 12,500 miles in all. He doesn't add in the totals for the British and Belgians and their German opponents, facing one another on what was that year the final tenth of the front. Tack on another twenty-five hundred miles—which gives the Western Front something like fifteen thousand miles of trenches, an extraordinary figure.

But it would seem that Barbusse and his character Cocon may have vastly underestimated the actual size of the trench system. At the end of 1915, French army statisticians calculated that there were twenty miles of trench for every mile of front; by summer's end, 1916, that had increased to thirty miles. Can we believe the figures? They would mean that there were almost fifteen thousand miles of trenches just on the Allied side of the Western Front. But we can't simply accord the Germans, those consummate moles, an equivalent fifteen thousand miles. A reasonable estimate might credit them with a third again as many trenches—five thousand miles—at least.

That would bring the combined total to perhaps thirty-five thousand miles of "hollowed lines"—and the war was only half over.

What was the final total? We can make a reasonable guess. In an address delivered on June 19, 1920, the president of France, Raymond Poincaré, estimated that "265 million cubic meters of trenches had to be filled up" on French soil alone, an estimate that translates to about fifty-five thousand miles. Add to that the intensely entrenched Belgian sector of the front, and the total for the entire Western Front might have been sixty thousand miles of trenches— almost two and a half times the circumference of the earth!

* * *

Think of the Western Front as the first strip city in history— not as long, as wide, or as thickly populated as what urbanologists call Bosnywash on the East Coast of the United States, but still immense enough. This perception came to me independently some years ago, but I have discovered since that I hold no monopoly on the urban analogy. People at the time saw it that way, whether it was Barbusse's Cocon or Lieutenant John Staniforth of the 7th Battalion, Leinster Regiment, who described the trenches as "an underground city with avenues, lanes, streets, crescents, alleys and cross-roads, all named and labeled and connected by telegraph and telephone. 'No. 3 Posen Alley' was my last address, and you reach it via 'Piccadilly,' 'Victoria Station,' and 'Sackville Street.'"

Later historians would agree. "That strange over-populated city," John Keegan called it. "After all, the Western Front was genuinely a *place*, however suddenly settled, however swiftly depopulated, with its own street plan, place-names, backwaters, dangerous turnings, local patriotisms, and emotional geography"—sectors such as the Ypres salient or Verdun having a heightened emotional charge for both sides. The Australian official historian C. E. W. Bean spoke of a system where men lived "as in the streets of a city":

> The elaborately constructed machine-gun and trench mortar positions, headquarters, observation and sniping posts, and dumps were the industrial establishments, and the nightly fatigue parties, dodging the light of flares and the stream of machine-gun bullets along the trench tramways, were the transport.

These "workers of war" (the phrase was coined by one of them, the German novelist Ernst Jünger) were the proletariat of a true revolution. War in its modern incarnation required a vast work force recruited to meet the needs of the assembly lines of mass destruction set up along the entire extent of the Western Front. Indeed, by 1916, military commentators were speaking of the "material battle."

But the millions of men and the machines they serviced could exist only in a concentrated urban setting, a martial version of the Ruhr or the Midlands.

Unreal the Western Front may have been—its total maleness, if nothing else, made it so. But a city it surely was. It had its boroughs and *arrondissements* (the army sectors); its distinct neighborhoods that ran the gamut from serene to perilous, from slummy to plush (but that were apt to go downhill precipitously); and its suburbs in the rear areas including those ultimate bastions of privilege, the châteaus where the staffs had their rooms at the top. (The peculiarly rigid urban design of the trenches encouraged a social and command structure that was hierarchical in the extreme, one that increasingly insulated the captains of this vast military industry from the workaday world they presided over.)

The strip city had its "avenues," the communication trenches that could extend for miles, with side streets and cul-de-sacs branching off. They took on names that were alternately picturesque (Dead Dog Avenue, Panama Canal, Queer Street) or grandly prosaic (Devon Avenue, Savile Row, Boyau d'Evian, Unter den Linden), names that recalled places that so many would never see again. The strip city had its long and intricate underground systems: one that the British occupied was an elaboration of existing coal mines and ran some twelve miles from Loos to Arras. The strip city had dugouts up to forty feet deep that could be, for officers, like the London clubs of St. James's; or, for enlisted men, like the Berlin tenements of Neükolln. The German writer Ludwig Renn described one tunnel on the Somme front where tiers of wooden bunks lined a narrow passageway seventy yards long: "Down below there hung a cold damp fog of wet clothes, tobacco smoke, and soot, making the candles burn reddish-brown. . . ." But the German dugouts could also exhibit a degree of luxury unknown on the Allied side of the line, with electric lights and ventilation pumps, water tanks, stoves and ovens, and varnished wood paneling, wallpaper, and rugs for the officers' quarters.

The strip city had its distinctive nighttime illumination: not neon, but Verey lights. Those were the hours when the activity of the trenches became positively bazaarlike. It had its nearby and all-but-built-in entertainment centers—towns like Lille and Laon and, until 1916, Verdun, where you could find cinemas, restaurants, and bordellos. (Directly behind the lines at Armentières, the British army had converted a brewery into a bathhouse, and once soldiers emerged from the vats-turned-hot tubs, they could wander back to browse in shops that were, in the first year of the war, still brightly lit.) The diseases of filth and exposure that men

suffered from were the urbanlike maladies endemic to their way of
life: trench foot (caused by mud and wet and cold), trench fever
(lice), scabies (nits), the liver ailment called Weil's disease (rats).
For every two men brought into casualty clearing stations with
battle wounds, three reported in with serious illness.

There was an undeniably cosmopolitan quality about the Western Front experience, and one that only great cities possess. In
1917, my father, an American Field Service volunteer, billeted behind the lines in the Chemin des Dames sector, observed a sight
that he would recall to me seventy years later:

> Sometimes for three days at a time, a column of men and
> guns wound through the village where we were quartered.
> Chasseurs slouching along in their dark-blue uniforms,
> canteens and helmets banging against their hips; a regi-
> ment of Senegalese, huge men with blue-black faces. . . .
> Behind them, dust rose from an interminable line of sev-
> enty-fives drawn by great bay horses, with very blond
> Flemish artillerymen riding the caissons. . . . Then, in
> horizon blue, an infantry regiment from Provence, three
> thousand men with sullen features.

Looking on with the American college boys like my father were
Annamite (as the laborers from the French colony of Indochina
were then called) road menders. "The long parade of races was a
spectacle which it was our privilege to survey, a special circus like
the exhibition of Moroccan horsemen given for our benefit on the
Fourth of July. . . ."

How many men populated this strip city? Erich von
Falkenhayn, the German chief of staff, estimated that early in July
1916 the combined total for both sides was 6.1 million. That would
have made the Western Front the largest metropolis in the world.

* * *

Changing tactics, more than anything, made continuous lines
obsolescent. In fact, the Western Front was never continuous. Defenders, especially on the German side, were no longer tied to their
frontline trenches; reluctantly, the Allies began to imitate their
opponents. Everyone was running perilously short of manpower,
and it was not until the middle of 1918 that the Americans would
arrive in numbers large enough to tip the balance. Elastic defense
of zone replaced rigid defense of a line, a deadly "invitation to walk
right in," as the Germans put it.

Until open warfare returned in 1918, there were, of course,
sectors that would have made veterans of the old-time volatile

stability feel at home. But major urban redevelopment was fast altering the look of the strip city. A close examination of that belt of metropolitan scar tissue would have revealed widely spaced outpost networks, machine gunners concealed in shell holes, counterattack troops sheltered in pillboxes, deep dugouts, or fortified localities, and more defenders lurking behind vast successive bands of barbed wire. (The Australian military historian and battlefield archaeologist John Laffin estimated from examination of aerial photographs that one of those bands in the Hindenburg Line was as much as two hundred yards wide.) The Germans even dug trenches that they left empty, on purpose, a bit like those vacant apartment buildings that abutted the Berlin Wall: when outposts gave the alarm for an Allied attack, reserve detachments could leave their comfortable reserve billets and march up in plenty of time to man the prepared lines.

The reverse of elastic defense was what you might call elastic offense, and as much as anything it brought the trench stalemate to an end. In the spring of 1918, German offensives gobbled up unimaginably huge chunks of Allied territory. They demonstrated that the biggest problem was no longer the tactical one of how to cross no-man's-land but the strategic one of what you did once you got beyond it. The Germans never did solve that problem.

The pattern of urban decline in the Western Front strip city was one that has become increasingly familiar. Decay, blight, ghettoization, anomie: all the trademark symptoms were present, even the brown inversion of smog. They were weirdly accelerated that final year. Old neighborhoods disappeared as a flight outward to new margins of action took place. Its purpose accomplished, the machinery of war that had given the city its brief squalid eminence ground to a halt. Its factory hands, that great underclass of cannon fodder who lived in its dugout tenements, would soon be out of work. But its dangerous toxic dumps, its fields seeded with poison gas and high-explosive shells, would remain.

Left behind, too, South Bronx-like, were the desert areas of former battlefields. Early in the fall of 1918, as the Western Front receded eastward, P. H. Pilditch wandered over the recent no-man's-land in the Aubers Ridge sector of south Flanders. Here, the lines had hardly budged for most of the war. Pilditch found that he could trace

> the various battles amongst the hundreds of skulls, bones and remains scattered thickly about. The progress of our successive attacks could be clearly seen from the types of equipment of the skeletons, soft cloth caps denoting the

1914 and 1915 fighting, then respirators, then steel helmets marking attack in 1916. Also Australian slouch hats, . . .

Pilditch's image leads us to a final point. During the 1,563 days of fighting on the Western Front, the average *daily* loss for all combatants in killed, wounded, captured, or missing was eight thousand—a total of about 12.5 million men. That figure exceeds the combined 1914 populations of London, Paris, and Berlin.

As the dark satanic mills of the Western Front shut down, the skeletons in the weeds waited to be collected. They were the true products of a new industrial revolution, an industrial revolution of war, and the ultimate reality of that unreal city.

Q&A

Q. How was the problem of solid waste disposal handled?

A. There were carrying cans that could be used for this purpose, but I think shell holes were used most often. Also there were side trenches branching off from the main trenches which served as latrines. But the troops had difficulties using these trenches because, from the air and in aerial photographs, they looked just like trench mortar sites, which made them a frequent target of enemy artillery.

Q. How did the troops deal with the gas that had settled into the trenches after a gas attack?

A. This was a problem. The masks made breathing difficult and it was difficult for the men to keep them on for a long time. The gas did tend to settle to the bottom of the trenches, and after awhile the troops just sort of went on with their business with the masks off and prayed that something wouldn't happen to them.

Q. What role did the ruined cities on the front play in the unreal city?

A. The front lines tended to go through villages, and the troops would convert them into fortified localities.

Q. What was the proportion of combat troops to support personnel?

A. [Dennis Showalter replies] In the French sectors it could be as high as three combat to one combat support, but just as in the American Civil War, the infantry were constantly called on for details and work parties. The British pioneers could never do enough, so the men who dug the trenches were usually infantrymen. The Germans and French both organized labor battalions, but these were composed of men who were physically unfit, in their forties, that sort of thing, and there were limits to what they could do.

A. [Robert Cowley] Dennis is quite right. Most of the work was actually done by the soldiers themselves, and they complained constantly about that. In the AEF, however, African-Americans were used widely as labor.

Q. *Could you comment on the rehabilitation of the front-line system after 1918?*

A. A lot of the entrenchments were filled in, especially the dugouts. In the Somme region, it was thought that the dugouts should be filled in quickly because the local authorities were afraid they would be used by bandits. But there are still great stretches of trenches that you can see today, and not just in places like Verdun. As a role of thumb, if you go to where the line went, you are almost certain to find trenches and shell holes. As you get farther south, some of which is rather poor country, the trenches haven't been filled in at all. In the Argonne, for instance, you can walk through trenches which are still quite high.

Q. *Many men who served in the trenches came from a rural back-ground and returned to it after the war was over. But many of them did not. Could you comment on this?*

A. I think it became a matter of how you're going to keep them down on the farm after they've seen Paris. And a lot of them didn't stay on the farm. In the United States, 1920 is the first year in which you have more people living in cities than in the country.

Q. *Following the war, how long did it take to return the ground to agricultural use?*

A. It depended. You can look at some places today and, except for the cemeteries, you could not believe that a war had ever been fought there. South Flanders is an example of this. Then you have places like the area around Verdun, which is impregnated with gas shells and duds.

Q. *Can you give us a rough estimate of the number of casualties suffered during the clearing of the battlefield, say, ten years after the conflict?*

A. There are figures on that, but I don't have them at hand. How-ever, I can tell you that people involved in that endeavor are still being killed. I think four men were killed when a shell ex-ploded near Ypres a couple of years ago. It's a dangerous task.

Comment

Paul Fussell: Robert Cowley's wonderful paper emphasized the old literary theme of the artificial versus the natural—a motif without which literature and most of our thinking and talking couldn't take place. I especially liked it because, after so much abstraction, which we've had a lot of here—all the talk about politics and economics and so on—it was a welcome descent to actualities, to spades and shovels and dirt and latrines and that sort of thing.

Tim Travers: Robert Cowley's talk reminded me right at the beginning of H. G. Wells. In *War of the Worlds* you could see that Wells was anticipating mechanized warfare, even tank warfare. And *The Time Machine* anticipated the trench system and a world with two levels of society, one living in the depths and one above ground.

In that regard, I wonder why the German trenches were better than the British or French trenches? You read accounts by British and French soldiers in which they always say something like, "The German trenches are marvelous. Wish we could live in them." I know the argument that the Germans were often on the defense and therefore needed to make good trenches because they knew they were going to stay in them. But I think there was something more to it than that.

Finally, what about the miners, Robert? I know you talked about going underground and those miners went even further underground and lived sort of a sub-subterranean life. Some of their stories are quite remarkable. There's one story out of Gallipoli about a man who was buried alive for three days, and he had this wonderful dream, at least in retrospect it's wonderful. He dreams of going back to his village in England, actually a mining village in the north, where he sees his mother. Then he starts to leave and his mother is waving at him and he thinks that this is the end of his life. Then he comes to, and is able, after three days, to get out of the mine and up top again.

Robert Cowley: Actually, I've written about this and it is a fascinating topic. On the Western Front the miners were, of course, used for digging those long shafts where they laid the underground mines, notably in the Hill 60 area. Some of the best miners were Australians, but many of the clay-kickers, as the miners were called, had worked on the London underground. But I think that the influence of coal mining may have been even greater than the influence of the underground and the metro because so many former coal miners found their way to the Western Front. They were the ones who built those long shafts at Loos. I know several people who went through the shafts; one of them was Rose Coombs, who wrote *Before Endeavors Fade.* She had gone down with some others into this tunnel and they'd been in there for most of the day when suddenly someone said, "Rosie, come here, I have something to show you." And there on the wall was a caricature of her own father. He had been a mining officer during the war, and one of his men had drawn a caricature in chalk of him.

Dennis Showalter: Robert Cowley brilliantly evoked the trench system of World War I not merely as a city but as an edge city. I found this interesting because, like the edge cities of late twentieth-century America, the edge city of World War I was devoted to a very limited purpose. His paper linked the trenches of World War I to Atlantic civilization generally and to the emergence of sieges and trenches. It also highlighted a couple of points that I think relevant, for example the notion that the war from 1914–1918 became an urban enterprise whereas, historically, war had been a rural enterprise fought by farmers mostly under rural conditions. Does that still obtain? Is war still an urban enterprise? Was Desert Storm? Or have we gone back to war as a rural enterprise. Desert Storm and Vietnam offer some very fruitful possibilities for discussion along these lines.

In a broader context, we may ask to what extent World War I reinforced a very common Western assumption of urban life as unnatural. This is particularly true in the United States. The city is seen in many ways as an unnatural place, a place that is appealing, but for all the wrong reasons.

And I think we can see how Rob's presentation and the other presentations opened questions that deal not only with the Great War but with the Great War in modern memory. In that context I think it's worth raising one more point from my perspective as something of an outsider. This conference offered a brilliant synthesis of macro- and micro-history. Now, there's a certain tendency to see these two approaches as being in opposition. On the one hand, you talk about an antiquarian interest in nuts and bolts and uniforms; on the other, sometimes there's talk about an elitist concern for generals and battles and the so-called high history. As a matter of fact, and in my opinion as a military historian, the relationship between macro- and micro-military history is symbiotic. The details of German coastal fortresses, for example, provide a link to a legacy of siege operations dating back to the Trojan War. The details of diplomacy and espionage in Eastern Europe from 1917 through 1919 shape the history of that region for the remainder of the twentieth century. And perhaps we can offer an analogy here, as Professor Travers's work particularly demonstrates, that all the combatants in the Great War had learned by 1918 that victory depended on combinations of infantry, artillery, engineers, aircraft, and armor all working together towards a common goal. I think that is not a bad image for those of us in the company of military historians to take away from what, for me, has certainly been one of the finest conferences of my experience.

Audience Member: What historical parallels, if any, to past wars did soldiers in the Great War feel or see?

Dennis Showalter: At Gallipoli some of the Brits, especially those in the Royal Naval Division, have this sense of destiny, this sense of going off to liberate classical antiquity from the new Hun.

Tim Travers: On the Western Front, I think there was a sense that the slums of the cities that people came from were actually very similar to the trenches. The common soldiers didn't see any great difference between the two, and it was only these rather unusual officers such as Robert Graves and Siegfried Sassoon who saw the historical parallels.

Audience Member: Did anyone see similarities to the fighting at Petersburg during the American Civil War?

Dennis Showalter: World War I was so generic to the men who fought in it that I think the search for historical analogies broke down almost from the beginning.

Paul Fussell: A lot of the more pretentiously and self-consciously educated soldiers and young officers at Gallipoli fancied their expedition as being a latter-day crusade, a Christian crusade against the Muslims. It's almost as if they thought they were coming to recapture Jerusalem from these horrible Moslem hordes. But nobody thought of it that way except men who had just come out of college or public school.

Robert Cowley: At the start of the war there was a sort of general expectation that this was going to be a Napoleonic enterprise with great charges and everything. The soldiers soon found out that it wasn't going to be that way. There's a wonderful book called *German Student Letters* in which a couple of the young men who were snuffed out pretty early in the fighting talk about how the war was not what they had expected, and how they felt sort of shocked and chagrined by this. But in general I think history went down the drain in the First World War, at least history as people were conscious of it.

Audience Member: I was stationed in Galveston, Texas, during World War II, and there was a huge coast artillery placement there. When were those built? Were they carried over from World War I?

Robert Cowley: Most of the coast defenses were put in place before the First World War, and then afterward the guns were upgraded. We began using railway guns, which we copied from the French and British. The Panama Canal zone in particular was beefed up heavily. The zone had sixteen-inch naval guns in some of the batteries.

Audience Member: At Fortress Monroe in Virginia there are a number of disappearing coast-gun emplacements. They were built during the Spanish-American War and upgraded during the First World War.

Robert Cowley: Some were built right after the Civil War. And some, such as Fort Adams in Newport, Rhode Island, were built in the 1830s and '40s and subsequently upgraded.

Paul Fussell: I think we've all been reminded, especially by Gerard Demaison's paper on Verdun and the Maginot Line, of how little we all know about fortifications, permanent concrete fortifications, and how much we should know about them. For example, the fortifications at Corregidor . . . the gun pits had no roofs, which strikes me as very odd, very odd indeed when contrasted with the forts at Verdun and the great works along the Normandy coast. You see on Corregidor and in Europe two totally different schools of thought about fortification and the way you protect a big gun. I'd like to know their origin.

Audience Member: The uncovered emplacements in the Philippines had twelve-inch mortars, and the whole idea was to lob shells at high angles that would come down on warships. When they were designed there was no possibility of air bombardment.

Audience Member: The United States made a tremendous investment in coastal defense in the late nineteenth and early twentieth century, one of the reasons being that with coastal defenses, all the money you spent stayed in the United States. The main weapon was the disappearing gun, and it was outmoded by World War I, although it took Congress thirty years to accept that. There's a funny story about the Spanish fleet in 1898, how it set out from Spain to fight the Americans in the Caribbean. But the ships' engineers were Scots, and they all quit when the war started, leaving them to the tender mercies of the Spanish engineers. The fleet took a long time crossing the ocean, and after a while nobody knew where it was. Consequently, there was terror in New York City. Before the war a Spanish warship had visited the city, and the captain used to point out that he had an eleven-inch gun installed on the forward deck. He said if he fired the gun from just below Manhattan, the shell would land in the Bronx. That was something people could understand. So there was terror along the East Coast. People thought the Spanish fleet would come into New York harbor and the Spanish would demand, oh, $100 million in gold or else they'd blow the city off the map. And that made it very easy to get appropriations to either build coastal fortifications or to modernize them.

Audience Member: Speaking of New York City, if you want a demonstration of the incongruity and unreality of military service . . . I was inducted into the army in December of 1942 and sent immediately from Camp Upton to Governor's Island, New York, which is right in the harbor, five minutes from Wall Street. And every other night we had to stand alert, which meant that we had to report to a central station with our helmets, packs, and gas masks. And I would look out over the water holding my gas mask, thinking of my girlfriend in Brooklyn, my parents in Manhattan, being totally exposed to enemy gas attack while I was protected. It was a very sad situation. I was safe and they were in such danger.

The Great War and Cultural Modernism
Paul Fussell

Ezra Pound was not always deranged. At one time, before he went in for eccentric economics, anti-Semitism, and wartime treason, he was a most original if often rude, critic, perhaps the most active international enthusiast for literary and cultural modernism. He once made an observation as brilliant as it is simple: "A yardstick," he said, "cannot measure itself."

That perception may suggest some of our difficulties in understanding what modernism was, or is. As heirs of modernism, no matter how unwilling or unconscious, we are the yardstick trying to describe and assess ourselves and trying to describe and assess the value of modernism as a cultural force. Surely our vanity, our satisfaction with what we have found to be the uses of modernism, will figure in our attempts to look objectively at the undeniably important but hard-to-define intellectual and artistic tendency we call modernism. Even if we designate ourselves "postmodern," it is through modernism that we have arrived at that similarly honorific state, and we are no less forced to measure ourselves as we aim at a quasi-scientific objectivity. Let us try regardless.

Modernism could once be seen as simply the adversary of bourgeois culture. As a premier modernist, James Joyce stigmatized Ireland as "an old sow that eats her farrow." Ireland's attitude towards him seemed equally hostile. But we are not the only ones who have become, willy-nilly, modernist. Ireland has too. Witness the new ten-pound banknotes just issued there. They bear, and proudly, the portrait of James Joyce. That filthy-minded subversive exile has been embraced as Stephen Hero indeed. Clearly, modernism has conquered. It has turned into modernist enclaves not just cultural consumers and critics but cities and countries, and what began as puzzling, paradoxical elements of poetic modernism are now largely integrated into the idiom of middle-class society. Eliot once challenged readers with the line "April is the cruellest month," but recently I heard on the radio that "April has been a cruel month for the tire business."

* * *

My topic is the relation of the Great War to Modernism. The first thing to recognize is that there are two opposite views about that relation. The traditional view is that the war was an important

248

cause of modernism, or powerfully advanced it. But it is also possible to consider the war as just another expression of modernism,
like the Bauhaus, Picasso, the Empire State Building, the melo-
dramatic rejection of the recent past, and the convention of sexual
outspokenness.

A holder of the view that the war is itself a work of modernism
is Modris Eksteins, a professor of history at the University of Toronto
and author of *Rites of Spring: The Great War and The Birth of the
Modern Age* (Houghton Mifflin, 1989). One of Eksteins's chief concerns is the *cause* of modernism. How, he wonders, did it happen
that writers as odd as Eliot and Joyce and Pound arose, all in such
a short period of time, to call into question the concerns and techniques of Hardy and Swinburne, Conrad and William Dean Howells?
Why did Picasso and Braque and Duchamp choose to puzzle and
outrage an audience comfortable in its appreciation of Van Gogh
and Gauguin and Renoir? Why did modernist architects decide to
reject conventional architectural decoration like triglyphs, acorns,
wreaths, and Palladian balustrades and sweep their buildings clean
of such to the past? Wyndham Lewis's magazine *Blast* appeared
first in June 1914, almost three months before the outbreak of the
Great War. What was he doing in this insolent challenge to contemporary artistic manners and taste? His curious behavior is no-
table because it defines the main relation of the post-Great War
modernist to his audience. That relation is predominantly
adversarial and provocative.

The model of that adversarial behavior was established,
Eksteins observes, in May 1913, in Paris, with the first performance
of the Stravinsky-Diaghilev-Nijinsky ballet. It occasioned a riot in
the theater. *The Rite of Spring* was about the ritual sacrifice of youth,
and it might be seen now as curiously prophetic of the actual sacrifice of the young that was to begin in later summer, 1914. At this
first shocking performance, fistfights broke out between
progressives and philistines in the audience. So much angry clamor
arose that the music was quite drowned out and Nijinsky had to
shout out from the wings the count for the dancers. The conservatives in the audience booed, hissed, and made animal noises, being scandalized by Stravinsky's modernist discords as well as by
Nijinsky's deliberately non-pretty flat-footed and knock-kneed cho-
reography. An eyewitness reported that

> One beautifully dressed lady in an orchestra box stood
> up and slapped the face of a young man who was hissing
> in the next box. Her escort rose and cards were exchanged
> between the two men. A duel followed next day. Another
> society lady spat in the face of one of the demonstrators.

An aristocratic lady, appalled at the artistic novelty of the ballet, stormed out of the theater with the words, "I am sixty years old, but this is the first time anyone has dared to make a fool of me." It was artistic warfare, and on that significant evening, says Eksteins, it became clear that the response of the audience "was as . . . important to the meaning of this art as the intentions of those who introduced it." Art had become, all of a sudden, "provocation and event." (And in more conservative London, before long Edith Sitwell's *Façade* gave similar intentional offense.)

For the first time in history, art had defined itself by locating an enemy, conceived as the respectable, passionless, moralistic middle class—the genteel automata spawned by decades of successful industrial production and identifiable by its complacency and by its emotional anemia. Art had now become a sort of surrogate religion, but a religion less of comfort than of shock, less of peace than of vitalism. It offered its own version of "resurrection," in which a new sensibility was born of the dying old one.

That *The Rite of Spring* seems implicated in succeeding events can be sensed from a French soldier's writing, after the war, "Often during the scientific, chemical, cubist warfare, I have thought of [*The Rite of Spring*]." And listening to the morning artillery barrage, a British soldier couldn't help noticing its kinship with the new modern music, "not," he emphasized, "a music of conventional melodies and harmonies, but a new music, the antithesis of all customary composition."

Although we might have to strain to call the Great War a cultural event, the wild enthusiasm that greeted its outbreak is like the excitement that the new art occasioned among its creators and enthusiasts. The war was welcomed most fervently in Germany— "the first modernist country," as Eksteins notes. Before long, it was possible for Germans to conceive of their British enemy very much as the cultural modernists conceived of theirs, and to imagine that thus the war gained powerful symbolic meaning. It would seem a struggle for a new authenticity, a battle against the exhausted, gentlemanly ideas and assumptions of the Entente Cordiale. German theorists managed to understand the fighting on the battlefield as a war against British hypocrisy and tyranny. The British were seen as fighting to preserve the status quo, while the Germans could be regarded as trying to set in motion something new—just as, a quarter-century later, they would seek to establish by force a New Order in Europe. (*Make It New* was the title of Pound's book of essays published in 1934, and his exhortation was addressed to both writers and critics.)

In the Great War it was the Germans, except for the belated British invention of the tank, who contrived such new weapons as poison gas and the zeppelin and the U-boat, analogous to the new techniques of modernist culture. And the Germans were still performing their modernist act in the Second World War with their flying bombs and V-2 rockets and snorkled submarines. The German modernist scorn for hypocrisy and gentility, which they associated not just with the British but with the other Allies as well, lay behind their contempt for the Versailles Treaty. And the modernist insistence that an "awakening" is urgently called for was aped in Hitler's injunction to Germans to stop slumbering like the rest of the world and wake up: as he put it, *"Deutschland Erwache!"* The modernist impulse was to break out to the future regardless of consequences, and the would-be artist Hitler—characterized in 1941 by his propagandist, Dr. Josef Goebbels, as "a totally modern man"—insisted that Nazism intended a breakout *(Aufbruch)* into new forms and modes. As Norbert Frie concluded in his recent study of National Socialism, "Nazism was an attempt to complete the project of the modern. . . ." The anger Hitler publicly manifested in pressing these points oratorically seems to illustrate Lionel Trilling's observation when he says that "The modern self is characterized by certain habits of indignant perception."

Once we observe the many analogies between political and artistic culture, it is hard not to notice the degree of "totalitarianism" of intellect and taste lurking in cultural modernism, with its accustomed tone of indignation—think of D. H. Lawrence and Pound and Joyce—and its disdain for the comfortable, the traditional, and the ordinary. Once we are awakened to the parallels between actual warfare and the world of art, we may notice the importance of the sixty-pound pack that weighed down the British infantry attacking at the Somme. It is emblematic of the excess baggage of useless traditional inhibitions and restraints associated, in the German view, with the British national style and the British wartime cause. And as we read such subversive postwar writings as *All Quiet on the Western Front* and *A Farewell to Arms* it is hard not to see the frontline troops as a literal *avant garde,* analogous, despite the troops' disillusionment, to the figurative avant garde in postwar writing, art, and music. Both the troops and the artists and the critics designated the rear "the enemy," the rear with its supposed insensitivity, its literal-mindedness, and its unearned privilege. It was the soldiers who first sensed the war's consummate absurdity, and awareness of the absurd is one of the elements not just of Dada but of fully developed artistic modernism in general. As Eksteins says,

In a war in which men buried themselves so as to live . . .
in which a dead carrier pigeon was decorated with the
Legion d'honneur, in which the British commander . . .
declared . . . the day before the "big push" at the Somme,
that "the wire has never before been so well cut," . . . in
such a war and such a world the jackal of Kilimanjaro
and the sniggering footman of Prufrock appeared to be
the only suitable inhabitants.

*   *   *

Whether we hold with Eksteins that the war was itself a work
of modernism or agree with a more traditional view that the war
was largely the cause of the consolidation of modernism in the
1920s and 30s, we'd have to notice that outcrops of something
very like modernism had been appearing since 1855, when Whitman
set forth the terms of his quarrel with the past, and in his free
verse and novel diction showed how that quarrel could be conducted and finally won by the poets of the future. Perceiving the
way modernism tends to define itself by oppositions and antagonisms, we can see Whitman's foreshadowing of Pound's modernist
opposition to the technical slush and didactic highmindedness of
Georgian poetry. "Tell me not," Pound adjures a poet of the preceding generation, "Tell me not in mournful wishwash / Life's a sort of
sugared dishwash." And there are many other nineteenth-century
anticipations, shall we say, of modernism. It wouldn't be easy to
find more despair anywhere in the modernist canon than in Arnold's
"Dover Beach" of 1867. And ten years later there occurred an artistic event that accurately defined the modern artist's attitude toward his audience. This was James McNeill Whistler's libel trial
against John Ruskin, who, in his review of one Whistler's exhibitions of paintings, had declared that Whistler, with his near-ab-
stractions, had "flung a pot of paint in the public's face." It was in
1879 that Oscar Wilde, in his essay "The Decay of Lying," called for
an end to narrative realism, foreshadowing and inviting the modernists' emphasis on geometrical forms and stylization rather than
on a vulgar, obvious, "photographic" representation.

Furthermore, the modernist adversary relation with the past, a
past conceived as destructively pious, genteel, and fatally mistaken,
was well under way by 1907, as Edmund Gosse's memoir *Father
and Son* indicates. And such modernist themes as Auden embraced
in his early poems, themes of unspecified menace, civil dissolution,
and sinister spies and terrorists, are to be found fully fledged in
1907 in Conrad's *The Secret Agent.* Since these modernist elements
were not caused by the Great War but were already there well before
it, perhaps the soundest thing to say about the relation between

the war and modernism is that the war accelerated prewar modernist impulses, provided them with telling examples, and strengthened them, making them fit to be passed on uncompromised.

* * *

It is clear regardless that the adversarial posture of modernism owes much to the realities of the trench war. "We" are all on this side, "they"—the enemy—are over there, and a no-man's-land divides us. Once one is accustomed to this sort of gross dichotomizing, it is natural to impose the adversarial pattern everywhere. For Wyndham Lewis, people who go in for old-style, prewar artistic products are the Enemy, and an unbridgeable divide separates the philistine from the knowing. As Siegfried Sassoon remarked, the war taught him to aspire to a world of "green chartreuse and Epstein sculpture" while his mother remained bogged down in her world of "G. F. Watts and holy communion." And of these two worlds, Sassoon adds emphatically, "They can't be mixed."

As the aforesaid suggests, the discrepancy between trench horrors and civilian incomprehension and optimism produced widespread estrangement between the troops on the line and the folks back home. Indeed, a favorite fantasy of the soldiers was somehow visiting violent and if possible agonizing death upon the complacent, patriotic, fatuous civilians at home. Sassoon would like to see them crushed to death by a tank plunging down the aisle of one of their cheery music halls, as he says in his poem "Blighters":

> The house is crammed; tier beyond tier they grin
> And cackle at the show, while prancing ranks
> Of harlots shrill the chorus, drunk with din;
> "We're sure the Kaiser loves our dear old Tanks!"

> I'd like to see a tank come down the stalls,
> Lurching to ragtime tunes, or "Home, Sweet Home,"—
> And there'd be no more jokes in music-halls
> To mock the riddled corpses round Bapaume.

Similarly, lying newspapermen and bellicose members of Parliament became special adversaries of the troops. In one poem titled "Fight to a Finish," Sassoon enacts a fantasy of the soldiers' postwar retribution. The war over, he posits that the army is marching through London in a victory parade, cheered along the way by writers for the jingoistic gutter-press. Suddenly, the soldiers fix bayonets and turn on the crowd, as they've wanted to do for years: "At last the boys had found a cushy job," says Sassoon. Leading grenade charges on the crowd, Sassoon cleans up the lying journalists, and then "With my trusty bombers turned and went / To clear those Junkers out of Parliament."

The poet Charles Sorley is not joking when he writes in a letter after only three months of frontline experience, "I should like so much to kill whoever was primarily responsible for the war." And one observer of soldiers temporarily home on leave found that "They hated the smiling women in the streets. They loathed the old men. . . . They desired that profiteers should die of poison gas. They prayed God to get the Germans to send Zeppelins to England— to make the People know what war meant."

Thus the British scene. Adversaries of an American kind are the demobilized soldier Harold Krebs and his mother in Hemingway's story "Soldier's Home." Harold has returned to his Midwestern town quite changed by the war. Instead of pursuing the life once felt appropriate for him—job, marriage, good behavior—he spends much time either sleeping or enjoying himself in the local poolroom. One pivotal scene in the story reveals the new adversarial relation between Harold and his mother. The conflict is not about art—this is the Midwest in the early 1920s—but about religion:

"Have you decided what you are going to do yet, Harold?" his mother said.
"No," said Krebs.
"Don't you think it's about time?"
"I hadn't thought about it," Krebs said.
"God has some work for every one to do," his mother said, "There can be no idle hands in His kingdom."
"I'm not in His kingdom," Krebs said.

Faced with this sort of incomprehension of the distinction between prewar and postwar, Krebs knows that he has only one recourse: flight. Like Hemingway himself escaping from his mother in Oak Park, Illinois, he decides to "go over to Kansas City and get a job." Krebs's mother, of course, represents the whole prewar era which has bumbled into the war blindly under a series of Victorian assumptions, to confront the troops with massed artillery fire, the mud of Flanders and Picardy, gas, and a prevailing vagueness about war aims and meanings. Even Rudyard Kipling, formerly an upholder of the old military traditions of sacrifice, obedience, and heroism, arrived finally at a position close to the skepticism and contempt for "leaders" so essential to the modernist posture. Before the war and during it, he had been a conspicuous patriot, but after his son, John, aged eighteen, became one of the twenty thousand British killed at Loos, he leaned towards the modernist pole, producing such writings as this self-castigating passage from "Epitaph of the War": "If any question why we died / Tell them, because our fathers lied."

As the war turned more and more disastrous, as Loos was followed by the misguided attempt to flank the whole thing at Gallipoli, then the attack on the Somme and the campaign at Passchendaele, one British writer in London watched it all with mounting horror and outrage. He was the essayist and belletrist Lytton Strachey, and as he watched he became convinced that the preceding generations were the self-righteous, unimaginative cause of all this. It was their moral rigidity, their intellectual mediocrity, their preposterous, bigoted piety that he set out to satirize in his book *Eminent Victorians,* which appeared in May 1918. It did not mention the war, but no reader could miss the similarity between the stubborn, witless General Sir Douglas Haig, presiding over the carnage on the Western Front, and Strachey's Bible-pounding Victorian General Charles Gordon, whose refusal to admit mistakes resulted in the brutal murder of his followers and himself in the Sudan. *Eminent Victorians* is one of the earliest modernist works of adversarial art directed against the war. As Michael Holroyd has said of the Great War, it was "a catalyst" in the writing of *Eminent Victorians,* occasioning Strachey's caustic, ironic "sifting of those Victorian pretensions that seemed . . . to have led civilization into such a holocaust." Strachey's position as an important modernist has been noted by Cyril Connolly, who comments, *"Eminent Victorians* is the work of a great anarch, a revolutionary text book on bourgeois society written in the language through which the bourgeois ear could be lulled and beguiled. . . ."

After igniting his bomb, Strachey remained in London, but it was flight that seemed to others than Krebs to be their only defense against wartime and postwar culture, with its lies, its protective compulsory patriotism, and its ignorance about what was actually happening on the battle fronts. Joyce fled to Paris and finally to Trieste and Zürich. Robert Graves uttered a resounding *Good-bye to All That* and fled to Majorca, resolved "never to make England my home again." D. H. Lawrence, shocked by the humiliations and condescensions he'd suffered at the hands of the conscription authorities, left England forever, bearing with him a hatred for his country so intense as to be almost unutterable. He tried to suggest its depths in his novel *Kangaroo.* There he wrote:

> In England, during the later years of the war . . . the criminal spirit arose in all the stay-at-home bullies who governed the country during those years. . . . The torture [they imposed] was steadily applied to break the independent soul in any man who would not hunt with the criminal mob.

Because he was married to a German wife and wore a beard and allowed himself to be overheard in rural pubs and teahouses stigmatizing the war as an indecent racket, Lawrence was assumed to be some sort of German spy. After one particularly humiliating physical examination at the local conscription center—it kept calling Lawrence back despite his obvious tuberculosis—he determined that he would "obey no more; not one more stride. . . . Never, while he lived . . . would he be at the disposal of society." Once the Armistice was proclaimed, he and his wife applied for passports and, saying goodbye to all that, they left for Italy, never to return. In enacting the modernist gesture of self-exile, Lawrence was merely one among many: Pound, Gertrude Stein, Aldous Huxley, Isherwood, and Auden are names that come to mind. Here one remembers Trilling's observation about modernist writing: that one of its functions has been "to make us aware of the particularity of selves, and the high authority of the self in its quarrel with its society and its culture."

* * *

But this adversarial impulse is not the only thing the modernist enterprise took from the Great War. Equally important is irony, said by Monroe Engel to constitute "the normative mentality of modern art." Seven years after the Armistice the Spanish philosopher José Ortega y Gasset observed, "I much doubt that any young person of our time can be impressed by a poem, a painting, or a piece of music that is not flavored with a dash of irony." Irony easily emerged as the only adult emotion appropriate to a war that was supposed to be over by Christmas 1914, and that finally, after more than four years of industrialized horrors, quite shockingly reversed the former century's faith that all was right with the world. Indeed, we sense that the word *tragic*, usually so loosely used, is for once suitable to apply to this war, not because its events are sad but because the war involves that indispensable Aristotelian tragic element, ironic reversal. In a book he tellingly titled *Disenchantment*, the journalist C. E. Montague describes the high hopes animating the young volunteers at the outset:

> All the air was ringing with rousing assurances, France to be saved, Belgium righted, freedom and civilization rewon, a sour, soiled, crooked old world to be rid of bullies and crooks and redeemed for straightness, decency, and good nature . . . What a chance!

Certainly, it was a chance no bright, optimistic, athletic young man of the Rupert Brooke-type would want to miss. But irony of situation, leering with tongue in cheek, was waiting for these eager youths who very early in the trenches came to experience such sardonic understandings as those hinted in Wilfred Owen's poem "The Last Laugh," written in 1918 after he'd come to know the real, rather than the ideal, war. Coarse sardonic laughter at human folly is the only possible reaction, a reaction shared by even the weapons of war themselves:

> "O Jesus Christ! I'm hit," he said; and died.
> Whether he vainly cursed, or prayed indeed,
> The bullets chirped—In vain! vain! vain!
> Machine-guns chuckled,—Tut-tut! Tut tut!
> And the Big Gun guffawed. . . .

And as the poem proceeds through two more stanzas, the falling shell fragments "titter" on their way down and the bayonets "grin."

Owen's poem overlaps into what a later age will term black humor, and in a book titled *Now It Can Be Told*, Philip Gibbs analyzed the relation of laughter to the irony:

> It was the laughter of mortals at the trick which had been played on them by an ironical fate. They had been taught to believe that the whole object of life was to reach out to beauty and love, and that mankind, in a progress to perfection, had killed the beast instinct, cruelty, blood-lust, the primitive, savage law of survival by tooth and claw and club and ax. All poetry, all art, all religion had breached this gospel and this promise.
>
> Now that ideal was broken like a china vase dashed to the ground. The contrast between That and This was devastating. . . . The war-time humor of the soul roared with mirth at the sight of all that dignity and elegance despoiled.

Those words of Gibbs's appeared in the early 1920s in a context of modernist irony provided once by the war and sustained now by Joyce's *Ulysses*, Cummings's *The Enormous Room*, Pound's *Mauberley*, Huxley's *Crome Yellow* and *Antic Hay*, Pirandello's *Six Characters in Search of an Author*, and Kafka's *The Trial*.

So accustomed were the troops to regarding the war and its elements as understandable only through irony that they came to use irony as their main mnemonic in recalling wartime events. The outrageous gap between the expected and the actual, indispensable for irony, is what obsesses Henry Williamson as, thirteen years after the event, he recalls the first day on the Somme:

> I see men arising and walking forward; and I go forward with them, in a glassy delirium wherein some seem to pause, with bowed heads, and sink carefully to their knees, and roll slowly over, and lie still. Others roll and

roll, and scream and grip my legs in utmost fear, and I have to struggle to break away, while the dust and earth on my tunic changes from grey to red.

And I go on with aching feet, up and down across ground like a huge ruined honeycomb, and my wave melts away, and the second wave comes up, and also melts away, and then the third waves merges into the ruins of the first and second, and after a while the fourth blunders into the remnants of the others, and we begin to run forward to catch up with the barrage, gasping and sweating, in bunches, anyhow, every bit of the months of drill and rehearsal forgotten, for who could have imagined that the "Big Push" was going to be this? (*The Wet Flanders Plain* [London, 1929], pp. 15–16).

What assists Williamson's recall is the ironic pattern ("Who could have imagined?") which subsequent vision has laid over the events.

Artilleryman Charles Bricknall, in an unpublished memoir held in Imperial War Museum (London), similarly calls on irony to remember many years later an event he's never going to forget. At one point his unit was being replaced by a battery fresh from England, "all spick and span," he remembers, "buttons polished and all the rest of it." The newcomers assembled on a road behind the trenches, but one which Bricknall and his buddies know is a favorite artillery target of the Germans. Bricknall and his friends warn the newcomers, but to no avail: "Up they went and the result was they all got blown up." Contemplating this sad denouement, Bricknall can comment only, "What a disaster! Which could have been avoided if only the officers had gone into action the hard way"—that is, overland, avoiding the road. "That was something I shall never forget," says Bricknall. It is the *if only* rather than the slaughter that helps Bricknall to "never forget" this. A slaughter by itself is too commonplace to recall as a separate incident. When it illustrates an ironic point it becomes memorable, just like the whole war.

* * *

In June 1917, a couple of weeks after the British attack at Messines, near Ypres, a twenty-nine-year-old civilian living in London sent a letter to the periodical *The Nation*. He said:

Sir—I enclose herewith an extract from a letter lately received from a young officer which I hope may interest some of your readers. I may add that the officer in question entered the Army directly from a public school, and began his service in the trenches before he was nineteen.

The letter from the boy officer—his identity is not known—reads in part as follows:

It is morally impossible for me to talk seriously of these things to people who cannot even approach comprehension. It is hideously exasperating to hear people talking the glib commonplaces about the war and distributing cheap sympathy to its victims.

Perhaps you are tempted to give them a picture of a leprous earth, scattered with the swollen and blackening corpses of hundreds of young men. The appalling stench of rotting carrion mingling with the sickening smell of exploded lyddite and ammonal. Mud like porridge, trenches like shallow and sloping cracks in the porridge—porridge that stinks in the sun. Swarms of flies and bluebottles clustering on pits of offal. Wounded men lying in the shell holes among the decaying corpses: helpless under the scorching sun and bitter nights, under repeated shelling. Men with bowels dropping out, lungs shot away, with blinded, smashed faces, or limbs blown into space. Men screaming and gibbering. Wounded men hanging in agony on the barbed wire, until a friendly spout of liquid fire shrivels them up like a fly in a candle.

But *these are only words*, and probably only convey a fraction of their meaning to their hearers. They shudder, and it is forgotten. . . .

The young writer of that letter is already laboring at the great modernist effort to find an appropriate language for a new reality, a language to replace "only words." The words of a former chivalry, of honor and heroism, even of patriotism will no longer do. And the man who made sure that the *Nation* received that letter is one whose career will be devoted to carving out the essential suitable forms and devising the suitable idioms of a truly modern mode of language. Indeed, he is said to have "invented modern poetry in English." At almost the same moment that he sent that young officer's letter to the *Nation* his first book was published. It was titled *Prufrock and Other Observations*. And five years later certain details from the young officer's letter found a place in the poem which is one of the monuments of modernism. As the historian Theodore Bogacz has said, the young officer's "despairing vision of modern war and of the necessity of seeing it directly, without 'poetic' defenses, is the unspoken background of Eliot's postwar masterpiece *The Waste Land*."

And perhaps more than the unspoken background. In the first section of *The Waste Land*, "The Burial of the Dead"—an odd title, surely—we hear of "A heap of broken images," "the dead tree" which gives no shelter, and "fear in a handful of dust." We encounter

Madame Sosostris, "famous clairvoyante," very like the cynical spirit mediums who exploited the pathetic postwar needs of bereaved parents and wives to get in touch with their dead sons and husbands blown to bits at the Somme or Gallipoli. Or their drowned sailor sons—"Fear death by water," she says. And later we hear of the drowned Phoenician sailor, now reduced to bones shifted by the undersea current, but who was once "handsome and tall as you." Elsewhere, our guide through these postwar scenes says of the crowd flowing over London Bridge, "I had not thought death had undone so many." The society lady who asks her companion, "What are you thinking of?" is answered with this equivalent of the words, "I think we are in an everlasting trench": "I think we are in rats' alley / Where the dead men lost their bones." This is followed by the scene of the working-class wives in the pub concerned with the possibly aborted affections of their newly demobilized men, some of whom have been "in the army four years" and who are therefore avid for "a good time." Soon, we are given nightmare images like "White bodies naked on the low damp ground," just what you'd see from the lip of a trench after three weeks of continuous rain. A poet aware that an early form of the gas mask was a gray chemical-impregnated fabric hood with ghostly eyepieces on the front is in a good position to ask, "What are those hooded hordes swarming / Over endless plains, stumbling in cracked earth," where we hear what might be an echo of the young officer's description of "trenches like shallow and sloping cracks in the porridge," the ubiquitous mud. And *The Waste Land* closes with references to both obituaries and memories, fit imagery for years of war marked with a countless number of both.

Eliot was propelling the new style so powerfully that it would dominate the postwar decades, satisfying especially those who had been taught by the trenches to be forever dissatisfied, as Bogacz says, "with banalities, half-truths, and outright lies disguised in a vapid abstract rhetoric that hid the realities not only of modern war but of the modern world as well."

* * *

But one problem remains. It is that we, as instinctive modernists, will find in the Great War only what we are looking for, using our yardstick to measure only ourselves while imagining that we are measuring external reality and all of contemporary history. Only superhuman humility and skepticism about our own interpretative techniques and habits will save us from making a fatal confusion between what we see and what we are.

Contributors

George Anastaplo is a professor of law at Loyola University of Chicago, lecturer in the liberal arts, The University of Chicago, and Professor Emeritus of political science and of philosophy, Rosary College. He has an abiding interest in the role of the Great War in twentieth-century history. His most recent book is *The Amendments to the Constitution: A Commentary.*

Edward M. Coffman received his doctorate at the University of Kentucky in 1959 and has been a professor of history at the U.S. Military Academy and universities in Tennessee, Ohio, and Wisconsin. He has published several well received volumes on American history and personalities, including *The War to End All Wars: The American Experience in World War I,* and *The Old Army: A Portrait of the American Army in Peacetime, 1784–1898.* A member of the Western Front Association, Dr. Coffman participated in the conference panel discussions.

Robert Cowley is the founding editor of *MHQ: The Quarterly Journal of Military History.* A graduate of Harvard University, he has been a magazine and book editor for nearly forty years. He is the author of numerous articles and books on the Great War, many of them focusing on the Western Front. He has traveled the entire extent of the Western Front as a research scholar and tour guide.

Gerard J. Demaison first visited the Verdun battlefield in 1934 with his father, who had fought there in 1916. He has revisited it many times, using period military maps to explore the entire battlefield area. He is a petroleum geologist with a science degree in geology from the Sorbonne and a master of sciences degree in geology from the Colorado School of Mines. He has published two books on French army weapons of the Great War and several scientific papers on aspects of oil exploration. He is a member of the Great War Society.

Aleks A. M. Deseyne was born in Zonnebeke, Belgium in 1947. After teaching school for eighteen years, he was appointed the first curator of the Zonnebeke Museum in 1988. He is curator of the Prince Charles Memorial and the Atlantic Wall Museums, and is the author of *Raversijde: History of the Royal Domain Raversijde 1914–1918* and *The Forgotten Winter 1914–1915.*

Paul Fussell is the Donald T. Regan Professor of English literature at the University of Pennsylvania. He has earned degrees

261

at that university and at Harvard. He is the author of several books on military and literary topics, the most prominent being *The Great War and Modern Memory*. During his distinguished career he has been accorded many academic and literary honors and fellowships to numerous prestigious institutions. Dr. Fussell was decorated for his combat service with the U.S. Army in World War II.

Sergey V. Listikov is senior researcher at the Institute of Universal History, Russian Academy of Sciences, Moscow. His academic focus is on Russian-American relations from 1914 through 1918. He has done extensive research on U.S. trade union and socialist movements in the early twentieth century and has written numerous books, essays, and articles on these subjects.

Dr. Viktor L. Mal'kov is the director of the Center for Historical Research and Analysis in the Institute of World History and a professor of history at Moscow State University. He has published numerous papers and books on the labor movement in the United States during the Great Depression, domestic politics and foreign policy during the Franklin D. Roosevelt years, and U.S.-Russian relations on the eve of the twentieth century. He has participated in many international conferences in the United States and Europe.

Philip Markham was born in England and served in the Royal Air Force in World War II. After the war he served in the Auxiliary Air Force and the Royal Canadian Air Force, and worked for the National Aeronautical Establishment and a naval architectural firm. In retirement he has been associated with the Canadian War Museum, the National Aviation Museum, and the [Canadian] National Film Board. Mr. Markham passed away in March 1996.

Daniel Moran received his undergraduate degree from Yale University and his doctoral degree from Stanford University. A member of the Phi Beta Kappa Society, he is an associate professor in the Department of National Security Affairs at the Naval Postgraduate School in Monterey, California. His most recent major publication is *Carl von Clausewitz: Historical and Political Writings*, which he co-edited with Peter Paret.

Desmond Morton received undergraduate degrees from the Royal Military College of Canada and Oxford University, his master's of arts from Oxford, and his doctorate from the University of London. He served in the Canadian army from 1954 through 1964. He is principal of Erindale College, University of Toronto, where he is also a professor of history. He is the author of numerous books, the latest publication being *When your Number's Up: Canadian Soldiers in the First World War*.

Edward F. Murphy, a graduate of Northern Illinois University, served in the U.S. Army from 1965 through 1968 and is the founder and president of the Medal of Honor Society. He is the author of several books, the latest being *Dak To: The 173rd Airborne Brigade in South Vietnam's Central Highlands, June–November 1967.*

Dennis E. Showalter received his undergraduate degree from Saint John's University and graduate degrees from the University of Minnesota. He is a professor of history at Colorado College and was Distinguished Visiting Professor, U.S. Air Force Academy, from 1991 through 1993. He has received many awards and fellowships and edits a number of military journals, the most recent being *War in History,* published in Great Britain. He is the author of several books on German military history, the latest being *Tannenberg: Clash of Empires,* which received the Paul Birdall Prize and was a Military Book Club Selection.

Richard B. Spence received his master's and doctoral degrees from the University of California at Santa Barbara and is an associate professor of history at the University of Idaho. He has written and edited several books focusing on Russian and Slavic subjects, including *Boris Savinkov: Renegade on the Left.*

Timothy Hugh Eaton Travers is a professor and former chairman of the University of Calgary's history department. After attending McGill University, he received his master's and doctoral degrees from Yale. He is internationally known as an author and lecturer. His books include *The Killing Ground: The Western Front and the Emergence of Modern Warfare, 1900–1918* and *How the War Was Won: Command and Technology in the British Army on the Western Front.* Dr. Travers was a participant in the conference panel discussions.

Betty Miller Unterberger received an undergraduate degree from Syracuse University and her master's and doctoral degrees from Harvard and Duke universities, respectively. She is Patricia and Bookman Peters Professor of History at Texas A&M University. She has taught at Charles University, Prague, Peking University in Beijing, the University of Hawaii, and Princeton University. Dr. Unterberger has written extensively on America's intervention in Siberia (1918–1920), Wilsonian diplomacy with Russia, the formation of Czechoslovakia as a nation, and Mohammad Ali Jinnah of Pakistan.

Dale E. Wilson received his master's and doctoral degrees from Temple University after service in Vietnam as an infantry officer. He has since taught at the U.S. Military Academy and other institutions. The former executive editor at Presidio Press, he is the author of several monographs and articles and the critically acclaimed book, *Treat 'Em Rough! The Birth of American Armor, 1917–1920.*

John F. Votaw is executive director of the Cantigny First Division Foundation. A graduate of the U.S. Military Academy and U.S. Army War College, he has served in Vietnam and Germany. He received his doctoral degree from Temple University and has taught at the U.S. Military Academy and other institutions. He has published numerous articles on military matters and is the author of a forthcoming book on U.S. military attachés.

Host and Sponsors

The First Division Museum is located in Wheaton, Illinois, on the grounds of Cantigny, the estate of the late Colonel Robert R. McCormick. Its state-of-the-art facility features innovative exhibits and presentations on the history of the division, a gallery for temporary exhibits, and the Colonel Robert R. McCormick Research Center. Containing more than forty-five hundred books, periodicals, microfilm, and other research materials, the center provides an environment for the serious study of the division and general military history and is open to the scholars, students, veterans, and persons interested in this subject area.

The Great War Society was founded in 1987 by a group of scholars at the Hoover Institution of War, Peace, and Revolution. Members subscribe to the belief that the First World War changed the course of twentieth-century history, and that every major event since then—the rise of communism and fascism, the Great Depression, World War II and the Cold War—have their origins in that conflict. Headquartered in Stanford, California, the Great War Society has three chapters in the San Francisco Bay area and members from the United States, Canada, and Europe. For more information, contact the Great War Society, Box 4585, Stanford, CA 94309.

The Western Front Association is an international organization dedicated to preserving the experience and memory of the First World War. The association offers publications, conferences, and annual seminars in the United States and Britain. Membership information can be obtained by writing Leonard G. Shurtleff, 6915 NW 49th Street, Gainesville, Florida 32653-1152.

Notes

Did Anyone "In Charge" Know What He Was Doing?
Thoughts on the Thirty Years' War
of the Twentieth Century
George Anastaplo

The notes for this paper were prepared after the paper was delivered. Useful suggestions were provided by Larry Arnn, president, The Claremont Institute; Laurence Berns, tutor, St. John's College; and Maurice F. X. Donohue, former dean, University College, The University of Chicago.

1. John, Viscount Morley, *Recollections* (New York: Macmillan Co., 1917), vol. 2, p. 88. See, also, Harry V. Jaffa, *Original Intent and the Framers of the Constitution* (Washington: Regnery Gateway, 1994), pp. 367–68. See, on John Morley, Winston S. Churchill, *Great Contemporaries* (London: Odhams Press Ltd., 1940), p. 69. See as well notes 13, 37, and 46, below.
2. See Anastaplo, "Clausewitz and Intelligence: Some Preliminary Observations," *Teaching Political Science* 16 (1989): 77, 84, n.17. (This was a paper prepared for delivery at the Conference on Intelligence and Policy sponsored by the Defense Intelligence College, Washington, D.C., August 26–28, 1986.) See, also, note 34, below. Ranking "high" among the other monumental catastrophes around the world to which the First World War eventually contributed was the Pol Pot tyranny in Cambodia. See Anastaplo, *The American Moralist: On Law, Ethics, and Government* (Athens: Ohio University Press, 1992), pp. 95–96, 171. The more or less immediate impact of the First World War has been described in this way:

   > In the First World War some 10 million men were killed, maimed, and wounded in combat alone. There were over 2 million casualties per year, 190,000 per month, and 6,000 per day. The trench warfare on the western front was particularly horrifying. In 1916 the battle of the Somme claimed 500,000 casualties in four months, the battle of Verdun 700,000 in ten months. This immense bloodletting, which contributed to inuring Europe to the mass killings of the future, was not due primarily to the deadliness of modern weapons such as automatic machine guns and field artillery. Rather, it must be attributed to the zeal with which swarms of officers and men kept "going over the top" in the face of impossible odds. This dutiful self-immolation was a measure of the extent to which, from the outset, the war of 1914 to 1918 was a secularized "holy war," even if its ideological reason was not fully revealed and articulated until 1917. With the Russian Revolution the interpenetration of international conflict and civil war which is characteristic of times of general crisis also began to surface. 1917 was also the year of the entrance of the United States into the war, which signaled the beginning of the end of Europe's long-standing ascendancy in the global economic and political system.
   >   The military, economic, and social stresses of the First World War and its aftermath gravely unsettled four of Europe's six major belligerents . . . This radical destabilization and change in all the major continental

powers, except France, went hand in hand with the thorough disloca-
tion of Europe's intramural balance of power.

Arno J. Mayer, *Why Did The Heavens Not Darken? The "Final Solution" in History*
(New York: Pantheon Books, 1988), p. 4. See, also, Winston Churchill, *The World
Crisis* (New York: Charles Scribner's Sons, 1923), vol. 2, pp. 1–5. See as well
notes 13, 26, and 43, below. See, on the casualties of the Second World War,
ibid., pp. 12–13.

3. Marshal Ferdinand Foch is quoted in Winston Churchill, *The Gathering Storm*
(Boston: Houghton Mifflin Co., 1948), p. 7. See, also, notes 19, 30, and 43, below.

4. Ibid., p. iii. Churchill spoke from the perspective of the only man to hold high
political office in both of the world wars.

5. See, on Thucydides's *History of the Peloponnesian War*, Leo Strauss, *The City and
Man* (Chicago: Rand McNally & Co., 1964), p. 139. See, on the uses and limita-
tions of history (partly with a view to understanding the First World War), Leo
Raditsa, "On the Past," *Gallatin Latin Review*, Winter 1992, pp. 19, 25, 26, 48.

6. See, e.g., *Encyclopedia Britannica*, 15th ed. (1993 printing), vol. 11, p. 711. See,
also, Arno J. Mayer, *Why Did The Heavens Not Darken?*, pp. 19–23, 30–33.

7. It is an historical curiosity that a Ferdinand was critical to the outbreak of both
of these extended pan-European wars—the aggressive Emperor Ferdinand II in
1619 and the assassinated Archduke Franz Ferdinand in 1914. See, also, note
30, below.

8. *Encyclopedia Britannica*, 15th ed. (1993 printing), vol. 11, p. 711.

9. See, e.g., Anastaplo, *The American Moralist*, pp. xvi, xix, xxi–xxii, 555–69; Jaffa,
Original Intent and the Framers of the Constitution, pp. 359–86.

10. See Anastaplo, *The American Moralist*, p. 586. See, also, note 45, below.

11. See ibid., pp. 225–44, 623. I was better able, in 1946, to observe the fervor of the
Europeans in Cairo than that of the Egyptians, although I volunteered to serve
as the officer in charge of armed vehicles which on more than one occasion took
supplies from our air base to the American Embassy while the city was generally
off-limits to American military personnel because of riots in the streets. (I particularly recall how peculiarly quiet those ordinarily vibrant streets were that we
ventured through.) The anti-English passion of the Egyptians is described in
Naguib Mahfouz's *The Cairo Trilogy*. See note 38, below.

12. Woodrow Wilson's powerful rhetoric promoted the unsettling doctrines of "open
covenants openly arrived at" and of "self-determination." See ibid., pp. 96–97,
330–31. See, also, Henry Grunwald, "Memorandum to Woodrow Wilson," *Time*,
Nov. 14, 1994, p. 104. See, as well, note 49, below.

13. See, e.g., Book Review, *Times Literary Supplement*, Feb. 22, 1968, p. 186. See, also,
notes 15 and 19, below. John Morley, upon resigning (in August 1914) from the
British Cabinet when the decision was made to go to war, prepared a memorandum (published only after his death in 1923) which included these observations:

> [Foreign Minister Sir Edward] Grey has more than once congratulated
> Europe on the existence of two great confederacies, the Triple Alliance
> and Triple Entente, as healthily preserving the balance of power. Bal-
> ance! What a beautiful euphemism for the picture of two giant groups
> armed to the teeth, each in mortal terror of the other, both of them
> passing year after year in an incurable fever of jealousy and suspicion!

John Viscount Morley, *Memorandum on Resignation* (London: Macmillan and Co.,
1928), p. 7. No doubt the Germans meant to win and thought they would do so
easily, gaining thereby glory and power. But what they and others soon found
themselves "obliged" to do was simply ghastly—and a prompt reconsideration of
both their goals and their methods was then the duty of all the belligerents,
instead of simply digging in "for the duration." See notes 19 and 37, below. Compare note 26, below.

14. Ethnic minorities in the Austro-Hungarian and German empires had become troublesome by 1914. Persistent revolutionary ferment was an eventual consequence of the general European settlement imposed by the Congress of Vienna in 1815. An adventurous American observer could see the origins of the First World War in this way:

> The cause of this war is found in the movements of the different races of Europe toward the formation of governments coextensive with their separate identities. This movement impinging against the existing order of things is in this century what the movement of liberalism against the existing order of things was in the last century, what the hatred of monarch against monarch was in the eighteenth century, what the movement for religious change was in the century before, and the movement against feudalism was the century before that—each one the great motive force of its age.

Robert R. McCormick, *With the Russian Army* (New York: Macmillan Co., 1915), p. 255.

15. A useful collection of the relevant documents here may be found in Imanuel Geiss, ed., *July 1914: The Outbreak of the First World War* (London: B. T. Batsford Ltd., 1967). See, for a review of the Geiss collection, note 13, above.

16. See Geiss, ed., *July 1914*, pp. 330–31. See, on the rules of war which Europeans once relied upon, Winston Churchill, *Marlborough: His Life and Times* (abridged edition) (New York: Charles Scribner's Sons, 1968), p. 277.

17. We saw this sort of thing satirized by the reliance upon a Doomsday Machine in the 1964 movie, *Dr. Strangelove. Or How I Learned to Stop Worrying and Love the Bomb.*

18. See Geiss, ed., *July 1914*, p. 119. See, also, D. A. Hamer, *John Morley: Intellectual in Politics* (Oxford: Clarendon Press, 1968), pp. 372–74; note 13, above.

19. In 1919 John Maynard Keynes assessed in this way the "contributions" by various nations to the disaster:

> Moved by insane delusion and reckless self-regard, the German people overturned the foundations on which we all lived and built. But the spokesmen of the French and British people have run the risk of completing the ruin, which Germany began, by a Peace which, if it is carried into effect, must impair yet further, when it might have restored, the delicate, complicated organization, already shaken by war, through which alone the European peoples can employ themselves and live.

Keynes, *Essays in Persuasion* (New York: W. W. Norton & Co., 1963), pp. 3–4. Keynes also spoke of the First World War as "the European Civil War." Ibid., p. 5.

20. Perhaps war would have been averted, or at least postponed, if it had been generally believed, before July 1914, that England would intervene on the side of France once Germany and France went to war. We can be reminded here of what happened in Korea in June 1950. See, on what Germany and Great Britain shared, Morley, *Memorandum on Resignation*, p. 19; Hamer, *John Morley*, pp. 360–61, 368. See, on the significance of the entrance of the United States into the First World War, note 2, above.

21. See Anastaplo, *The Amendments to the Constitution: A Commentary* (Baltimore: Johns Hopkins University Press, 1995), epigraphs (drawing on Ulysses S. Grant's *Personal Memoirs*, chapter 20). See, also, Anastaplo, "Natural Law or Natural Right?," *Loyola University of New Orleans Law Review* 38 (1993): 915.

22. This professor was Malcolm P. Sharp of The University of Chicago Law School. See Anastaplo, *The American Moralist*, p. 621. Another teacher of mine, in graduate school, could speak of the insanity in Germany in the following generation, which was "led politically by Hitler." See Leo Strauss, *What Is Political Philosophy?* (Glencoe, Illinois: The Free Press, 1959), pp. 240–41. Is an instinct of aggression in the human species exhibited in all this? See Malcolm P. Sharp, "Aggression: A Study of Values

and Law," *Ethics* 57 (1947): 1. See, on Leo Strauss, Anastaplo, *The Artist as Thinker: From Shakespeare to Joyce* (Athens; Ohio University Press, 1983), pp. 249–72.

23. The movie made from the Buchan story, decades later (in 1935), is quite different in significant respects from the original novel. Colonel Buchan's history of the origins of the First World War includes sentiments that had colored his wartime novels:

> Great events spring only from great causes, but the immediate occasion may be small. . . . The events of that June [1914] morning at Sarajevo . . . in their sequel must rank among the fateful moments of history. They brought to a head the secular antagonism between Slav and Teuton, and awoke the dormant ambitions and fears of every Power in Europe. . . .
> . . . For more than a year the rulers of Germany had made up their minds for war—war, if possible, in installments, but war which in the last resort would give them a world hegemony. She seized, like Austria, on the pretext of Sarajevo, but with a far wider purpose. . . . All [of Germany's] statesmen were at one on the war with Russia and France, but many would have fain postponed the reckoning with Britain to a more convenient day. . . . It must be recorded that it was only by accident that the right course was taken [by Britain]. The tone of the press at the time, and the discussions in the Cabinet up to 3rd August [1914], showed how ignorant and unprepared were our people. The true political issue was not understood save by a few, and had the issue remained only political it is to be feared that Britain would have long hesitated, and might have fatally compromised the fortunes of [Russia and France] by her delay. But the outrage on Belgium raised a *moral* issue which swept away every doubt. It is not too much to say that the honour and liberty of our race were saved by the martyrdom of their little neighbour.

John Buchan, *A History of the Great War* (London: Thomas Nelson and Sons Ltd., 1921), vol. 1, pp. 7, 79–80 (author's emphasis). See note 49, below.

24. The Germans did not do themselves the good they believed they would with their resort to punitive terror in Belgium and France. Their brutal violation of Belgium neutrality, and later their depredations on the high seas, contributed (along with such German follies as meddling in United States-Mexico relations) to the eventual American entry into the war.

25. See C. S. Forester, *The General* (Annapolis: The Nautical & Aviation Publishing Company of America, 1947), p. 227. One can also be reminded of the devastation of the continent-wide witch hunts which probably reached their climax four centuries ago. See, on the European witch trials, Anastaplo, "Church and State: Explorations," *Loyola University of Chicago Law Journal* 19 (1987): 65–86.

26. See, on the antipathy to a negotiated settlement of the First World War, Anastaplo, *The Constitutionalist: Notes on the First Amendment* (Dallas: Southern Methodist University Press, 1971), pp. 784–85. See, also, Winston Churchill, *Thoughts and Adventures* (London: Odhams Press, Ltd., 1949), pp. 106–9, 113–16; Hermann Hesse, *If the War Goes On . . .* (New York: Farrar, Straus and Giroux, 1971), pp. 3 ("the bloody absurdity of the war"), 15–16, 33f; note 2, above, note 43, below. Compare Arno J. Mayer, *The Persistence of the Old Regime: Europe to the Great War* (New York: Pantheon Books, 1981), p. 305 (emphasis added): "Throughout most of the nineteenth century Europe's civil and political societies had gone to war for limited, well-defined, and *negotiable* objectives." Compare notes 13 and 19, above, note 37, below.

27. See, on how the Battle of Verdun can still be regarded by a few, Anastaplo, "On the Use, Neglect, and Abuse of Veils: The Parliaments of the World's Religions, 1893, 1993," in *Great Ideas Today*, vol. 1994, pp. 30, 48–49 (1994) (quoting from Harry Neumann, *Liberalism* [Durham: Carolina Academic Press, 1991], pp. 292–94). See, also, note 38, below.

28. Forester, *The General*, p. 27.

29. Ibid., p. 205. See, also, note 2, above.
30. See, for an appraisal of Ferdinand Foch, Churchill, *Great Contemporaries*, p. 143. See, on the "staleness of [Foch's] military grousings," Georges Clemenceau, *Grandeur and Misery of Victory* (New York: Harcourt, Brace and Co., 1930), p. 8. See, as well, note 7, above, note 43, below.
31. See Geiss, ed., *July 1914*, p. 10. Compare ibid., p. 365: note 19, above.
32. See, e.g., Anastaplo, *Human Being and Citizen: Essays on Virtue, Freedom, and the Common Good* (Chicago: Swallow Press, 1975), pp. 8, 203 (discussing Plato's *Apology* and *Crito*).
33. See, e.g., Anastaplo, *The Artist as Thinker*, pp. 15–28.
34. The Kaiser was a nephew of King Edward VII and a grandson of Queen Victoria. The calamities of the First World War included the destruction visited upon the Russian, Austro-Hungarian, and German royal houses:

> If for a space we obliterate from our minds the fighting in France and Flanders [during the First World War], the struggle upon the Eastern Front [during the same war] is incomparably the greatest war in history. In its scale, in its slaughter, in the exertions of the combatants, in its military kaleidoscope, it far surpasses by magnitude and intensity all similar human episodes.
>
> It is also the most mournful conflict of which there is record. All three empires, both sides, victors and vanquished, were ruined. All the Emperors or their successors were slain or deposed. The Houses of Romanov, Hapsburg, and Hohenzollern woven over centuries of renown into the texture of Europe were shattered and extirpated. The structure of three mighty organisms built up by generations of patience and valour and representing the traditional groupings of noble branches of the European family, was changed beyond all semblance.

Winston Churchill, *The Unknown War: The Eastern Front* (New York: Charles Scribner's Sons, 1931), p. 1. See on the precariousness of the house of Windsor today, "An Idea Whose Time Has Passed," *The Economist*, October 22, 1994, p. 15; "Labour to Strip Queen of Political Power and Slim Down Monarchy," *Sunday Times*, December 4, 1994, p. 1; "Most Britons Feel the Monarchy is Doomed," *Manchester Guardian Weekly*, January 15, 1995, p.1.
35. Still, it can be salutary to recognize how the Germans could regard themselves even during the Nazi era. See, e.g., Milton Mayer, *They Thought They Were Free* (Chicago: The University of Chicago Press, 1955). See, on the Nuremberg trials, Anastaplo, "On Trial: Explorations," *Loyola University of Chicago Law Journal* 22 (1991): 765, 977–94.
36. See, on this campaign, Jeffrey D. Wallin, "Politics and Strategy in the Dardanelles Operation," in Harry V. Jaffa, ed., *Statesmanship: Essays in Honor of Sir Winston Spencer Churchill* (Durham: Carolina Academic Press, 1981), p. 131. See, also, Churchill, *Great Contemporaries*, pp. 268–69.
37. See, e.g., Morley, *Memorandum on Resignation*, p. 21 ("the adventurous energy of Winston"). See, also, ibid., pp. 5, 26. Churchill's principal contribution to the war on the Western Front was probably his sponsorship of the armored tank. See, e.g., Churchill, *The World Crisis*, vol. 2, pp. 7–8. Churchill did consider the war, as it was fought, a disaster. See ibid., pp. 1–2. This could have been avoided, he believed, by the classic response: strategy raised to the level of statesmanship. But what should have been done when it became apparent, even during the opening months of the war, that the war would not be fought sensibly on either side? See note 13, above. Compare note 26, above. See, on the mass effects in modern life which are touched upon in this paper, Churchill, *Thoughts and Adventures*, p. 192. See, also, McCormick, *With the Russian Army*, pp. 287, 298–99. See as well note 43, below.

38. Basil Liddell Hart, "The Military Strategist," in A. J. P. Taylor, ed., *Churchill Revised: A Critical Assessment* (New York: Dial Press, 1969), p. 225. Churchill was always an exceptional "romantic," entranced by opportunities for the exhibition of extraordinary bravery and of the ability to lead effectively in the most threatening circumstances. A very pale contemporary reflection of, if not yearning for, this kind of temperament (albeit a half century ago) may be glimpsed in note 11, above. See, also, the end of note 49, below. What the young Winston in turn looked up to, more than a century ago, may be glimpsed in Churchill, *Marlborough*, p. 283.

39. John Van Doren, of the Institute for Philosophical Research (Chicago, Illinois), has provided this distillation from my paper: "The First World War seems to have involved a failure of imagination on all sides, and the question, the main question, is how that could have come about. Somehow the European mind had lost the sense of tragedy, had become blind to the possibility of failure, of destruction." Consider also this 1921 observation by John Maynard Keynes *(Essays in Persuasion*, p. 46): "It is the method of modern statesmen to talk as much folly as the public demand and to practice no more of it than is compatible with what they have said, trusting that such folly in action as must wait on folly in word will soon disclose itself as such, and furnish an opportunity for slipping back into wisdom . . ." See note 43, below.

40. Maurice F. X. Donahue has noticed that a number of American regiments suffered, because of their leaders' blunders, larger single-encounter losses in the Civil War than Tennyson's fabled Light Brigade. See, on the First World War practice of going "over the top" in the face of impossible odds, note 2, above, note 43, below.

41. See note 11, above. See, on the supposed revitalization of the morale of the American army by the Gulf War, Anastaplo, "On Freedom: Explorations," *Oklahoma City University Law Review* 17 (1992): 465, 626–28.

42. Desmond King-Hall, *Shelley: The Man and the Poet* (New York: Thomas Yoseloff, 1960), p. 372.

43. The turmoil, both psychic and social, that Europeans had to confront may be glimpsed in the grand novels of Marcel Proust and in such musical works as Arnold Schoenberg's *Five Pieces for Orchestra*, Op. 16 (1909). See, also, on "the great debauch which periodically affects mankind," McCormick, *With the Russian Army*, p. 252. Particularly intriguing here is the unfortunate influence in prewar imperial Germany of someone as learned as Kurt Riezler. See, e.g., Geiss, ed., *July 1914*, pp. 12–13, 33–35, 39, 60, 74, 340, 364–65, 369, 398. Compare Leo Strauss, *What Is Political Philosophy?*, p. 233. See, as well, note 39, above. (Martin Heidegger may have attempted, before the Second World War, to play the role in Germany that Kurt Riezler had played there before the First World War. See, e.g., Anastaplo, *The American Moralist*, p. 144.) The consequences of attempting to "work out," through the First World War, whatever was "wrong in the European soul" have been described in this way in Great Britain by a former Minister of State at the Ministry of Defense (1989–1992):

> The end of deference, the degradation of patriotism, the exposure of Christianity—all these became, in the fullness of time, not just accepted but industrialised, integrated into the new world. The vanquished nation states produced Lenin and Hitler; the "victorious" democracies, a train-load of mediocrities. And the cards were marked up for another huge ritual slaughter. . . .
>
> What frightful conceits and brutality of intellect caused the High Command to ignore—not once, twice, or five times, but ten thousand times—the "lesson" that muffling machine-gun fire with human flesh is a wasteful technique. "Hammer away," said Marshal Foch to the British commander, "hammer away, and you will get there" . . .

The Great War also exemplified a massive social betrayal. The elders of the ruling class expended all the loyalties and obligations of the feudal system—and the lives not only of the villeins but of their younger sons—in obstinate pursuit of their avid vanities. The "Home Front," too, changed out of recognition with the emancipation of women, and the final shift in industrial power from guilds to trade unions.

Alan Clark, "Social Betrayal in the Flanders Mud," *Guardian Weekly*, Oct. 2, 1994, p. 28. See further, on "the end of deference," A. A. Milne's one-act comedy, *The Boy Comes Home* (1918). See, also, notes 2 and 37, above.

44. See Forester, *The General*, pp. 172–73. See, also, Churchill, *The World Crisis*, vol. 2, p. 5. H. H. Asquith, the prime minister who took Great Britain into the First World War, played bridge recklessly. See A. F. Alington, *The Lamps Go Out: 1914, and the Outbreak of War* (London: Faber and Faber, 1962), p. 117. (The Alington book provides a useful simplified account of the beginning of the First World War. See, for a more elaborate introduction, Martin Gilbert, *The First World War: A Complete History* [New York: Henry Holt, 1994].)

45. The anti-colonialism passion to which I also referred in my 1946 letter (quoted in Section I of this paper), to the extent that this passion did not depend upon the Cold War, has still to be reckoned with, drawing as it does upon sentiments (both high and low) that go back to the American and French Revolutions and that found worldwide application in the Wilsonian doctrines of the First World War. See note 12, above.

46. It seems that the Russian economy, which may have been about to "take off" before the First World War, was crippled by the 1917 Bolshevik Revolution and its aftermath. That aftermath included such abominations as the slaughter of the Kulaks and the Gulag terrors. See Anastaplo, "On Freedom," pp. 630–43. See, on Germany as a bulwark (before the First World War) against the threat to European civilization of Russian barbarism, Morley, *Memorandum on Resignation*, p. 6; Hamer, *John Morley*, pp. 363, 367. Aleksandr Solzhenitsyn's *August 1914* (1983) argues that there were wholesome elements in Russia that could have so reformed the country as to save the army from defeat and the monarchy from revolution. See, e.g., Vladislav Krasnov, "Wrestling with Lev Tolstoi," *Slavic Review* 45 (1986): 707.

47. Controversies with respect to the risks undertaken by the United States during the Cuban Missile crisis have yet to be resolved. See, e.g., Anastaplo, *The American Moralist*, pp. 233–34, 607.

48. See, e.g., Anastaplo, "On Freedom," pp. 645–65.

49. Related to these problems is how we equip ourselves to talk about the issues that we confront as a people. A recent case in point was the 1994 prospect of an invasion of Haiti by the United States. An American secretary of state, upon being asked whether the administration would secure Congressional approval for an invasion of Haiti, spoke of presidential power in this way: "We can't tie the hands of the President. The President may have to act in a situation very quickly and on his own constitutional authority." Niel A. Lewis, "Aides Say Clinton Doesn't Need Vote in Congress to Invade Haiti," *New York Times*, Sept. 12, 1994, p. 1A. The secretary could say this despite the obvious fact that there had been, by the time he spoke (on September 11, 1994), more than enough time to have had a proper debate in Congress with respect to what the basic American policy toward Haiti should be. Similarly, during the Gulf War, the proper time to secure the required Congressional authorization was in November 1990, not in January 1991 when Congress was confronted with a fait accompli by an ultimatum-brandishing president. See, e.g., Anastaplo, "On Freedom," pp. 613–16. The Germans and Austro-Hungarians, as well as others, would probably have conducted themselves more sensibly in July 1914 if their constitutional arrangements had required and permitted responsible public

discussion of the measures being considered. Compare note 23, above. See, on the proper powers of the president, Anastaplo, *The Constitution of 1787: A Commentary* (Baltimore: Johns Hopkins University Press, 1989), pp. 89–123. See, on the effects of broadcast television upon the souls of Americans, Anastaplo, *The American Moralist*, pp. 245–74. See, also, Anastaplo, "On Crime, Criminal Lawyers, and O. J. Simpson: Plato's *Georgias* Revisited," *Loyola University of Chicago Law Journal* 26 (1991): 456. See, on current debates about the conditions of American souls, Robert L. Stone, ed., *Essays on "The Closing of the American Mind"* (Chicago: Chicago Review Press, 1989), e.g., pp. 225, 267. See, on the case for constitutionalism and personal sacrifice, Roger K. Newman, *Hugo Black: A Biography* (New York: Pantheon Books, 1994), pp. 502–7 ("We must not be afraid to be free.").

The German Soldier of World War I: Myths and Realities
Dennis E. Showalter

1. The best example is Holger Herwig's "The Dynamics of Necessity: German Military Policy During the First World War," in *Military Effectiveness*, vol. 1, *The First World War*, ed. A. Millett, W. Murray (Boston, 1988), pp. 80–115.
2. Cf. Heiger Ostertag, *Bildung, Ausbildung, und Erziehung des Offizierkorps im deutschen Kaiserreich 1871 bis 1981: Eliteideal, Anspruch und Wirklichkeit* (Frankfurt, 1990); and Bernd Schulte, *Die deutsche Armee 1900–1914. Zwischen Beharren und Verändern* (Düsseldorf, 1977).
3. Cf. Peter Scholler, *Der Fall Löwen und das Weissbuch* (Köln, 1958); Geoffrey Best, *Humanity in Warfare* (New York, 1930), 225 ff.; and James F. Willis, *Prologue to Nuremberg: The Politics and Diplomacy of Punishing War Criminals of the First World War* (Westport, Conn., 1982).
4. Ulrich Trumpener, "The Road to Ypres: The Beginnings of Gas Warfare in World War I," *Journal of Modern History* 47 (1975): 460–483.
5. Wolfram Wette, "Ideologien, Propaganda und Innenpolitik als Voraussetzungen der Kriegspolitik des Dritten Reiches," in *Das Deutsche Reich und der Zweite Weltkrieg*, vol. 1, ed. W. Deist, et al. (Stuttgart, 1989), 25 ff., is an excellent overview. Cf. Jay W. Baird, *To Die for Germany: Heroes in the Nazi Pantheon* (Bloomington, Ind., 1990).
6. See Dennis E. Showalter, "Army, Status, and Society in Germany, 1871–1914: An Interpretation," in *Another Germany. A Reconsideration of the Imperial Era*, ed. J. R. Dukes and J. Remak (Boulder, Colo., 1988), pp. 1–18.
7. Joseph Hlagus, "The Bavarian Soldier, 1871–1914: Efforts to Use Military Training as a Means of Strengthening Consensus in Favor of the Existing Order," Ph.D. Dissertation, New York University, is a modern case study. Ludwig Seckendorff, "Die allgemeine Wehrpflicht und ihr sozialer Wirkungsbereich in den Jahren 1888–1914," Ph.D. Dissertation, Heidelberg, 1934, provides still-useful ideas.
8. Criticisms of maneuvers held at harvest time and loss of sons' labor described in, inter alia, David Blackbourn, *Class, Religion and Local Politics in Wilhelmine Germany* (New Haven, Conn., 1980), p. 208, can also be interpreted in terms of army service as a perceived threat to parental and pastoral control over the next generation.
9. An excellent example is Karl Unruh, *Langemarck. Legende und Wirklichkeit* (Koblenz, 1906).
10. Thomas Rohrkrämer, *Der Militärismus der kleinen Leute. Die Kriegervereine im Deutschen Kaiserreich 1871–1910* (Munich, 1990).
11. There is as yet no German counterpart to Jacques Becker's work on French public morale at the outbreak of war. Jeffrey T. Verkey, 'The Spirit of 1914'; The Myth of Enthusiasm and the Rhetoric of Unity in World War I Germany," Ph.D. Dissertation, University of California, Berkeley, 1991, is an excellent beginning.

Cf. as well Margret Stickelberg-Eder, *Aufbruch 1914, Kriegsroman der späten Weimarer Republik* (Zürich, 1983).

12. Unruh, p. 19 passim, offers a survey based largely on the regimental histories of the new units—volumes unlikely to overstate problems, hardships, and fiascoes caused by the military system.

13. Cf. Peter Simkins, *Kitchener's Army. The Raising of the New Armies, 1914–1916* (Manchester, 1988). Jacques Becker, *Les Français dans la Grande Guerre* (Paris, 1980); and P. J. Flood, *France 1914–1918. Public Opinion and the War Effort* (New York, 1990).

14. Martin van Creveld, *Supplying War: Logistics from Wallenstein to Patton* (Cambridge, 1977), 109 ff.; H. von Kühl and J. von Bergmann, *Movements and Supply of the German First Army during August and September 1914* (Ft. Leavenworth, Kans., 1920).

15. Erwin Rommel, *Attacks*, tr. J. R. Driscoll (Athena, Va., 1979), 3 ff.; Walter Bloem, *The Advance from Mons*, tr. G. C. Wynne (London, 1930).

16. Sewall Tyng, *The Campaign of the Marne 1914* (New York, 1935), p. 85; and the accounts by participants in *Das Ehrenbuch der Garde. Die preussische Garde im Weltkrieg 1914–1919* , ed. E. V. Eisenhart-Rothe, M. Lezius (Berlin, 1931).

17. Hans von Seeckt, *Aus meinem Leben* (Leipzig, 1938), 85 ff.; Hans Meier-Welcker, *Seekt* (Frankfurt, 1967), 43 ff.

18. Friedrich Seeselberg, *Der Stellungskrieg 1914–1918* (Berlin, 1928), p. 103; Wilhelm Balck, *Development of Tactics—World War*, trans. H. Bell (Ft. Leavenworth, Kans., 1922) p. 18.

19. Werner Beumelberg, *Loretto*, vol. 17 of *Schlachten und Treffen des Weltkrieges* (Berlin, 1927), eloquently conveys a sense of the nature of the fighting in a period and sector that remains neglected.

20. Lyn Macdonald, *1915. The Death of Innocence* (New York, 1995), 514 ff., offers a vivid description of what the shocked Germans called "the corpse-field of Loos."

21. G. C. Wynne, *If Germany Attacks*, reprint ed. (Westport, Conn., 1976) p. 97; Balck, p. 55. Martin Samuels, *Doctrine and Dogma. German and British Infantry Tactics in the First World War* (Westport, Conn., 1992), 59 ff., surveys the tactical concepts that underlay specific doctrines and methods.

22. Helmuth Gruss, *Die Deutsche Sturmbataillonen im Weltkrieg* (Berlin, 1939); and Bruce Gudmundsson, *Stormtroop Tactics* (New York, 1939), are the standard accounts.

23. Gerald D. Feldman, *Army, Industry and Labor in Germany. 1914–1918* (Princeton, 1966), remains the definitive study. Cf. as well Jürgen Kocka, *Facing Total War: German Society 1914–1918* (Leamington Spa, 1984).

24. Robert Whalen, *Bitter Wounds: German Victims of the Great War, 1914–1939* (Ithaca, N.Y., 1984), p. 53 passim.

25. Richard Bessel, *Germany After the First World War* (Oxford, 1993), p. 14.

26. Whalen, pp. 49, 111 ff.

27. See Lothar Burchardt's survey, "Die Auswirkung der Kriegswirtschaft auf die deutsche Zivilbevölkerung im Ersten und im Zweiten Weltkrieg," *Militärgeschichtliche Mitteilungen* 15 (1974): 65–97.

28. Wilhelm Deist, "Der militärische Zusammenbruch des Kaiserreiches. Zur Realität der 'Dolchstosslegende'," in vol. 1 of *Das Unrechtsregime: Internationale Forschung über den Nationalsozialismus*, ed. U. Bittner et al., (Hamburg, 1969); Eric Leed, *No Man's Land* (New York, 1978), 83 ff., deals with the disillusion of the volunteers. Hermann Kantorowicz's *Der Offiziershass im deutschen Heer* (Freiburg, 1919) emphasizes the contributions of the officer corps to the process.

29. Cf. Bessel, 8 ff.; Bruno Thoss, "Menschenführung im Ersten Weltkrieg und in Reichswehr," in *Menschenführung im Heer*, ed. Militärgeschichtliches Forschungsamt (Herford, 1982), p. 113 passim; Dieter Dreetz, "Methoden der Ersatzgewinnung für das deutsche Heer 1914—1918," *Militärgeschichte* 16 (1977):

701–706; and Hermann Gauer, *Von Bauerntum, Bürgertum und Arbeitertum in der Armee* (Heidelberg, 1936).

30. Michael Salewski, "Verdun und die Folgen: Eine militär- und geistgeschichtliche Betrachtung," *Wehrwissenschaftliche Rundschau* 65 (1976): 39–96. German Werth, *Verdun. Die Schlacht und der Mythos* (Gladbach, 1979), vividly describes the process of attrition.

31. Heige, p. 291 passim. Konstantin vom Altrock, *Vom Sterben des deutschen Offizierkorps* (Berlin, 1922), especially stresses the impact of the loss of the regulars on the army's routine and morale.

32. G. Krumeich, "Le Soldat allemand sur la Somme," in *Les Sociétés Européénnes*, pp. 367–374.

33. Ernst Jünger, *Im Stahlgewittern* (Berlin, 1922) remains the prototypical statement of this world view. Cf. Modris Ekstein's *Rites of Spring. The Great War and the Birth of the Modern Age* (New York, 1989); and Leed, p. 115 passim.

34. Bernd Hüppauf, "Langemarck, Verdun and the Myth of a New Man in Germany After the First World War," *War and Society* 6 (1983): 84–96.

35. Cf. Feldman, 149 ff.; Michael Geyer, "German Strategy in the Age of Machine Warfare," in *Makers of Modern Strategy*, ed. P. Paret (Princeton N.J., 1986), 537 ff.; and as a case study, John Morrow, *German Air Power in World War I* (Lincoln, Neb., 1982).

36. Cf. Timothy Lupfer, *The Dynamics of Doctrine: The Changes in German Tactical Doctrine During the First World War* (Ft. Leavenworth, Kans., 1981), 7 ff.; Gudmundsson, 77 passim; and George Bruchmüller, *Die Deutsche Artillerie in den Durchbruchschlachten des Weltkrieges* (Berlin, 1922). The quotation is from Lupfer, p. 15.

37. Dieter Dreetz, "Zur Unerfüllbarkeit der personellen Ersatzanforderungen der deutschen militärischen Führung für das Feldheer im Ersten Weltkrieg," *Revue Internationale d'Histoire Militaire* 62 (1985): 51–60.

38. Thoss, 112 ff.; Samuels, 105 ff.; and Ostertag, p. 292 passim, offer recent scholarly introductions to a subject that will repay in-depth research.

39. Omer Bartov, *Hitler's Army. Soldiers, Nazis, and War in the Third Reich* (New York, 1991), pp. 95–96.

40. Martin Hobohm, "Soziale Heeresmisstände im Ersten Weltkrieg," in *Der Krieg des kleinen Mannes. Eine Militärgeschichte von Unten*, ed. W. Wette (Munich, 1992), pp. 136–45.

41. Herwig, pp. 101–2; and Gudmundsson, pp. 151–52, survey this development and its consequences. Related to this was the growing alienation of the Bavarians. The Royal Bavarian Army's active and first-line reserve divisions had maintained on the whole sufficiently high levels of effectiveness to be regarded as assault troops, somewhat in the fashion of the British Expeditionary Force's (BEF's) Scottish divisions. As a result their morale, while usually described as high in Allied intelligence reports, was also commonly described as anti-Prussian. Cf. the specific entries in *Histories of the Two Hundred and Fifty-One Divisions of the German Army Which Participated in the War (1914–1918)*, ed. General Staff, American Expeditionary Forces (AEF) (Washington, D.C., 1920).

42. The figures are from Wilhelm Deist "Verdeckter Militärstreik im Kriegsjahr 1918?," in *Krieg des kleinen Mannes*, pp. 146–67. Cf. also Deist, "Militärischer Zusammenbruch," 111 ff.

43. A point well established in Bessel, *Germany After the First World War*.

44. James M. Diehl, *Paramilitary Politics in Weimar Germany* (Bloomington, Ind., 1977). In this respect the *mentalité* of German veterans of the Great War significantly resembles that of their Union counterparts as described in Gerald F. Linderman's *Embattled Courage: The Experience of Combat in the American Civil War* (New York, 198), 266 ff.

45. F. Scott Fitzgerald, *Tender Is the Night* (New York, 1951), pp. 117–18.

46. Leonard V. Smith, *Between Mutiny and Obedience. The Case of the French Fifth Infantry Division During World War I* (Princeton, 1993), is suggestive. Cf. as well Jeffrey Greenhut, "The Imperial Reserve: The Indian Infantry on the Western Front, 1914-15," Ph.D. Dissertation, Kansas State University, 1978.

Sidney Reilly, Master Spy:
A Reappraisal of His Role in the Lockhart Plot
Richard B. Spence

1. Although very limited in their source material and often inaccurate in their interpretations and conclusions, the two main biographies of Reilly are Robin Lockhart's *Ace of Spies* (New York, 1967) and its 1987 sequel, *Reilly: The First Man*, plus Michael Kettle's *Sidney Reilly* (London, 1983), the latter being the more scholarly work. Reilly's supposed "memoirs," *The Adventures of Sidney Reilly* (London, 1933), although likely inspired by some of Reilly's accounts, particularly those relating to 1918, were not written by him, but by his last wife with the aid of a ghostwriter.

2. Accusations that Reilly spied for Russia and Japan in 1904-05 came from several sources, most of them British, and most of these persons connected to intelligence matters. See, for instance, the statements contained in U.S. National Archives (NA), Bureau of Investigation (BI), Investigative Case File OG 39368 (largely based on Office of Naval Intelligence—ONI—reports, thus, hereafter BI/ONI), 17 Oct. 1917 report from Bond to Hunnewell quoting Capt. Abbott, 6 Sept. 1918 memorandum to Smith and Hunnewell quoting N. M. Rodkinson, and 23 Aug. 1918 memorandum to Lt. Irving quoting an unnamed British officer.

3. Some standard accounts can be found in M. Ia. Latsis, *Dva goda bortba na vnutrennem fronte* (Moscow, 1920); P. G. Sofinov, *Ocherki istorii Vserossiiskii Chrezvychainoi Komissii (1917-1922)* (Moscow, 1960); F. D. Volkhov, *Krakh angliiskoi politiki interventsii i diplomaticheskoi izolatsii Sovetskogo gosudarstva, 1917-21 gg.* (Moscow, 1954); and the same author's "Zagovor poslov' i provokatsionnaia rol' Briusa Lokkarta," *Novaia i noveishaia istoriia*, no. 5 (1976), 112-127. Another valuable source is Iakov Peters "Vospominaniia o rabote v VChK v pervyi god revoliutsii," *Proletarskaia Revoliutsiia*, no. 10/33 (1924), p. 532.

4. Richard K. Debo, "Lockhart Plot or Dzerzhinski Plot?", *Journal of Modern History* (Sept. 1971): 413-439.

5. Edward Van Der Rhoer, *Master Spy* (New York, 1981). The author, a former U.S. Naval Intelligence officer, concludes that Reilly acted as a Soviet double agent in 1918. Pimenov's work, "Kak ia iskal shpiona Reilli," Radio Liberty Samizdat Archive, MSS no. 1089 (Leningrad, 1968) is a somewhat tongue-in-cheek analysis focusing on the inconsistencies in standard Soviet accounts.

6. Allen and Rachel Douglas, "The First Chapter of the Trust: The Lockhart Plot," *Executive Intelligence Review* (Nov. 1988), pp. 1-15. The authors and *EIR* are partisans of Lyndon LaRouche, a controversial and intensely anti-British American political figure. While their theories of Anglo-Bolshevik collusion are carried to extremes, their approach does ask questions hitherto overlooked or ignored and points out the inadequacies of earlier accounts.

7. Lockhart described his adventures in Russia, before and during 1918, in *British Agent* (London, 1932). His initial view of the Bolsheviks is noted on pp. 104-5 (1961 paperback edition). See, also, Great Britain, Public Record Office, Kew (PRO), Foreign Office (FO), 371/3332, no. 92708, cover minutes to 17 May 1918 report from Lockhart to FO.

8. The new MI1c (MI6) station chief in Russia, Boyce reportedly was "disgusted" by Lockhart's appointment. See Edgar Sisson, *One Hundred Red Days* (New Haven, 1931), p. 294, also Christopher Andrew, *Her Majesty's Secret Service* (New York, 1985), pp. 212, 530 n.33. Boyce's predecessor, Capt. Stephen Alley, was removed from the post, in part because of his refusal to work with Lockhart.

9. Albert Resis, ed., *Molotov Remembers: Inside Kremlin Politics* (Chicago, 1993), p. 142. Trotskii abstained in the vote.

10. BI/ONI, 11 Oct. 1918 report from Bond to Hunnewell in which Samuel Vauclain notes Reilly's "tremendous political backing" reaching into the imperial court, and the 12 Sept. 1918 Memorandum no. 7 quoting like statements by Samuel Pryor. See also the similar conclusions of a later White Russian intelligence report, HIA, P. N. Vrangel; Collection, Box 110, File 22, "Rossiskii voennyi agent v Konstantinople, Report # 7," (n.d.), pp. 1–4.

11. See the above White Russian report, 1, and BI/ONI, Memorandum 9, Bond to Hunnewell, 27 Sept. 1918, noting Reilly's past connection to an Okhrana agent.

12. R. Lockhart, *Ace*, pp. 60–62, and Kettle, p. 18.

13. For Orlov's recollections, see his *Underworld and Soviet* (New York 1931).

14. For Fride's presence in prewar Petersburg, see, e.g., *Ves' Peterburg, 1912*, p. 948 and *1913*, p. 668.

15. Reilly's American dealings are detailed in my article "Sidney Reilly in America, 1914–1917," scheduled for publication in an upcoming issue of *Intelligence and National Security*. Many of my current references are drawn from this article.

16. Hoover Institution Archives (HIA), Stanford, Cal., R. H. B. Lockhart Collection, Box 6, translation of a Soviet report on "Case: Lockhart," 1, describing trial testimony.

17. The relationship between Reilly, Jahnke, and Hintze is discussed in the above article dealing with Reilly's wartime stint in America.

18. On Kalamatiano and his relationship to American intelligence the most thorough treatment is David S. Foglesong, "America's Secret War against Bolshevism: United States Intervention in the Russian Civil War, 1917–1920" (Ph.D. dissertation, UC Berkeley, 1991), pp. 298–363 and passim, and the same author's "Xenophon Kalamatiano: An American Spy in Revolutionary Russia?", *Intelligence and National Security*, vol. 6 (Jan. 1991). See also William R. Corson and Robert T. Crowley, *The New KGB: Engine of Soviet Power* (New York, 1985), pp. 47–64. Kalamatiano's 1917 assistance to Reilly is noted, very obliquely, in Wiseman's "Intelligence and Propaganda Work in Russia, July to December 1917," in the William Wiseman Papers, Folder 261, Stirling Library, Yale University.

19. Weinstein's brother, Gregory (Grigorii) was the paper's business manager. On Weinstein's other connections, see BI/ONI, Memorandums of 23 Aug. and 6 Sept. 1918, and MID, File 9140-6073, MIB to Biddle, 12 March 1918 and MIB to MI5, 20 April 1918.

20. "Record of Service of the Late 2nd Lt. Sidney George Reilly" (Pi 21220) MC, Ministry of defense, RAF Personnel Management Centre, Innsworth, England.

21. Ibid.

22. The Germans soon did just that in Ukraine, where, in April, they toppled the leftist *Rada* government and substituted a compliant military dictatorship under Gen. P. Skoropadskii.

23. G. L. Owen, "Budberg, the Soviets, and Reilly," unpublished manuscript, pp. 7–8.

24. NA, Military Intelligence Division (MID) File 9728182/1, Military Contre-Espionage, Report from A.D.6, 14 March 1918, and E. H. Carr, *The Bolshevik Revolution, 1917–1923*, vol. 3 (New York, 1953), p. 314.

25. Carr, pp. 314–15.

26. Ibid., pp. 85, 315

27. Alley to Robin Lockhart, 13 May 1966. A copy of this letter was graciously provided by Mr. Lockhart. Another copy may be found in Box 6 of the Lockhart Collection in the HIA. In his account of this episode, Robin Lockhart claims that Reilly's coded messages were for his father, but Alley's letter mentions nothing about their content or destination.

28. PRO, Admiralty Records (ADM), 137/HS1388, telegrams of 20 Nov. and 31 Dec. 1917.

29. B. Lockhart, p. 273, and Reilly, p. 12.
30. M. D. Bonch-Bruevich mentions his contact with Reilly in his *From Tsarist General to Red Army Commander* (Moscow, 1966).
31. B. Lockhart, pp. 161–62.
32. Ibid., pp. 136–37.
33. PRO, Foreign Office (FO) 371/3332, no. 92438, Lockhart to FO, 16 May 1918, and no. 95039, Lockhart to FO 26 May, 30 May, and 12 June 1918.
34. BI/ONI, Memorandum 3 to Irving, 28 Aug. 1918, 3, noting the arrival of a telegram from Murmansk which listed Reilly's return address as the British consulate in Moscow.
35. *Vserossiiskaia chrezvychainaia komissiia, VChK.*
36. V. F. Kravchenko, *Pod imenem Shmidkhena* (Moscow, 1973), p. 13.
37. The best biography of Peters is Valentin Shteinberg's *Ekab Peters* (Moscow, 1989).
38. It is natural to suspect the veracity of any confession derived under circumstances such as those prevailing in Russia in 1937. However, given that Peters's statements were never made public and had no real value as evidence in other cases (Karakhan had already been shot), why would anyone have bothered to concoct a story about something that had no obvious bearing on recent events? As for Peters, he had nothing to lose by confessing such past misdeeds and nothing to gain. Most importantly, however, Peters's version (see below) *fits* the circumstances.
39. Internationale Instituut voor Social Geschiedenis, Amsterdam, B. V. Savinkov Archive, Box 37, "Liste de Bolcheviks," p. 12.
40. See, for instance, the conclusions of Donald Rumbelow, *The Houndsditch Murders and the Siege of Sidney Street* (London, 1973).
41. George Hill, *Go Spy the Land* (London, 1932), pp. 90–115, 189–93. See also George Leggett, *The Cheka: Lenin's Political Police* (Oxford, 1981), p. 301.
42. On Savinkov's actions in the period, see my *Boris Savinkov, Renegade on the Left* (Boulder, Colo., 1991), pp. 185–210. On his relationship with Reilly, see my "The Terrorist and the Master Spy: The Political 'Partnership' of Boris Savinkov and Sydney Reilly," *Revolutionary Russia*, vol. 4, no. 1 (June 1991), pp. 111–31.
43. PRO, FO 371/3108, no. 5751, Spring-Rice to FO, 8 Jan. 1917.
44. See Lockhart's account in PRO, FO 371/3332, no. 97708, Lockhart to FO, 17 May 1918. Their first meeting was 15 May.
45. Spence, *Savinkov*, pp. 198–99, and Andrew Angarsky, *Eighty-Seven Days* (New York, 1963), pp. 197–201.
46. Kettle, 47, quoting a 10 Nov. 1918 MIIc report to the WO.
47. Contrary to the version presented by Robin Lockhart (*Ace*, 82-83), based on Reilly's own account, there is no evidence that he employed the surname "Constantine" (Konstantin) in Moscow. Rather, as Berzin's deposition suggests, Reilly used Konstantin as a codename in his Moscow dealings while operating as Konstantin Massino in Petrograd. See Kravchenko, *Pod. . .*, pp. 146–47. This is also noted in the *Protokol* of E. P. Berzin, 18 Sept. 1918 (to Ia. Peters), 303305, and *Zakliuchenie sledstvennoi komissdi pri VsTsIK*, 310311, pp. 318. Both documents are from the Cheka dossier on the Lockhart case and were provided to me and authenticated by Dr. Lev Bezymenskii, *Novoe Vremia*, Moscow.
48. See also Orlov's synopsis of his career, "Memorandum 9639," 30 June 1920, attached to NA, US Dept. of State, File 861.0-1055, Hurley to Hoover, 20 April 1921, and Douglas, 10. George Hill, pp. 236–38, also states that Reilly held a Cheka pass.
49. Orlov, *Underworld*, p. 117.
50. And why would Reilly have bothered to cover up Peters's role after the fact? Because their cooperation continued long after 1918. That, however, is another story.
51. Orlov continued to work for Bartels until the late 1920s. Bartels testified about their 1918 liaison as part of a later Berlin criminal case involving Orlov, See NA, USDS, File 811.44 Borah, Enclosure 1, "Protokoll des Prozesses Orlow und

Genossen vor dem Schoffengericht Berlin-Schoneberg vom 1. bis 6. Juli 1929," Protocol of 10 July, p. 10.

52. Orlov, *Underworld*, p. 104.
53. Volodarskii's assassin was an SR with links to Savinkov's organization. Writing in 1920, the Chekist writer Latsis (pp. 23–24) attributed the killing to Savinkov and linked it with the later attacks on Uritskii and Lenin. Curiously, however, Savinkov never claimed credit for Volodarskii although he later admitted trying to kill Lenin.
54. Molotov, perhaps not the most objective judge, characterized Iagoda as a "scoundrel" and "a filthy nobody who wormed his way into the Party." See *Molotov Remembers*, p. 237, and passim.
55. N. Ipat'ev, *Life of a Chemist* (Stanford, 1946), p. 264. On Iagoda's background see also Roman Gul', *Dzerzhinskii: Menzhinskii—Peters—Latsis—Iagoda* (Paris, 1936), pp. 165-74, E. H. Carr, *Socialism in One Country*, vol. 2 (New York, 1960), p. 430 n.3., and Alexander Orlov, *The Secret History of Stalin's Crimes* (New York, 1954), p. 260. Many of my assumptions about Iagoda's relationship to Reilly in 1918 derive from evidence relevant to their later dealings in the 1920s.
56. "Case: Lockhart," pp. 1–2. Also, Berzin, pp. 305–6 and *Zakliuchenie. . .*, p. 314.
57. See, in particular, Debo's article, and *Krasnaia kniga VChK* (Moscow, 1920), pp. 129, 194–198.
58. Kravchenko, pp. 109–113, and Van Der Rhoer, p. 53.
59. B. Lockhart, p. 86.
60. For a summation of Bliumkin's Dzerzhinskii links, again see Debo, passim, Douglas, pp. 4–6, and Van Der Rhoer, p. 103. On links to Hill, see Leggett, p. 293, and Bruce Lockhart, p. 298. Bliumkin lived in the same hotel as Hill and Lockhart—next door to the latter!
61. This action would later cause Lockhart no end of embarrassment, particularly as some of the checks continued to surface as late as 1929. See PRO, FO 371 / 14048, #N1966 / 1966 and FO 371 / 9371, #5825. According to Robin Lockhart, this scheme ultimately raised more that 8 million rubles (about £240,000), *Ace*, p. 89.
62. *Zakliuchenie . . .* , p. 318.
63. Berzin, p. 305.
64. For Lockhart's initial recollection of these events, which differs in some details from his later memoirs, see FO 371/3348, #190442, Lockhart to SIS, 5 Nov. 1918.
65. Spence, *Savinkov*, pp. 189, 194, 201–10, passim.
66. Berzin, p. 303.
67. See also the 8 Sept. 1918 report of K. A. Peterson to the All-Russian Central Executive Committee in A. S. Pokrovskii, comp., "Kistorii zagovora R. Lokkarta (1918 g.)," *Istoricheskii arkhiv*, #4 (1962), pp. 234–37. The first public account of the plot, the report emphasizes the aggressive and farsighted role of Peters in uncovering the affair, and has Berzin contacting Shmidkhen, rather than the other way round. In his 1924 memoir (p. 22), Peters takes full credit for unmasking the plot.
68. Berzin, p. 305.
69. Reilly, pp. 31–32. See also Marchand, *Allied Agents in Soviet Russia* (London, 1918), for his version of events. Marchand was a convenient (and willing?) scapegoat because of his later admission of pro-Soviet sympathies. Reilly could not have revealed the true source of his suspicion without compromising his own connection to the Cheka, connections that remained useful to him for years to come.
70. The following account is based on "Iz Protokola pokazaniia E. Petersa ot 18 ianvaria 1938 g.," and "Protokol . . . E. Petersa, 27 dekabria 1937 g." Copies of these documents, and additional information (Shteinberg to G. L. Owen, 5 Sept. 1993), were provided by Dr. V. Shteinberg and G. L. Owen.

71. One of the most convincing aspects of Peters's account is his description of Reilly's anger, something that only exploded in full fury when he felt betrayed.
72. Uritskii's assassin, Leonid Kannegisser, also was "spared" a lengthy interrogation or public examination. He also had personal links to Savinkov's organization. For a standard Soviet view of this and the Kaplan case, see D. L. Golinkov, *Krushenie antisovetskogo podpol'ia v SSSR (1917–1925 gg.) (Moscow*, 1975), pp. 200–3, 578.
73. Recent research on the Kaplan case, including copies of the interrogations arranged by Peters, can be found in Evgenii Danilov, "Za chto kaznili Fanii Kaplan?," *Ogonek*, #35 (Sept. 1993), pp. 10–16. I also am grateful to Dr. L. Bezymenskii for his insights into the Kaplan case.
74. Reilly, pp. 58–59.
75. On British uncertainty about Cromie's role in the plot, see FO 371/3336, #153837, Clive to FO, 8 Sept 1918.
76. Diary of Bruce Lockhart, 31 Aug.–2 Oct. 1918, entry of 30 Sept. This diary, in Lockhart's handwriting, is in the possession of Robin Lockhart and is quoted with his permission.
77. The Soviet court also sentenced Reilly and Vertemont to death en absentia. Kalamatiano's sentence was later suspended, so the unfortunate Fride became the only person to die for his part in the plot. Perhaps not incidentally, he was also one of the least important and most expendable of the conspirators.

Canadian Fannigans in the Kaiser's Clutch: Canadian Prisoners of War, 1914–1919
Desmond Morton

1. *Daily Express*, January 4, 1919. See Maria Tippett, *Art in the Service of War: Canada. Art and the Great War* (Toronto: University of Toronto Press, 1984), pp. 65, 81–87.
2. National Archives of Canada (NAC) Kemp Papers, vol. 133, Statement "In the Matter of 'Canada's Golgotha.'"
3. Mary M. Moore, *The Maple Leaf's Red Cross: The Wart Story of the Canadian Red Cross Overseas* (London: Skeffington & Son, 1919), p. 107.
4. Desmond Morton, *Silent Battle: Canadian Prisoners of War in Germany, 1914–1919* (Toronto, Lester Publishing, 1992).
5. On numbers see *Report of the Overseas Military Forces of Canada* (London: n.p., n.d. [1919]), pp. 58, 469, and NAC, R.G. 9, III, vol. 1123, P-48–4.
6. See Henri Béland, *My Three Years in a German Prison Camp* (Toronto: William Briggs, 1919). On civilian internment, J. D. Ketchum, a musician turned academic sociologist by his experiences, wrote *Ruhleben: A Prison Camp Society* (Toronto: University of Toronto Press, 1965). See also *Report of the Royal Commission . . . to investigate and report upon all claims which may be submitted to the Commission for the purpose of determining whether they are within the First Annex to Section l; or Part III of the Treaty of Versailles* (Ottawa: King's Printer, 1928), 2:511–41 passim.
7. On the suspected deserters, see NAC, R.G. 24, vol. 6992, and John Cooke in Royal Commission for the Investigation of Illegal Warfare Claims and for the Return of Sequestered Property in Necessitous Cases (McDougall Commission) *Report of the Commission on Reparations, 1930–31: Further Report on the Maltreatment of Prisoners of War* (Ottawa: King's Printer, 1933), p. 36.
8. On the battle, see G. W. L. Nicholson, *Canadian Expeditionary Force, 1914–1919: The Official History of the Canadian Army in the First World War* (Ottawa: Queen's Printer, 1962), pp. 66–83. On casualty figures, see NAC, R.G. 24, vol. 1874, file 211.
9. NAC. M.G. 30, E-376, Lt. Col. Ussher's account.

10. Cited in Reid, Gordon, ed., *Poor Bloody Murder: Personal Memoirs of the First World War* (Oakville: Mosaic Press, 1980), p. 83.
11. Coleman Phillipson, *International Law and the Great War* (London: T. Fisher Unwin, 1916), p. 252.
12. Hauptstadtarchiv Stuttgart, M1/11/Bn 800. Copy of remarks made in the course of a conversation with the Canadian Brigadier General Victor Williams by Captain Tettenborn, translated by Stephen Brown. To be fair, Williams had suffered from severe head wounds.
13. See McDougall Commission, *Maltreatment of Prisoners of War* (Ottawa: King's Printer, 1931), p. 39.
14. T. M. Scudamore, "Lighter Episodes in the Life of a Prisoner of War," Canadian Defense Quarterly 7, 3 (April, 1930), pp. 395–96.
15. George Pearson, *The Escape of a Princess Pat. . .* (New York: George Doran, 1918), p. 81.
16. J. W. Gerard, *My Four Years in Germany* (New York: George Doran, 1917), pp. 172–74; see also Robert Jackson, *The Prisoners. 1914–18* (London and New York: Croom Helm, 1989); Daniel McCarthy, *The Prisoner of War in Germany: The Care and Treatment of the Prisoner of War with a History of the Development of the Practice of Neutral Inspectorate* (New York: Moffat, Yard, 1918); Richard Speed, *Prisoners, Diplomats and the Great War: A Study in the Diplomacy of Captivity* (New York: Greenwood [1990]).
17. Morton, *Silent Battle*, pp. 15–20.
18. See McCarthy, *Prisoners of War*, pp. 45–46, 54–55.
19. See, for example, W. F. and M. Chambers, "The Unwilling Guest," unpublished manuscript in possession of George Chambers, p. 2; Morton, *Silent Battle*, pp. 48–50.
20. Ibid., pp. 50–56.
21. Major Peter Anderson, *I, That's Me: Escape from German Prison Camp and Other Experiences* (Ottawa: Bradburn Printers, n.d.), pp. 89–90.
22. McDougall Commission, *Maltreatment*, pp. 139–40.
23. The Hague Convention, Chapter II, Article 6 (amended 1907), in James Brown Scott, ed., *The Hague Conventions and Declarations as of 1899 and 1907. . . .*, 3rd ed. (New York: Oxford University Press, 1918) p. 109.
24. On work, see Morton, *Silent Battle*, pp. 66–77.
25. McDougall Commission, *Maltreatment*, p. 209.
26. On defiance and punishment, see Morton, *Silent Battle* pp. 71–83.
27. Ibid., pp. 112–23; see also NAC, R.G. 9, vol. 4739, folders 155–60; McDougall Commission, *Maltreatment*, pp. 251, 292.
28. On Bokelah incident, NAC, M.G. 30 E–204, Henry Howland "Come March With Me" (unpublished manuscript), pp. 183–97; McCarthy, *Prisoner of War*, pp. 101–3.
29. Howland, "Come March With Me," p. 216.
30. McDougall Commission, *Reparations. 1932: Final Report* (Ottawa: King's Printer, 1933), p. 102.
31. McDougall Commission, *Maltreatment*, pp. 212–13.
32. Morton, *Silent Battle*, pp. 83–87.
33. NAC, M.G. 30 E-33, Major Gillies Wilken papers, "Short Record of My Captivity," p. 16.
34. Statement of Claude Allan Beesley, NAC R.G. 9 III, vol. 4737, file 36-1-B. On "behind the lines prisoners," see Morton, *Silent Battle*, pp. 89–93.
35. McDougall Commission, Maltreatment, pp. 40–41; NAC, R.G. 9 III, vol. 2921, Maj. J. E. L. Streight to G.O.C., May 21, 1918.
36. Nellie McClung, *Three Times and Out as told by Private M. C. Simmons* (Toronto: Thomas Allen, 1918), pp. 165–66.

37. On his escape attempts see J. C. Thorn, *Three Years a Prisoner in Germany: The Story of Major J. C. Thorn. A First Canadian Contingent Officer who was captured by the Germans at Ypres on April 24th, 1915. Relating His Many Attempts to Escape (Once Disguised as a Widow) and Life in Various Camps and Fortresses with Illustrations* (Vancouver: Cowan & Brockhouse, 1919).
38. On exchanges, see Morton, *Silent Battle.* pp. 118–31.
39. NAC, R.G. 9 III, OS file 10-12-59, Lt. Col. Gerald Birks to the Hon. Edward Kemp, October 29, 1918.
40. McDougall Commission, *Maltreatment*, p. 291.
41. Conn Smythe, *If You Can't Beat 'Em in the Alley* (Toronto: McClelland & Stewart, 1981), pp. 142–43.
42. McDougall Commission, case 2185, p. 262. See also Howland, "March With Me," pp. 337–38.
43. Michael Moynihan, *Black Bread and Barbed Wire: Prisoners in the First World War* (London: Leo Cooper, 1978), p. x.

The Emergence of the Great Nation: The United States, Past, Present, and Future As Viewed by the Russian Liberal Press During the Great War
Sergey V. Listikov

(Note: Some references give two dates: the "old style," derived from the Julian calendar, and the "new style" (in parentheses), derived from the Gregorian calendar used in the West. The latter, which is thirteen days ahead of the Julian calendar, was officially adopted by the nascent Soviet state in February 1918.)

1. *Russkoye Slovo*, January 26, 1917.
2. *Rech*, January 11 (24), 1917; *Novoie Vremia* January 12 (25), 1917.
3. *Utro Rossii*, March 12, 1917; *Novoie Vremia*, June 17 (30) 1917; *Russkoye Slovo*, February 25, 1917.
4. *Novoie Vremia*, June 17 (30) 1917; *Utro Rossii*, August 6, 1917.
5. *Novoie Vremia*, July 23 (August 5), 1917.
6. *Novoie Vremia*, July 15 (28) and July 23 (August 5), 1917.
7. *Russkoye Slovo*, March 15, 1917.
8. *Novoie Vremia*, February 22 (March 7), 1917.
9. *Utro Rossii*, June 14, 1917.
10. *Russkoye Slovo*, March 24, 1917.
11. *Utro Rossii*, July 4, 1917.
12. *Russkoye Slovo*, January 12, 1917.
13. *Novoie Vremia*, March 10 (23), 1917.
14. *Novoie Vremia*, February 23 (March 8) and May 17 (30), 1917.
15. *Utro Rossii*, August 19, 1917.
16. *Novoie Vremia*, June 17 (30), 1917.
17. *Novoie Vremia*, May 10 (23), 1917 and August 9 (22), 1917.
18. *Novoie Vremia*, July 2 (15) and August 25 (September 7), 1917.
19. *Utro Rossii*, December 15, 1916; *Novoie Vremia*, January 12 (25), 1917.
20. *Rech*, January 23, 1917; *Russkoye Slovo*, January 12, 1917; *Novoie Vremia*, January 17 (30), 1917, etc.
21. *Rech*, January 8 (21), 1917; *Russkoye Slovo*, January 11, 1917.
22. *Novoie Vremia*, January 17 (31), 1917.
23. *Russkoye Slovo*, March 23, 1917, and April 23, 1917; *Novoie Vremia*, January 11 (24), 1917.
24. *Utro Rossii*, April 22, 1917; *Novoie Vremia*, April 28 (May 11), 1917.
25. *Rech*, May 13, 1917, and May 30, 1917.
26. *Rech*, May 31, 1917; *Novoie Vremia*, May 20 (June 2), 1917.
27. *Utro Rossii*, April 22, 1917.

A Wilsonian View of Self-Determination for Eastern Europe and Russia
Betty Miller Unterberger

1. Clyde Eagleton, "The Excesses of Self-determination," *Foreign Affairs* 31 (July 1953): 594.
2. John Locke, *Treatise of Civil Government*, Book 2.
3. J. D. Richardson, ed., *A Compilation of the Messages and Papers of the Presidents, 1789–1897* (Washington, D.C. ,1869–1899), 1:213 ff.
4. John Catanzariti, et al., eds., *The Papers of Thomas Jefferson*, 25 vols. to date (Princeton, N.J., 1950–), 25:367. For an elaboration of these views, see also 24:632–33, 800.
5. The discussion above is drawn from Betty M. Unterberger, "National Self-Determination," in Alexander DeConde, ed., *Encyclopedia of the History of American Foreign Policy*, 3 vols. (New York, 1978), 2:635–650.
6. For example, Russia could hardly support the principle of nationality and the "right of the peoples to determine their own fate—principles in the name of which dissolution of the Dual Monarchy was called for—because this constituted a precedent which could detach from Russia all of her heterogeneous ethnic population." Ján Papánek, *La Tchécoslovaquie histoire politique et iuridique de sa creation* (Prague, 1923), p. 33. For conflicting evidence regarding the Tsar and Foreign Minister Sergei D. Sazonov's views toward self-determination, see Merritt Abrash, "War Aims Toward Austria-Hungary, The Czechoslovak Pivot," in *Russian Diplomacy in Eastern Europe, 1914–1917*, edited by Alexander Dallin (New York, 1963), pp. 86–91, 96–100; Edvard Benes, *Souvenirs de guerre et de revolution, 1914–1918*, 2 vols. (Paris, 1929), 1:314; Karel Kramar, "M. Krámar et la politique slave," *Le Monde Slave*, November 1926, p. 294; Gifford D. Malone, "War Aims Toward Germany" in Dallin, ed., *Russian Diplomacy in Eastern Europe*, p. 142–43; Maurice Paléologue, *La Russie des tsars pendant la grande guerre*, 2 vols. (Paris, 1921–22), 1:93–94, 246–47; Sergei D. Sazonov, *Fateful Years, 1909–1916* (London, 1928), pp. 273–74; William Renzi, "Who Composed 'Sazonov's Thirteen Points'? A Reexamination of Russia's War Aims of 1914," *American Historical Review*, 88 (April 1983): 349–50. For British and French views regarding self-determination and the breakup of empires see Betty Miller Unterberger, *The United States, Revolutionary Russia, and the Rise of Czechoslovakia* (Chapel Hill, N.C., 1989), pp. 9–11.
7. For example, see Arno J. Mayer, *Political Origins of the New Diplomacy. 1917–1918* (New Haven, Conn., 1959), pp. 75, 341–44; Michla Pomerance, "The United States and Self-Determination: Perspectives on the Wilsonian Conception," *The American Journal of International Law*, 70 (1976): 2.
8. "An address on Preparedness to the Manhattan Club," November 4, 1915, in Arthur S. Link, David W. Hirst, et al., eds., *The Papers of Woodrow Wilson*, 68 vols. (Princeton, N.J., 1966–1993), 35:168, hereafter cited as *PWW*.
9. H. W. V. Temperley, *A History of the Peace Conference of Paris*, 2 vols. (London, 1920–24), 1:217. For the view of Wilson as "the spokesman for humanity the world over," and the first president to universalize the Jeffersonian ideal of democracy, see Merrill D. Peterson, *The Jeffersonian Image in the American Mind* (New York, 1962), pp. 344–46.
10. *PWW*, 30:248-55; Arthur S. Link, *Woodrow Wilson: Revolution, War, and Peace*, (Arlington Heights, Ill., 1979), pp. 4–6.
11. *PWW*, 37:115.
12. Arthur S. Link, *Woodrow Wilson and the Progressive Era, 1900–1917* (New York, 1954), pp. 107–44.
13. Woodrow Wilson to Lindley M. Garrison, August 8, 1914, *PWW*, 30: 362; see also John Reed, Draft Article Based on Interview with Woodrow Wilson, June 30, 1914, ibid., pp. 231–38.

14. A Draft of an Address to a Joint Session of Congress, June [26], 1916, *PWW*, 37:303.
15. *PWW*, 37:115.
16. Pomerance, "Perspectives on the Wilsonian Conception," 18; Morton H. Halperin and David J. Scheffer, *Self-Determination in the New World Order* (Washington, D.C., 1992), pp. 16–18.
17. *PWW*, 40:533–39.
18. Robert Kerner, "Brief Memorandum," No. 308, Inquiry Archives, Record Group 256, Department of State, National Archives, hereafter cited as *RG* and *DSNA*; Jusserand to Aristide Briand, n.d., received March 7, 1917, Guerre 1914–1918, Etats-Unis, 505:280–81, French Foreign Ministry Archives, hereafter cited as *FFM-Ar*; *PWW*, 41:354–57.
19. U.S. Department of State, *Papers Relating to the Foreign Relations of the United States, 1917* (Washington, D.C., 1926), pp. ix, xvi, hereafter cited as *FRUS*.
20. *FRUS, 1918, Russia*, 3 vols. (Washington, D.C., 1931–33) I:253. Wilson agreed that this formula "expresses the instinctive judgment as to the right of plain men everywhere." He had added "that a wrong use has been made of a just idea is no reason why a right use should not be made of it." *FRUS, 1917*, p. xvi.
21. *PWW*, 45:411–14.
22. Jan Smuts to Lloyd George, December 26, 1917, CAB 1/25, Public Record Office, hereafter cited as PRO.
23. Victor S. Mamatey, *The United States and East Central Europe. 1914–1918* (Princeton, N.J., 1957) pp. 150–52; CAB 23/13, War Cabinet 308(a)157, Draft Minutes of the Meeting on December 31, 1917, PRO.
24. CAB 23/5, War Cabinet 312/13, Minutes of Meeting on January 3, 1918, at 11:30 A.M., PRO; Llewellyn Woodward, *Great Britain and the War of 1914–1918* (London, 1967), p. 401; Mayer, *Political Origins of New Diplomacy* (New Haven, Conn., 1959), pp. 13–28.
25. CAB 23/5, War Cabinet 313/13, Minutes of Meeting on January 3, 1918, at 5:00 P.M., PRO; CAB 23/5, War Cabinet 314/13, Minutes of Meeting on January 4, 1918, PRO.
26. CAB 23/5, War Cabinet 314/13, Minutes of Meeting on January 4, 1918, PRO. For the full address, see *FRUS, 1918, Supplement 1, World War*, 2 vols. (Washington, D.C., 1932), 1:4–12, and David Lloyd George, *War Memoirs of David Lloyd George*, 6 vols. (London, 1933–37), 5:63–73. See also *PWW*, 45:487–88, n.2.
27. *FRUS, 1918, Russia*, 1:244, 253, 258, 405-8.
28. Wilson to Lansing, January 1, 1918, Woodrow Wilson Papers, Library of Congress, Washington, D.C.
29. Frank William Taussig to Wilson, January 3, 1918, Woodrow Wilson Collection, Princeton University Library, Princeton, N.J.; *PWW* 45:440–41; John Wheeler-Bennett, *Brest-Litovsk: The Forgotten Peace. March 1918*, 2nd ed. (New York, 1956), p. 121; Charles G. Fenwick, "Notes on International Affairs," *American Political Science Review* 12 (November 1918), pp. 706–7.
30. Wheeler-Bennett, *Brest-Litovsk*, pp. 127–36; Morgan Phillips Diary, *My Reminiscences of the Russian Revolution* (London, 1921), p. 199; William Phillips Diary, January 4, 1918, in Journal and Notes of a Diplomatic Courier, Harvard University Library, Boston, Mass.
31. *FRUS, 1918, Russia*, 1:405–8.
32. Lansing to Wilson, January 2, 1918, *PWW*, 45:427–30.
33. Ibid., pp. 428.
34. Ronald Hugh Campbell to House, January 2, 1918, Wilson Collection, Princeton. The full report is printed in Lloyd George, *War Memoirs*, 5:21–36.
35. Stephen L. Gwynn, ed., *The Letters and Friendships of Sir Cecil Farina Rice*, 2 vols. (Boston, 1929), 2:422–25.
36. Spring Rice to Balfour, January 4, 1918, Arthur J. Balfour Papers, PRO; *PWW*, 45:454–58.

37. Ibid., 45:454–58.
38. Unterberger, "Woodrow Wilson and the Russian Revolution," in Arthur S. Link, ed., *Woodrow Wilson and a Revolutionary World* (Chapel Hill, N.C., 1982), pp. 52–53.
39. Unterberger, *America's Siberian Expedition* (New York, 1969), pp. 22–25; Memorandum from Robert Cecil to the British Embassy, January 1, 1918, *PWW*, 45:420.
40. H. R. Wilson to Lansing, December 28, 1917, DF 763.72119/10068, *DSNA; PWW*, 45:415–17; Mamatey, *United States and East Central Europe*, p. 174; Woodrow Wilson to Lansing, January 1, 1918, DF 763.72119/10068, *DSNA; PWW*, 45:415–17; Heinrich Bendikt, *Die Friedensaktion der Meinlgruppe 1917–1918*, (Graz and Cologne, 1962) Introduction, and p. 308. See also Leo Valiani, *The End of Austria-Hungary* (New York, 1973), pp. 267–85.
41. Italics inserted. Balfour to House, January 2, 1918, Wilson Collection, Princeton. This latter phrase was quoted verbatim to Count Albert von Mensdorff in the Smuts-Mensdorff conversations and again quoted specifically to Wilson when Balfour informed him of those conversations two weeks later. The phrase appeared without alteration in Wilson's Point Ten.
42. *PWW*, 45:481–82, 485, 514; Balfour to House, January 2, 1918, Wilson Papers, Washington, D.C.
43. Lansing Diary, January 7, 1918, in Robert Lansing Papers, Library of Congress, Washington D.C.; House Diary January 9, 1918, *PWW*, 45:550-59; Memorandum on Subject of the President's War Aims Address on January 8, 1918, Which are Open to Debate, January 10, 1918. Selected Papers of Robert Lansing, Princeton University Library, Princeton, N.J.; Robert Lansing, *War Memoirs of Robert Lansing, Secretary of State* (Indianapolis, 1935), p. 261.
44. *PWW*, 45:534–39; Unterberger, "Woodrow Wilson and the Bolsheviks: The 'Acid Test' of Soviet-American Relations." *Diplomatic History* 11 (Spring 1987), pp. 71–72.
45. Paul Mantoux, *The Deliberations of the Council of Four (March 24–June 28, 1919): Notes of the Official Interpreter*, translated and edited by Arthur S. Link, vol. 1 (Princeton, 1992), p. 67.
46. House Diary, January 29, 1918; *PWW*, 46:167–68, 183–93; *New York Times*, January 22, 1918; Oswald Villard, *Fighting Years: Memoirs of a Liberal Editor* (New York, 1939), pp. 340–41; Wheeler-Bennett, *Brest-Litovsk*, pp. 201–04.
47. *FRUS, 1918, Supp. 1, World War*, pp. 54–59.
48. Ottokar Czernin, *In the World War* (London, 1919), pp. 188–89.
49. For a detailed examination of these efforts, see Unterberger, *The United States, Revolutionary Russia and the Rise of Czechoslovakia* (Chapel Hill, N.C., 1989), pp. 99–119.
50. Ibid., pp. 164, 166, 256.
51. Unterberger, "Woodrow Wilson and the Bolsheviks," pp. 78–90.
52. Unterberger, *America's Siberian Expedition*, pp. 232–33. As it turned out, there was no mention of the principle of self-determination in the Covenant of the League of Nations. Report of the International Committee of Jurists, *League of Nations Official Journal*, Special Supplement 3 (October 1920), p. 5.

Index

A

Abenheim, Donald, 32–33, 192, 203
AEF (American Expeditionary Forces), 154, 159–61, 242
aerial activity, 47
African-Americans, 154, 242
aircraft carriers, 32
airplanes, 25, 75
  DeHaviland DH-4, 153
  Fokker Dr.I, 103, 105–9, 110, 112
  Sopwith Camel, 105–6
Albert, King of the Belgians, 49
Alekseev, N., 196, 200
alienation of farmers; soldiers; workers, 65–66
All Quiet on the Western Front, 63, 251
Alley, Stephen, 131–32
Allied agents, 140–41
Allied blockade, 82, 97–99
Allied invasions, 48–49, 52–53
Allies, 10, 49, 63, 130–31, 135, 138
  and Russia, 198–99, 200, 202, 207–13, 220–22, 224, 226–27
America, 95–96, 190, 195, 197, 229. *See also* United States
American Civil War, 11, 31, 149–50, 155–56, 195, 217–18, 222, 234, 241, 245–46
American Federation of Labor (AFL), 197
American Legion, 5
American Revolution, 216–18
Americans, 4, 9, 12–13, 64, 134, 141–42, 144, 162, 166–67
  in Russian eyes, 195–99, 200, 212–13, 217
Amiens, France, 104
ammunition, 23–24, 26, 45–46, 51–52. *See also* guns
Anastaplo, George, 15, 188
Anderson, Peter, 185, 188–89
Anglo-French offensive (Somme), 74
antiaircraft, 47
anti-Bolshevik, 126–27, 133–35, 138–39
antitank guns, 28, 29, 164, 166. *See also* guns

antitank mines, 167
Antwerp, Belgium, 40, 43, 49
Archangel, Russia, 135, 188, 200
archetype, 74–75, 84
archives
  Australian, 113; French, 23–24; Soviet, 204, 206
Ardennes, 27–28
Armenia, 229
Armentières, France, 238
Armistice, 3, 15, 82, 97, 159, 176, 186, 211, 256
Armstrong, Fred ("Tiny"), 183
Arnold, Matthew, 252
Arras, France, 210, 238
artillery, 19, 21, 23–24
  in forts, 21, 23, 25, 43
  mobile, 22–24, 28, 166
artillery bombardment, 20–24, 28, 47–48, 52
artillery shells, 20–21, 24, 31, 48, 51
artillery, use of, 31
  at Verdun, 19–23, 28, 31
Artois, France, 70, 236
assault battalions (German), 76
Association for the Research of the Great War, 208
Atlantic Wall, 50, 53
atomic bomb, 191
Auden, W(illiam) H., 14, 252, 256
Australia, 104, 106
Australian Field Artillery, 103, 105, 107–8
Australian War Memorial Museum, 113
Australians, 84, 113–14, 243
Austria, 13, 210, 224
Austria-Hungary, 6–7, 14, 209, 221–22, 225–26
Austrians, 13, 15, 97, 223
Austro-Hungarian Empire, 220, 225–26, 228
Austro-Hungarians, 209–10, 211, 220
autonomous states, 219, 223, 225–26
Avocourt, France, 19